P9-CFP-445

Wall Street Made Simple

Merle E. Dowd

Edited and prepared for publication by The Stonesong Press, Inc.

A MADE SIMPLE BOOK

DOUBLEDAY

NEW YORK LONDON TORONTO SYDNEY AUCKLAND

Edited and prepared for publication by The Stonesong Press, Inc.
Executive Editor: Sheree Bykofsky
Editor: Sarah Gold

Published by Doubleday, a division of
Bantam Doubleday Dell Publishing Group, Inc.
666 Fifth Avenue, New York, New York 10103

MADE SIMPLE and DOUBLEDAY are trademarks of Doubleday,
a division of Bantam Doubleday Dell Publishing Group, Inc.

ISBN 0–385–41786–1
Copyright © 1992 by Doubleday, a division of Bantam Doubleday Dell Publishing Group, Inc.

All Rights Reserved
Printed in the United States of America
August 1992
First Edition

Library of Congress Cataloging-in-Publication Data

Dowd, Merle E.
    Wall Street made simple / Merle E. Dowd.—1st ed.
      p.   cm.
    "A Made simple book."
    1. Investments—United States. 2. Wall Street. I. Title.
  HG4910.D68 1992   91–40427
  332.6'0973—dc20   CIP

CONTENTS

PART TWO: INVESTING

Welcome to the world of finance, investment, and money. Although the name refers to a short street near the tip of Manhattan Island in New York City, Wall Street is mainly a state of mind. Wall Street covers the broad range of investment opportunities that offer potential for increasing your wealth.

Knowledge is a key factor in investment success. Probably the single biggest problem small investors face in attempting to deal with Wall Street is the lack of confidence that results from a lack of understanding. If you wonder whether you are doing the right thing in moving from low-yielding bank or savings and loan savings accounts into more rewarding investments, don't throw up your hands in frustration and turn your money affairs over to a professional. A broker's interest in making a living might not mesh with your interest in building personal wealth. And even if you elect to consult with a financial planner or broker, you must learn enough to ask the right questions and understand the answers. Remember, no one has a deeper interest in your financial affairs than you.

If you believe that investing in stocks or bonds is not worth the risk, worry, and trouble, consider these statistics: $1 invested in U.S. Treasury bills (T-bills) in 1925 would have grown to $9.67 by the end of 1989, before taxes. Adjusted for inflation, the real return of $1 invested in T-bills would have grown to only $1.38, before taxes. And T-bills pay more interest than bank savings accounts. On the same basis, long-term U.S. Treasury bonds would have grown to $17.30. However, $1 invested in common stocks of major blue-chip, large capitalization companies would have grown to $534.45, and an investment of $1 in the shares of small companies would have grown to $1,628.59—168 times more than the dollar investment in T-bills. These figures include the declines during the depression of the 1930s and other market collapses, including the free-fall in October 1987 when the Dow Jones Industrial Average fell 508 points in one day.

The message is: Returns from low-risk, insured investments are so small, they guarantee a loss in terms of purchasing power, after inflation and taxes. You're better off accepting some level of risk to gain a chance to break even or profit with stocks, bonds, or mutual funds.

The objective of *Wall Street Made Simple* is to help you understand the world of investments and money and to help you gain enough confidence to undertake a long-term program of wealth building. Some chapters, such as those on commodities, futures, and options, are aimed at helping you understand the operations and the jargon; once you understand these areas and their risks, you will probably avoid them as investments.

Helping you to learn StreetSpeak, the mumbo jumbo of specialized vocabulary popularly known as Wall Street jargon, is a special objective of this book. Don't be put off by jargon; learn to use it to expand your know-how and ability to function comfortably and profitably on Wall Street. The glossary in the back of this book pro-

vides definitions for key terms outlined in bold within each chapter.

Wall Street Made Simple is divided into two parts: Part One will acquaint you with the securities of Wall Street—stocks, bonds, mutual funds, commodities, futures, options, and others. Part Two explores investment strategies, how to track your investments' performances, and how to manage your money.

Learning about money, investments, and wealth-building strategies can become a fascinating hobby as well as a profitable adventure. Learning to think for yourself in this realm may be the biggest boost your capital-building program could experience. Investing is highly competitive, but you need not be the absolute best to be a winner—just better than you would be with a safe program of no-risk or low-risk investments.

CHAPTER ONE

Wall Street—What Is It?

KEY TERMS FOR THIS CHAPTER

markets	options	limited partnerships
exchange	market makers	equity
securities	pink sheets	yield
liquidity	make-out basis	appreciation
listed	open outcry	tax-advantaged
seats	program trader	tax-deferred
arbitrage	volatility	IRA
specialist system	beta	Keogh plan

Wall Street is the center of financial activities in the United States. It encompasses stock, bond, commodities, futures, and options markets; institutions serving investors; and the people associated with the financial community. Internationally, Wall Street functions on a par with money centers in the City of London, Switzerland, Hong Kong, Singapore, and Tokyo. Nowhere is globalization more firmly established than in the world's financial markets, which are already closely intertwined and getting cosier every day.

Markets form the core of Wall Street—the center where money and people come together with the vibrant energy of free enterprise. If money makes the world go-round, then Wall Street and similar centers in other countries form the hub on which it rotates. What happens on Wall Street drives governments—ours and others around the world. What happens to the people of Wall Street makes news—good and bad. What happens on Wall Street affects all of us, whether we are active investors or merely trying to survive on salaries or wages: it drives inflation up or down, generates or cuts out jobs, and forms the financial base for the United States.

No one should underestimate the influence of Wall Street and its power to shape major elements in our lives. The more you know about Wall Street, the better you can manage your personal finances.

The Stock Markets

Wall Street's heart is at 11 Wall Street, the home of the New York Stock Exchange (NYSE). From this center of financial activity, communication lines extend to other exchanges in New York, as well as to exchanges in other cities of the United States and around the world. Although the New York Stock Exchange is the biggest and most powerful American market, it is not the only one. Numerous exchanges operate in both general and special arenas, mutual funds flourish in cities all over the United States, and over-the-counter markets reach into every city and town with a broker's office.

An **exchange** is a place where buyers and sellers get together in person, by telephone, or by computer terminal to trade stocks, bonds, commodities, options, futures contracts, and other **securities.** An exchange may be an edifice of brick and mortar or a network of computers interconnected to facilitate the offers to sell and bids to buy from individuals or institutions.

Exchanges provide **liquidity,** the ability to buy and sell shares quickly and inexpensively at their fair market value. If you believed you would have difficulty selling shares in a company, you might not invest in it. An exchange removes that hesitancy. Knowing a market for shares exists, and that you can get a fair price if and when you sell, generates confidence; and confidence underlies all viable markets.

The market for stocks and other securities is no different in concept from the public market where growers display their produce on counters and consumers come to buy; only the products are different. To understand how Wall Street functions, you must understand the markets and how they interact with each other and with the millions of investors who engage in financial transactions.

The New York Stock Exchange

History has it that what is now the New York Stock Exchange began on May 17, 1792, when 24 brokers, meeting under a buttonwood tree at what is now 68 Wall Street, signed an agreement that organized the first stock market in New York. Originally the New York Stock & Exchange Board, the name was changed to the New York Stock Exchange on January 29, 1863. On November 7, 1988, the NYSE went international when it opened a London office to help European companies gain access to the United States capital market through listings on the exchange.

On April 5, 1979, the New York Futures Exchange (NYFE) was incorporated as a wholly owned subsidiary of the New York Stock Exchange (see page 18).

The New York Stock Exchange, now at 11 Wall Street, is known as the "big board." The stocks and bonds of the biggest and most prestigious U.S. corporations trade on the floor of the NYSE. The NYSE includes member securities firms and dealers, individual and institutional investors, and more than 1,700 **listed** companies, whose securities trade on the exchange. The motives of participants vary:

Companies use the exchange to raise capital; individuals buy and sell stocks and bonds, hoping to make money; and the securities dealers and brokers act as intermediaries to earn personal income.

Prices and volumes for the NYSE and seven other U.S. markets are consolidated for consistent reporting. Out of these eight markets, the NYSE is by far the dominant exchange, trading about 85 percent of the share volume. Average daily volume for 1987, the all-time record year, was 188,938 million shares; the value of securities traded totaled $1.87 trillion. The crash of October 1987 created the heaviest volume of trading in the exchange's history—a record 608,148,710 shares traded in one day. The Dow Jones Industrial Average fell a record 508 points.

Member firms, brokerages, and securities dealers own the NYSE. **Seats** (memberships) on the exchange trade at auction like the shares of other corporations. The price of a seat depends on supply and demand, with demand dependent on how profitable ownership of the seat is perceived to be. Seats can cost over $1 million. A seat on the exchange permits the firm's employees to buy or sell shares on the trading floor on their own behalf and on behalf of their clients. Member firms may invest their own money, engage in a process known as **arbitrage** (the simultaneous buying and selling of similar products in different markets to take advantage of different prices in the various markets), and risk their own capital to facilitate trading and maintain liquidity.

The NYSE operates under a **specialist system.** Specialists perform a role similar to that of an air traffic controller. They operate at posts on the trading floor, maintaining a fair and orderly market in the securities assigned to them by the NYSE. To trade shares in a specific stock, brokers representing buyers and sellers congregate around the specialist assigned that stock. All trades move through the specialist's book of shares offered for sale and shares bid (offers to buy). At times the specialist may actively buy and sell shares. For instance, when so many shares are offered they begin to flood the market and drive prices down wildly, the specialist may buy shares for his own account. To maintain an orderly market when bids to buy threaten to swamp the market and drive prices too far up, the specialist may sell his shares. The specialist's intermediary role causes the stock market to differ from a true auction market.

The NYSE operates the largest corporate and government bond market in the United States, listing more than 3,000 issues of U.S. government, U.S. corporation, foreign government, foreign corporation, and international bank bonds. To be listed on the NYSE, a corporation must meet certain financial qualifications. The most important are as follows:

1. Earnings before federal taxes must be at least $2.5 million during the most recent year.
2. The market value of publicly held shares must exceed $18 million.
3. A total of 1,100,000 common shares must be held in public hands.
4. At least 2,000 shareholders must hold a minimum of 100 shares each, and the average monthly volume of trading in the company's shares must exceed 100,000 shares over a six-month period.

5. The corporation must agree to keep shareholders fully informed on a regular basis and to be bound by the rules of the NYSE.

Each application for listing is considered on its own merits and includes a judgment of the company's position in the industry, its perceived stability, and whether it appears to be expanding its position in the industry.

The American Stock Exchange

The American Stock Exchange (Amex) originally traded shares outdoors on New York's docks shortly after the revolutionary war. Outdoor trading of stocks later moved to Wall and Broad streets and then again farther south on Broad. Called the New York Curb Agency in 1908, the organization became the New York Curb Market Association in 1911. In 1921 the association moved to 86 Trinity Place and shortened its name to the New York Curb Market. It wasn't until 1953 that the name was changed to the American Stock Exchange.

After the NYSE, the Amex is the second largest single-floor exchange trading stocks. In terms of volume of trading, however, the Amex is far smaller than the over-the-counter market for unlisted stocks. The Amex also operates through specialists who function much the same as specialists on the NYSE, acting as brokers' brokers and maintaining a book of orders to buy and sell at a range of prices.

Listing requirements for the Amex are substantially less demanding than those for the big board. Each company's application is considered on its overall merits, but the following guidelines must be met:

1. Pretax income must exceed $750,000 for the latest fiscal year or in two of the most recent three years.
2. The market value of the shares in public hands must exceed $3 million. The price per share must exceed $3.
3. At least 800 stockholders must hold a minimum of 100 shares each.

Amex management also looks at the nature of a company's business, its markets, its management reputation, its historical record of operations and growth, its financial integrity, and its future outlook.

About 900 companies are listed on the Amex, but the number changes as companies move up to the NYSE or are delisted for failing to meet qualifications. A company whose stock trades over-the-counter may move up to the Amex to gain visibility and to make trading in the shares easier and less expensive.

The Amex is heavily involved in **options.** An option is a contract that entitles, but does not obligate, the holder to buy (call) or sell (put) a fixed number of shares of an underlying security at a stated price on or before a fixed expiration date (see Chapter 7 for a full discussion of options). The Amex introduced call options in 1975, put options in 1980, options on the Major Market Index (MMI) in 1983, and the Institutional Index Option in 1986. The Amex also trades options on the Computer Technology Index and the Oil Index. The Amex offers trading in call and put options on more than 140 listed and over-the-counter stocks plus options on U.S. Treasury bills and notes and options on stock indexes.

Other Exchanges

Regional and niche exchanges operate in a number of cities around the United States. Some of these exchanges participate in the Intermarket Trading System (ITS), which enables brokers and specialists to represent clients and interact with other markets to gain the best prices available. If a lower price for a multiple-exchange stock (a stock that trades on more than one exchange) is available on a regional exchange, the broker can make the trade through the ITS for the advantage of the client. Contacts are made through a sophisticated electronic communications network with the approval and encouragement of the Securities and Exchange Commission (SEC). The ITS began in April 1978 and has expanded continuously; at the end of 1989 it included 2,082 multiple-exchange stocks. The eight markets aligned through the ITS are the New York, American, Boston, Cincinnati, Midwest, Pacific, and Philadelphia stock exchanges and the National Association of Securities Dealers and Automated Quotation over-the-counter system.

Each of the regional exchanges functions similarly to the NYSE and the Amex. They are simply smaller and may trade the stocks of companies located in the regions, plus commodities, futures, or options unique to their exchange. If you have a specific interest in one of the regional stock exchanges, write the exchange for more information (see Resources for addresses).

• The Boston Stock Exchange (BSE) dates from 1834 when local business leaders decided to facilitate capital acquisitions and foster trade by forming an organized securities exchange. The BSE was the first organized exchange in the United States to admit foreign broker-dealers as members (in 1968). It currently operates an electronic link with the Montreal Stock Exchange in Canada. The BSE does not engage in futures, options, or commodities trading. During 1989 the BSE traded 900,529,000 shares or about 1.57 percent of the shares traded on the ITS.

• The Midwest Stock Exchange (MSE) is the result of two mergers—one in 1949 and one in 1960—that combined the exchanges in Chicago, St. Louis, Minneapolis-St. Paul, Cleveland, and New Orleans. A combination of listed and unlisted stocks trade on the exchange to build volume that in 1990 included trades of 2.44 billion shares. The MSE currently trades no commodities, futures, or options.

• The Pacific Stock Exchange (PSE) combines former regional exchanges in Los Angeles and San Francisco with two divisions and trading on exchange floors in both cities. The PSE's roots extend back to September 1882 when The Stock and Bond Exchange was founded in San Francisco. The Los Angeles Oil Exchange began in 1899, and its name was changed to the Los Angeles Stock Exchange one year later. The two merged in 1957. Volume is about 9 percent of the volume of the NYSE. The PSE offers the advantage of trading hours that extend beyond the close of the NYSE for stocks listed on the NYSE and the Amex. The PSE trades options on the Financial News Composite Index (FNCI), a price-weighted index of 30 large NYSE stocks. The FNCI (pronounced fancy) is maintained by the Financial News Network/Consumer News and Business Channel (FNN/CNBC). The PSE also offers extended-term options on a number of listed stocks with expiration dates as long as two years into the future.

• The Philadelphia Stock Exchange (PHLX) is the oldest organized exchange in the United States, having started in 1790. The PHLX is active in the options market and is the world's major exchange for foreign currency options. PHLX operates a subsidiary, the Philadelphia Board of Trade, for trading futures in seven major currencies of the world, including the European Currency Unit (ECU).

• The Cincinnati Stock Exchange (CSE) began in 1858. Securities on the CSE are traded by the National Securities Trading System (NSTS), the nation's first automated auction market for listed securities. The NSTS was developed under experimental status with the approval of the SEC and became permanent in 1982. The NSTS is a visible auction system, in contrast to the usual audible auction system, that includes bids and offers posted on electronic media and visible on computer screens. These bids and offers appear on the ITS. The CSE trades over 1,500 issues and was the original listing exchange for many of the major U.S. companies that are now listed on the NYSE.

Of three former niche stock exchanges in the western part of the United States, only the Spokane Stock Exchange remains. The exchanges traded mainly in the stocks of oil, gas, and metals mining companies.

• The Spokane Stock Exchange specializes in small mining company stocks. It began on January 18, 1897, during a mining boom in southern British Columbia, Canada. The Spokane Stock Exchange is near the silver and gold ore bodies of the Coeur d'Alene district, site of some of the biggest silver mines in the United States. A major expansion of the exchange in 1988 added computerized trading. Many of the stocks traded with the exchanges function as a centralized market maker are penny stocks (stocks with prices less than $1 per share).

• Two Canadian stock exchanges actively trade in some U.S. stocks as well as those of Canadian companies. Although technically not part of Wall Street, the proximity of these exchanges and the close ties between Canadian subsidiaries of U.S. corporations and Wall Street call for including them among exchanges of interest.

The Toronto Stock Exchange (TSE) operates a "Market-By-Price" electronic real-time market that, in effect, provides an open "specialist book" for all listed stocks, including 200 that are dual-listed on United States and international markets. An electronic market is one where open orders to sell or buy are exhibited on a computer screen, and trades are executed off the screens minute by minute. In a real-time market, changes are posted after each trade, as opposed to at the close of the day.

The Vancouver Stock Exchange (VSE), known as Canada's mining exchange, began in 1907 with five member firms to help raise venture capital for western Canada's burgeoning mining industry. The VSE continues to specialize in mining company issues in both Canada and the United States with investors from many of the Pacific-rim nations. In 1989 companies listed on the VSE raised $642 million in new capital with 65 percent of that money invested in initial public offerings of mining companies. More than 2,150 companies' stocks are listed on the VSE, including many U.S. issues. Electronic links permit rapid access to VSE stocks from both Canada and the United States.

Over-the-counter Markets

Over-the-counter (OTC) markets exist all around the country in brokers' offices rather than in a central facility. More than 500 securities firms in every corner of the United States trade shares of unlisted corporations. A stock that is unlisted can only trade OTC, and investors access this wide-ranging market through their brokers. Not all stocks traded OTC are those of companies too small to meet exchange minimum requirements—many companies simply prefer not to be listed on exchanges because they do not want to be bound by the rules and regulations of those exchanges. Such companies range from corporations with only a few employees to giants, such as Microsoft, Apple, and Nordstrom, with thousands of employees.

The OTC market trades more shares of stock on a typical day than any of the exchanges except the NYSE, and on rare occasions, the share volume traded OTC has even exceeded the share volume traded on the NYSE. In a recent year the OTC market traded nearly 30 billion shares of more than 4,500 corporations.

The OTC market is divided into two distinct divisions—the National Association of Securities Dealers and Automated Quotation and the National Quotation Bureau, Inc.

• The National Association of Securities Dealers and Automated Quotation (NASDAQ) functions as an electronic marketplace. A mammoth telephone-link communications system headquartered in Trumbull, Connecticut, connects individual market makers and securities firms nationwide. Quotations appear on more than 3,000 computer screens connected to the central computer complex and with each other by 80,000 miles of wire. NASDAQ connections exist in the United States and in 36 other countries; it is truly an international market.

Market makers are securities firms that function much like mini-exchanges in one or a number of stock issues. Many securities firms may choose to make a market in the shares of large corporations. The market maker, through his NASDAQ connection, posts the highest prices he is willing to pay for a limited number of shares and the lowest prices at which he is willing to sell. Larger numbers of shares must be negotiated. Prices for a corporation's shares may be called up on any participant's NASDAQ screen. A broker interested in trading can compare prices from several market makers to find the one best price, either buying or selling, for his or her client.

When an order for an OTC stock from the market maker's own firm reaches the trading desk—a central point under the direction of one or more experienced employees (known as traders) who work from computer screens and are trained to match buy-and-sell orders and set prices according to their judgment and the availability of shares—the trader may go in either of two directions. If the firm maintains an inventory of shares, the trader may sell shares out of that inventory or buy shares to build that inventory, but only if prices are equal to or better than prices being offered by other market makers through the NASDAQ system. If the shares are sold out of inventory, the firm charges a fee. If the trader finds lower bids or higher offers elsewhere after consulting his computer screen, he contacts the outside market maker and completes the trade. A Small Order Execution System (SOES) completes trades of 1,000 shares or less automatically at the best available price throughout the NASDAQ system. The SOES selects the market maker with the best prices by surveying all offers and bids. Executions (completions of orders) can be confirmed in 60 seconds or less on SOES.

The NASDAQ system began operations in February 1971 and includes companies of all types and sizes within and outside the United States. Many foreign corporations, including well-known corporations in England, Japan, and Australia, trade their securities in the OTC market. Nearly 200 foreign securities and 100 American Depositary Receipts (ADRs) accounted for about 2.5 billion shares traded annually.

Firms that want to trade their stocks on the NASDAQ system must qualify for participation by meeting minimum limitations on the number of shareholders, net worth, and assets. Typically, a company must have sold stock to at least 1,000 shareholders and issued at least 2 million shares of stock. This limitation aims to avoid stock manipulation. Companies need not prove profitability to meet NASDAQ requirements.

Nationally traded NASDAQ issues are reported daily in *The Wall Street Journal* and *Investor's Daily*. Local newspapers may report prices for issues of local interest only rather than all issues on NASDAQ.

● The National Quotation Bureau, Inc. issues bid (the price a buyer is willing to pay) and asked (the price an owner is willing to sell for) prices for publicly traded corporations too small to meet NASDAQ minimum listing requirements. Daily quotes are distributed to subscribing brokers on long, narrow sheets of pink paper, which give the bureau its slang name of **"pink sheets."** The pink sheets list corporations alphabetically along with the names of those securities dealers who make a market in that corporation's stock. A broker wishing to buy or sell shares of a corporation listed on the pink sheets must contact one or more of the market makers directly; there is no computer link to display prices on a screen. If more than one securities dealer makes a market in the company's stocks, the broker must check at least three dealers to be sure he finds the best prices. The National Quotation Bureau also issues a series of yellow sheets for bonds, listing the market makers dealing with the specific issues of bonds.

While a listing on the pink sheets affords a corporation some visibility by alerting brokers to market makers, having to call for information rather than pulling the data onto a computer screen reduces the off-NASDAQ market's efficiency. As a result, executing a trade for a stock listed on the pink sheets may require more than a few minutes and possibly as long as several days. In addition, due to the difficulties brokers encounter in locating market makers with shares available, trading costs tend to be higher. Market makers may not hold shares of small companies in their inventory. They may operate on a **make-out basis;** that is, they may compile a list of shareholders willing to sell shares or buyers willing to buy if prices are right. When an order comes in, the broker contacts those shareholders or buyers to see if a trade can be arranged. Not holding inventory slows the trading process but it reduces the capital needed by the market maker. A round-trip execution—that is, a buy and a subsequent sell—incurs three costs: the buy commission, the spread (or difference) between bid and offer prices, and the sell commission.

Commodities, Futures, and Options Exchanges

Commodities trading began in post-revolutionary war times. It prospered because it served the economic interests of growers and users of produce and other commodities. Futures contracts and listed options trading are more recent developments, dating only to the early 1970s, in response to an economic need for risk management.

A basic element of the commodities, futures, and options markets is the **open outcry** auction system of bringing buyers and sellers together, a distinctly different system than the stock exchange's specialist system. Arrayed in elevated steps around a center, called the pit, traders call or shout offers to buy or sell as they attempt to find someone willing to take the opposite side of an offered trade. If you have visited an auction market or seen one on TV, you are familiar with the apparently chaotic shouts, raised arms, and hand signals. During spirited sessions, the trader who shouts the loudest may be the one who makes the trade. The continuous action moves swiftly and efficiently.

The open outcry market has been compared to a scale. Offers to buy move the market to a level where sellers are willing to sell; offers to sell move the market to a level where buyers will buy—old-fashioned supply and demand meeting head-on. Trades are made and recorded within seconds and transferred almost instantaneously to participants off the floor. Futures for commodities, currencies, and stock indexes have proved risky but enormously popular. They are mainly for professionals and institutions. Individuals participate in these fast-moving markets much less than in the markets for stocks and bonds.

There are eight major markets in commodities, futures, and options.

● The Chicago Board of Trade (CBOT) trades commodities and financial futures and options. A group of 82 financiers, traders, and farmers gathered in 1848 to form the CBOT, the first organized U.S. futures exchange. In 1865 the CBOT set up standard sizes and specifications for commodities agreements, called futures contracts. For example, grains are traded at a specified number of bushels. The CBOT also initiated the margin system requiring traders to put up a certain amount of cash (the margin) as evidence of good faith to assure that buyers and sellers would honor these futures contracts. Over the years, trading expanded from the basic grains, wheat, corn, and oats, to U.S. Treasury instruments, energy, stock indexes, metals, and foreign currencies. Volume expanded rapidly with financial futures and options trading nearly 100 million contracts in 1987.

The CBOT consists of more than 3,000 individuals representing brokerage firms, financial and banking institutions, commercial grain exporters and processors, and independent trading firms. A staff of more than 500 people work at the exchange to ensure efficient and orderly markets. All trades at the CBOT are settled by the Board of Trade Clearing Corporation (CC), an independent organization that assures the integrity of the marketplace by reconciling member accounts daily. U.S. government surveillance is handled by the Commodity Futures Trading Commission.

Affiliated with the CBOT are the Chicago Rice and Cotton Exchange (CRCE) and the MidAmerica Commodity Exchange (MidAm). The MidAm affords an opportunity for smaller players to engage in commodities trading.

Rough rice is traded on the CRCE as part of the CBOT. Since rice is the staple grain for about 2.5 billion people in countries around the world, rice trading is truly global. About 40 percent of the rice grown in the United States is exported, mainly in trades through the CRCE.

• The Chicago Mercantile Exchange (Chicago Merc) trades futures and options in agricultural commodities, foreign currencies, interest rates, and the Standard & Poor's 500 Index (S&P 500). Agricultural commodities include cattle, hogs, and lumber; financial futures and options include contracts on interest rates and the S&P 500.

The Chicago Merc began in May 1874 as the Chicago Produce Exchange to provide a market for butter, eggs, poultry, and other farm products. A dissident group of traders split off in 1895 to form the Chicago Butter and Egg Board. This market expanded to include other commodities and changed its name to the Chicago Mercantile Exchange in September 1919. The Chicago Merc Clearing House also appeared in 1919 but operates as a separate entity, similar to the CC. It wasn't until after World War II that the Chicago Merc began trading in turkeys and then added apples, egg futures, and iron and steel scrap. On September 10, 1961, the Chicago Merc began trading futures in pork bellies (frozen slabs of uncured, unsliced bacon). Live cattle and hog contracts were added in the 1960s, and financial futures began trading in the 1970s.

Chicago's two major commodities, futures, and options exchanges, the CBOT and the Chicago Merc, account for about 75 percent of the futures trading in the United States. Of the 313 million contracts traded in the United States in 1989, 243 million were traded on the floors of the CBOT and the Chicago Merc. Globex, an international expansion of Chicago's commodities, futures, and options trading, is an integrated network of 165,000 terminals in 118 countries that ties markets together wherever they exist. Through the Chicago Merc and Globex, trading goes on throughout the world 24 hours a day.

• The New York Futures Exchange (NYFE) is one of the newest exchanges in the United States. The NYFE was incorporated as a wholly owned subsidiary of the NYSE on April 5, 1979, and began trading on August 7, 1980. Its most successful product is the NYSE Composite Index Futures (NYSE CIF). Currently the NYFE trades five contracts:

1. NYSE CIF, the second most heavily traded futures contract on U.S. markets. The NYSE CIF is based on the NYSE Composite Index.
2. Options on the NYSE CIF, another way to trade on anticipated moves of the general market.

3. Commodities Research Bureau (CRB) Index Futures, based on the CRB's Price Index.
4. Options on CRB Index Futures, another way to trade on anticipated moves of the commodities markets.
5. U.S. Treasury Bond Futures, a hedging mechanism and a trading opportunity for anticipated changes in the interest rates on U.S. Treasury securities.

Futures and options on futures of broadly based stock indexes permit major institutions, such as pension funds and bank trust departments, to hedge the value of the portfolios in the same way that the miller hedges the price of wheat by locking in to the current price in a futures contract. **Program traders** trade groups of securities against a futures contract for those securities, an arbitrage strategy limited to sophisticated professionals with complicated computer programs and millions of dollars at their disposal for short periods. Program trading is not for individuals.

• Commodity Exchange, Inc. (COMEX) is the world's most active metals market. It is the dominant exchange for gold, silver, and copper futures and options trading in the United States, and it is the only U.S. exchange trading aluminum futures. The COMEX is a major force in the world's gold market and holds a prominent place in international markets. In addition to their usual role of hedging and speculating, metals futures markets provide a visible gauge for prices of gold, silver, copper, and other metals.

The COMEX, a relative old-timer among specialty exchanges, started on July 5, 1933. The COMEX resulted from the merger of four older exchanges—National Metal Exchange, Rubber Exchange of New York, National Raw Silk Exchange, and New York Hide Exchange. Like the other exchanges, the COMEX has its COMEX Clearing Association, Inc. for the clearance of every trade executed on the trading floor and to assure the integrity of the COMEX market. The auction market uses the open outcry method for sellers to get together with buyers at mutually agreeable prices. As an intermediary, the COMEX Clearing Association itself becomes the ultimate buyer to every seller and seller to every buyer.

A total of 772 seats on the COMEX are held by individuals acting for firms who must pledge adequate financial backing to assure integrity of the market. The COMEX shares its 22,000-square-foot trading floor in the World Trade Center with four other futures exchanges: New York Mercantile Exchange; Coffee, Sugar, and Cocoa Exchange; New York Cotton Exchange; and New York Futures Exchange.

• The New York Mercantile Exchange (NYMEX) was founded in 1872, primarily to market agricultural products. A move to diversify brought in a platinum futures contract in 1956 and a palladium contract in 1968. Expansion took off rapidly when the NYMEX moved into oil and oil products, offering its first futures contract for heating oil in 1978. Just as the COMEX is heavily into metals, the NYMEX offers energy futures in crude oil, gasoline, heating oil, propane, residual fuel oil, and natural gas. The NYMEX also trades options on crude oil, heating oil, and gasoline. Due to the preeminence of oil as a primary energy source in the world, the NYMEX is now the third largest futures exchange in the

United States. NYMEX ownership is shared among 816 memberships, or seats.

• The Coffee, Sugar, and Cocoa Exchange, Inc. (CSCE) began in 1882 as the Coffee Exchange of the City of New York. It began trading sugar futures in 1914 and changed its name to the New York Coffee and Sugar Exchange in 1916. Separately, the New York Cocoa Exchange was founded in 1925 to trade cocoa futures. In 1979 the two exchanges merged. The CSCE began trading options on futures for sugar in 1982 and added similar options on cocoa and coffee in 1986. In addition to its contract for raw sugar, the CSCE added a futures contract on refined (white) sugar in 1987 because of the price variability between raw and refined sugar.

In 1989 the CSCE expanded into financial futures with a contract based on the International Market Index (IMI). Volume has grown rapidly, with the CSCE trading 11,217,844 contracts in 1989, almost double the number of contracts traded only three years before.

• The New York Cotton Exchange (NYCE), a mini-conglomerate exchange, is the oldest commodities exchange in New York, founded in 1870 by a group of cotton brokers and merchants. In addition to cotton futures and options, the NYCE trades frozen concentrated orange juice futures and options through an affiliate, the Citrus Associates. Another division of the NYCE is FINEX, organized in 1985 as a financial futures and options market.

FINEX trades futures and options in two international currency indexes, the United States Dollar Index (USDX) and the ECU. The USDX provides the most accurate statistics available on the value of the U.S. dollar, using a weighted average of 10 world currencies: German deutsche mark, Japanese yen, French franc, British pound, Canadian dollar, Italian lira, Netherlands guilder, Belgian franc, Swedish krona, and Swiss franc. The USDX spot value (instantaneous market value) is updated continuously 24 hours a day. Exporters and importers use the USDX in multinational trading to hedge currencies for risk control.

The ECU is a basket of 12 currencies of the 12 member nations of the European Economic Community. In addition to the major countries represented in the USDX, the ECU includes the currencies of Luxembourg, Denmark, Greece, Ireland, Spain, and Portugal. The ECU is also a weighted average, with Germany, France, and England carrying the major percentages of the ECU's value. The ECU futures contract affords the opportunity for hedging currency value changes between the United States and Europe and will probably assume an important role in trading when the European Economic Community integrates in 1992.

FINEX also trades Five-Year U.S. Treasury Note (FYTR) futures and options and Two-Year U.S. Treasury Note (2YTN) futures. Futures trading of U.S. Treasury Notes enables institutions to hedge interest rates.

• The Kansas City Board of Trade (KCBT) claims to be the world's predominant marketplace for the hard red winter wheat that grows in the plains of the Midwest and provides much of the flour for bread baked around the world. The KCBT also trades sorghum and sorghum futures. The KCBT uses the KCBT Clearing Corporation for matching trades and assuring that buyers' and sellers' records agree.

The KCBT began in 1856 when a group of Kansas City merchants assembled as a chamber of commerce. Operations halted during the Civil War but picked up again in 1869. In 1982 the KCBT began trading Value Line Index financial futures and a year later added a Mini Value Line Index futures contract. Options on Kansas City wheat futures were offered in 1984 and sorghum futures began trading in 1989.

Small auction markets continue to operate in communities around the United States. Livestock auctions occur regularly in many local arenas. Specialty markets for seeds and small crops of peas or beans may also function to serve specific needs. While these limited local markets bring buyers and sellers together, they are not generally a part of Wall Street.

Assessing the Risks and Returns of an Investment

Investors who buy stocks, bonds, commodities, futures, and options engage in transactions with varied levels of risk that can be measured several ways.

Volatility

The **volatility** of a security's price is a measure of risk. A security's price runs up when buyers bid for shares and declines when sellers offer more shares than buyers are willing to accept. The high-low range for prices of stocks appears daily in financial newspapers, indicating the difference between the extremes. A recent 12-month range for General Motors common stock was $50\frac{1}{2}$ high and $30\frac{3}{8}$ low. The position of a current price in relation to the high-low range offers investors some idea of how risky an investment might be. A price of 40 for General Motors on a specific day would indicate a middle position.

Beta is another measure of volatility. Beta is an index that relates a stock's or mutual fund's volatility to the volatility of the S&P 500, which is a measure of how the market is moving. The base of the beta index is 100. For example, if a stock's volatility rates a beta of 120, the stock is likely to rise 20 percent faster than the S&P 500 during an uptrending, or rising, market and decline 20 percent faster than the S&P 500 during a downtrending, or declining, market. A stock with a beta of .80 moves up and down more slowly than the S&P 500. Calculations of volatility and beta are available in Standard and Poor's reviews of individual stocks and mutual funds. The American Association of Individual Investors (AAII) also publishes betas of mutual funds in their annual *The Individual Investor's Guide to No-Load Mutual Funds* (see Resources).

Volatility introduces the risk that you might buy a stock or other security at a high price and see that price decline. Most volatility risks are relative; that is, you may lose or gain some portion of an investment according to the direction of prices, but you are unlikely to lose all of your investment.

Loss Potential

Loss potential represents the risk of losing all of one's investment. More options, for example, expire worthless than deliver a profit. When an option remains unprofit-able at its expiration, it no longer has any value. Stocks of companies that go bank-rupt may also become worthless, but the chances of stocks losing all of their value are less than with options and futures. **Limited partnerships** may turn up worth-less, as they represent an **equity,** or own-ership interest, in real estate, oil drilling, and similar deals. Most partnerships are highly leveraged; that is, a small part of the value may be equity and the remainder is debt. When a partnership goes sour, and many do, debt positions are secured by whatever assets the entity may own, and little is left over for the partners.

Yield, Appreciation, Cost, and Liquidity

Characteristics of securities vary, and risk is only one. Four other characteristics that influence security transactions and inves-tor interest are yield, appreciation, cost, and liquidity.

Yield represents a regular return on a security without reference to any potential gain in capital value. **Appreciation** rep-resents the potential for gain or loss of cap-ital without regard to any regular income the security might provide. Cost is the ex-pense incurred in acquiring a security. Li-quidity is a measure of how quickly a se-curity may be sold or redeemed at a reasonable price without disturbing the market.

In Table 1A a number of potential in-vestment opportunities are rated accord-ing to the five characteristics on a numer-ical scale from 1 through 10. A rating of 1 indicates a good rating. A rating of 10

means the security fares poorly relative to that characteristic. For example, the risk of a bank savings account that is insured by the Federal Deposit Insurance Corpo-ration (FDIC) is minimal and rates a 1—no risk. It rates a 10 for appreciation, how-ever, as the capital value cannot increase. A bank savings account rates a 1 in cost because the bank charges nothing for tak-ing your deposit. Buying shares of a stock incurs a commission, and that is a cost; therefore the cost rating is higher. A sav-ings account rates a 1 for liquidity because money can be withdrawn at any time the bank is open without cost and without af-fecting the rate of interest the bank pays on similar accounts.

The ratings compiled by the author in Table 1A are for illustration only. Ratings are highly judgmental for their absolute value and their value relative to other se-curities. While there are no right or wrong answers, the ratings provide a rough guide to help investors select securities for investment. Generally, investments with low total scores have more favorable char-acteristics than investments with high to-tal scores. However, if you are looking for more income or total return, you may be willing to assume higher risks or less li-quidity in exchange for more yield and/or appreciation. Obviously, differences of opinion affect every aspect of the market, and it is the consensus of opinions that drives the market up or down.

Investments and Taxes

Tax-advantaged investments come in two varieties—those that offer totally tax-free benefits and those that offer tax-deferred

TABLE 1A	RISKS AND BENEFITS: RATINGS OF INVESTMENT VEHICLES*					
	CHARACTERISTIC					
	Risk	Yield	Appreciation	Cost	Liquidity	Score
Bank/S&L Savings Account	1	7	10	1	1	20
EE-Bond	1	5	10	1	3	20
U.S. Treasury Bond	3	4	8	3	2	20
Corporate Bonds	6	3	4	6	4	23
Common Stocks—Listed	5	8	3	4	3	23
Common Stocks—OTC	7	9	2	6	5	29
Mutual Funds, Load	4	6	4	8	2	24
Mutual Funds, No-Load	4	6	4	1	2	17
Mutual Funds, No-Load with Timing**	3	6	3	1	2	15
Preferred Stocks	5	5	5	4	4	23
Real Estate	10	8	1	8	10	37
Stock Options	10	10	1	3	4	28
Futures Options	10	10	1	3	4	28
Commodities	8	10	1	3	4	26
Gold	8	10	4	6	6	34
Limited Partnerships	10	4	10	10	10	44
Insurance, Cash Value	3	8	10	8	10	39
Insurance, Tax-deferred Annuity	3	5	10	8	10	36

* Sample evaluations of risks and benefits.
** Market timing is a defensive strategy for limiting market losses.

benefits. Both can be advantageous to investors.

Totally tax-free benefits can accrue to investors who buy municipal bonds (muni-bonds). Interest from muni-bonds is not subject to tax at the federal level and is free of state tax for investors who reside in states without personal income tax. In exchange for their tax-free status, the yields from muni-bonds are lower than taxable bonds with comparable risks.

Tax-deferred investments are those sheltered under one of the umbrellas set up to encourage savings. An Individual Retirement Account, popularly known as an **IRA,** is not an investment; it is merely an umbrella that protects a variety of investments from income taxes for specified periods. Investments under the IRA umbrella may be stocks, bonds, mutual funds, and some forms of real estate but not collectibles, such as gold coins. A **Keogh plan** is similar to an IRA but is limited to self-employed persons. Both an IRA and a Keogh are administered by a trustee who holds the securities. You, as an investor with an IRA, may elect to manage the portfolio, in which case, the IRA is self-directed. Or, you may simply turn your contributions over to a trustee who manages the account and decides where your money will be invested. Many banks, financial planners, mutual funds, and insurance companies can offer information on these shelters. IRS Publication 590, available free from IRS offices and form distribution centers, details the rules and tax consequences for IRAs.

Companies may allow employees to defer income and avoid taxes on that income until withdrawal under a 401(k) plan. Typically, an employee agrees to defer receipt of a portion of his income, usually in the range of 1 percent to 10 percent, and the company matches that contribution with a 50 percent, or other percentage, amount. The 401(k) fund may offer options for investment in fixed-income, equity, or a mixed bag of securities. The company manages the 401(k) fund for participants.

Nonprofit and government organizations may offer a 403(b) plan to employees that is similar to the 401(k) plans for corporations. The plan for both deferred compensation programs is the same: to defer income tax until it is withdrawn at retirement or termination.

Tax-deferred income grows (compounds) faster because a tax bite is not taken out of the proceeds each year. Tax-free compounding, rather than immediate deductibility, is the major benefit of IRAs, Keoghs, and deferred compensation programs. Since the money that goes into these tax-deferred programs is not taxed at the outset, all withdrawals of original contributions plus earnings, are fully taxed. All of the tax-deferred programs include requirements for mandatory withdrawals, usually beginning in the year participants reach $70\frac{1}{2}$ years of age. The purpose of the mandatory withdrawals is to permit the IRS to tax the funds, based on the individual's federal and state personal tax rates. Tax-deferral from whatever source is a major benefit for investors. Plan to use these shelters if you expect to profit from Wall Street.

Conclusion

Wall Street functions as a metaphor for financial activity. Markets in New York and other places around the United States are part of Wall Street—a convenient term that embodies millions of persons and their money. At times Wall Street is blamed for the ills that sometimes afflict our economy. At other times Wall Street leads the way in economic forecasting and movement of the economy.

PART ONE

SECURITIES

CHAPTER TWO

Stocks

KEY TERMS FOR THIS CHAPTER

stock certificate	*convertible*	*arbitrageur*
shareholder	*P/E ratio*	*discounting*
common stock	*buy-back*	*ADRs*
dividends	*float*	*stock split*
preferred stock	*tender offer*	*penny stocks*

The basic element of the stock market is stock. Simple enough, but what is it? What you see is a piece of paper called a **stock certificate,** which represents ownership of a share or many shares in a corporation. If you own shares in ABC Corporation, you own a fraction of that company. You and other stockholders, who may be individuals or institutions, own the corporation. Another term for stockholder is **shareholder;** that is, a person who holds one or more shares of stock in a corporation. Whatever the corporation owns, you buy a piece of it when you buy stock.

Why Stocks?

A business may be as small as one person, often called a sole proprietorship. Many small businesses may employ a few or many employees and take in thousands, possibly millions, of dollars. Sole proprietorships, however, generally remain small businesses because their access to capital is limited to the resources of the owner. Proprietorships are popular among professionals who offer services, such as doctors, accountants, landscape architects, house painters, or any number of other trades. Service-oriented businesses require little capital to get started, and proprietorships are simple to start. You simply proclaim your intent to do business. You may need to get a tax number or a license for certain kinds of services, but then you're set.

As the needs for capital expand beyond the resources of one person, two or more people may join in a partnership. Partnerships can create problems, but they offer access to more capital.

Big business and big organizations require immense quantities of capital. A single person would experience great difficulty in rounding up enough money to build a steel plant, start an airline, or open a department store. So, an entrepreneur creates a corporation and sells shares to acquire the capital needed to build the business. Each person who invests receives an ownership share in the business. With an almost unlimited number of people able and willing to buy stock, the new corporation can raise millions, even billions, of dollars. Here is an example that illustrates the steps for building a corporation.

How a Company Goes Public

Bill D. is an engineer with a burning ambition to become his own boss. He uses his engineering talent to search for a product he can manufacture and sell, and finally he creates a device which he calls the Blipp. The Blipp is a useful tool likely to interest every homeowner, and the potential market for sales is enormous. As Bill develops the first Blipps in his basement workshop, he begins thinking about the steps needed to build more Blipps and about how to market them. He takes the first dozen Blipps to local hardware stores to test the market. The Blipps sell right away, and the stores order more. Bill is on to a hot product, but he has spent a big chunk of his available savings getting the test products to market.

Bill needs more money to buy machinery for manufacturing the Blipps, to rent or buy a building in which to produce them, to hire a salesperson to contact hardware stores all over the country, and to pay for all the other costs of expanding the business, so he forms a corporation. A corporation must be chartered by the state government; that is, the state creates what amounts to a synthetic person who can sell products, pay employees, sell shares to raise capital, and generally function as if the corporation were a real person. Bill hires an attorney who prepares the forms and paperwork needed for a charter and applies to the secretary of state where he lives. Once he receives the charter to operate his corporation, Bill contacts his friends to offer them shares in the new Blipp, Inc. Bill is permitted to offer only limited numbers of shares to original investors. These friends, or others with money looking for a chance to profit if Blipp, Inc. prospers, may buy shares; but they cannot resell them until the corporation goes public.

Using the funds from the sale of shares, Blipp, Inc. buys machinery and expands the business. Profits (the money left over from sales after all expenses have been paid) are plowed back into the business to expand it further. A business that grows by reinvesting its profits is said to "pull itself up by its bootstraps."

Blipp, Inc. continues to grow. In addition to Blipps, Bill develops Glipps and Klipps. The firm needs more capital to expand. Bill's circle of friends decline to invest any more of their savings for a variety of reasons. Bill would like to take some of his ownership interest or equity out of the business, so Blipp, Inc. decides to go public.

In order to sell shares to the general public and create a market for Blipp shares, Bill hires financing specialists who document the purposes and history of Blipp, Inc. and develop a prospectus for submission to the Securities and Exchange Commission (SEC). Prior to the official offering date, the selling group, a collection of brokerages, issues a "red herring," a preliminary prospectus with all the details of the offering except the share price, date, and disposition of proceeds from the sale (see box, pages 30–31). The purpose of the preliminary prospectus is to drum up interest among potential buyers of the stock. When the SEC approves the proposal, including the wording of the prospectus, the shares of stock become registered and available for sale to the public.

Bill originally issued 2,000 shares: 750 to himself, 250 to his friends, and 1,000 in reserve. Since he owns 75 percent of Blipp, Inc., Bill decides to sell 200 of his shares plus 800 unissued shares. He hires a stock brokerage firm to underwrite the new stock, called an Initial Public Offering (IPO). The underwriter, who purchases the stock with a view to offering it to the public, may contact a number of similar firms to collect a selling group.

Before the stock is sold, the Blipp, Inc. Board of Directors votes to split the stock 1,000-for-1—that is, one of the original shares is now 1,000 shares and the total number of shares available for sale is 1,000,000 (200,000 shares owned by Bill and 800,000 shares of previously unissued stock). Other owners do not participate in the sale, although their shares are also split 1,000-for-1. As part of the recapitalization, the number of new split shares may be expanded to 10 million shares. The IPO may be 1,000,000 shares with 800,000 shares being sold by the company and 200,000 shares coming from Bill's original ownership shares. If the IPO is priced at $10 per share, Blipp, Inc. acquires $8 million of new capital and Bill ends up with $2 million in cash.

When the new shares are bought by clients of the underwriter, a market appears for the shares. Some of Bill's friends may then decide to sell their shares, and they contact a stockbroker to offer their shares for sale. By doing this, they may get some or all of their money out of the corporation, hopefully at a substantial profit, but Blipp, Inc. does not benefit directly from the sale of this stock. One of the essential objectives of the IPO, to establish a market for the stock of Blipp, Inc., has been accomplished.

Different Types of Stock

As corporations grew, stock markets expanded, more investors flooded into the market, and a demand for different kinds of stock arose. Corporations issue different classes of stock for a variety of reasons, and various investors may be interested in these stocks, also for different reasons. Two basic types of stock are available: common stock and preferred stock.

PROSPECTUS

**SUBJECT TO COMPLETION
DATED MONTH 00, 1992**

1,000,000 Shares

BLIPP, Inc.

Class A Common Stock

Of the 1,000,000 shares of Class A Common Stock offered hereby, 800,000 are being offered by the Company and 200,000 by the Selling Shareholders. See "Principal and Selling Shareholders." The company will not receive any proceeds from the sale of shares by the Selling Shareholders. Prior to this offering, there has been no public market for the Common Stock of the Company. It is currently estimated that the initial public offering price will be between $10.00 and $12.00 per share. See "Underwriting" for information relating to the determination of the initial public offering price.

Blipp has only outstanding Class A Common Stock.

**THESE SECURITIES HAVE NOT BEEN APPROVED OR DISAPPROVED BY THE
SECURITIES AND EXCHANGE COMMISSION OR ANY STATE SECURITIES
COMMISSION NOR HAS ANY SUCH COMMISSION PASSED UPON THE
ACCURACY OR ADEQUACY OF THIS PROSPECTUS. ANY REPRESENTATION TO
THE CONTRARY IS A CRIMINAL OFFENSE.**

	Price to Public	Underwriting Discount	Proceeds to Company (1)	Proceeds to Selling Shareholders (2)
Per Share . . .	$	$	$	$
Total (2)	$	$	$	$

(1) Before deducting expenses payable by the Company and the Selling Shareholders, estimated at $ and $, respectively.

(2) The Selling Shareholders have granted the Underwriters a 30-day option to purchase up to 100,000 additional shares to cover over-allotments, if any. If the option is exercised in full, the total Price to Public, Underwriting Discount, and Proceeds to Selling Shareholders will be $, and $, respectively.

The Class A Common Stock is offered by the Underwriters when, as, and if delivered to and accepted by them and subject to their right to reject any order in whole or in part. It is expected that delivery of the certificates for the Class A Common Stock will be made on or about , 1992 through Blank Trust Company or at the offices of Brokers & Brokers, Incorporated, Some Town, USA.

Brokers & Brokers, Inc.

(Continued on p. 31)

The date of this Prospectus is Month 00, 1992.

"Red herring"
notification

Information contained herein is subject to completion or amendment. A registration statement relating to these securities has been filed with the Securities and Exchange Commission. These securities may not be sold nor may offers to buy be accepted prior to the time the registration statement becomes effective. This prospectus shall not constitute an offer to sell or the solicitation of an offer to buy nor shall there be any sale of these securities in any State in which such offer, solicitation, or sale would be unlawful prior to registration or qualification under the securities laws of any State.

Common Stock

Common stock represents ownership interest. Owners of common stock own the corporation. They may vote on numerous decisions affecting the corporation (including a decision to sell or merge with another corporation) and elect a board of directors, who, in turn, hire managers to run the business.

A majority shareholder is one who owns over 50 percent of the outstanding (issued) shares in a corporation and, thus, can call the shots. All other shareholders are minority shareholders. With ordinary common stock, the standard is one share, one vote.

In large corporations no single person or organization owns anywhere near a majority interest. In large, publicly owned corporations a shareholder with as little as 10 percent of the shares may control the corporation effectively. If things go badly, a coalition of so-called dissident shareholders may gather enough votes to replace the existing board of directors; the new board may fire the existing manage-

ment and bring in their own management team.

Dividends, a distribution of the firm's earnings, may be paid on common stock at the option of the board of directors. Every dividend, whether paid in cash or additional shares of stock, must be declared—that is, passed in a resolution at an official meeting of the board of directors—even if a dividend has been paid every quarter for the past 50 years. Many companies with stock outstanding pay no dividends, preferring to expand operations by reinvesting earnings instead of borrowing, floating (or issuing) bonds, or issuing more shares of stock. Ordinarily, as a corporation grows and matures, it will pay dividends; that is one reason investors buy stock.

Companies may issue more than one class of common stock; each class carries a different set of privileges. The classes are usually noted as Class A, Class B, and Class C. A Class A common stock may include full voting privileges. A Class B stock issued by the same company may participate in dividends but not be eligible to vote on the election of board members or other issues. A Class C stock may be issued for some special purpose. Limiting the voting rights to certain shareholders keeps control within a family or entrenched management and may be a tool to prevent takeovers. Different classes of stock will probably exhibit a wide variation in market prices for shares; for instance, Class A stock may sell at twice the price of Class B stock.

Preferred Stock

Preferred stock offers investors a different type of security and may be issued only after common stock has been issued. The term "preferred" applies to two conditions.

1. Preferred stockholders gain preferential treatment in the matter of dividends; that is, they receive a fixed rate of dividends prior to the payment of dividends on common shares.
2. If the company goes out of business or liquidates, preferred stockholders are closer to the front of the line than common stockholders when distributing the company's assets. In line ahead of preferred stockholders are secured creditors and bondholders.

A preferred stock may be issued in a par amount, for example, $100 par with a percentage figure for the fixed dividend, as in Par 100, 12 percent—a $12 dividend yearly on a Par 100 preferred stock. Par is a term useful mainly in determining the book value of a company, one method of valuing how much a corporation is worth. The dividend may also simply be stated as a specified amount per share. However stated, the amount payable does not change regardless of what may happen to the share price.

If the company runs into hard times, there may be no cash to pay the preferred dividend, and the board will refuse to authorize payment. A preferred stock may be noted as cumulative, however, which means that dividends not paid in the past must be made up before any dividends are paid to common stockholders. If a preferred stock is noncumulative, any past dividends are lost forever. Even though a dividend is fixed, the board of directors must pass a motion to pay it each time. Share prices vary according to the risk that the dividend might not be paid and the general interest rate environment.

Solid, creditworthy corporations may issue preferred stock, which assumes the status of a bond, by which a corporation borrows money with one difference—bond interest must be paid or the issue is in default. (See Chapter 3 for definition of bonds.) A continuing default on a bond issue could throw the corporation into involuntary bankruptcy. Unlike bond issues, preferred stock dividends will not affect the company's operations or solvency if not paid, but a nonpayment would likely affect the price of the preferred stock.

Preferred stock may also be **convertible.** Under some conditions, such as a stated conversion price (common stock at $50 per share, for example) or within a stated time limit, a share of preferred stock may be converted into one or more shares of common stock at a prescribed ratio. Why would anyone want to convert from an advantaged position as the owner of preferred stock to a lesser position as a common stockholder? If the company has prospered, earnings on the common stock may exceed those fixed payments assigned to preferred shares. As earnings mount, so does the price of the common shares. At some point, switching from preferred stock to common stock could sharply increase the dollar value of one's holdings.

Corporations may issue a number of different preferred stocks, each with a different dividend or different features, such as a cumulative dividend and/or conversion feature. Corporations add on the cumulative or conversion features to enhance the marketability of the issue. Utility companies, particularly, are prone to float different issues as their need for capital to expand production facilities seems never ending. Each issue is distinguished by its dividend rate and specific features. In 1991 the Pennsylvania Power & Light Co., for example, had one class of common stock outstanding and three issues of preferred stock, all listed on the New York Stock Exchange (NYSE). The three issues of preferred stock paid dividends of $4.40, $4.50, and $8.60, with share prices on one day at $49, $48.75, and $90.25, respectively. Investors were buying income at slightly different rates, according to that day's quotes, in the same way that a bank patron buys income of $60 by investing in a certificate of deposit costing $1,000 and paying 6 percent.

Stock Prices

How much is a stock worth? Whatever a buyer will pay for it. Supply and demand are the final determinants of price. The number of buyers in the market and how much stock is available determine the price at which a specific trade occurs. A high price brings out more shares for sale, and a large supply depresses prices. The following two anecdotes say it all: When asked what the market was likely to do, J. P. Morgan was said to have commented, "It will fluctuate." Another market watcher was asked why the market declined on a certain day. His comment—"More sellers than buyers."

The overall market and its actions affect individual stocks. The cliché of Wall Street is that "a rising tide lifts all boats." Overall market action may result from a real or perceived change in interest rates, a forecast by an acknowledged economist, major political action in some part of the world (such as the invasion of Kuwait by Iraq in the summer of 1990), a report that the president has had a heart attack, or some anomaly like the January effect, a well-documented tendency for stock prices to rise in January.

Despite the many explanations forthcoming from learned pundits and market watchers, no one really knows why prices advance or retreat—the market appears to have a mind of its own. Stock analysts tend to agree that about 70 percent of an individual stock's price movement may be due to the overall market level of prices on any specific day, with 30 percent of the price movement due to the characteristics of the individual stock itself. In any day's trading, some stocks rise and some fall. Prices reflect the sum total of millions of individual buying and selling decisions. Every transaction involves a buyer and a seller, each with obviously different perceptions of the value of a specific stock. If this difference of opinion didn't exist, there would be no trading. A particular stock's price reflects a number of perceptions of its value by traders and investors:

• Price/earnings ratio, or **P/E ratio,** is a common measure of a stock's value. A stock's P/E ratio is the price of the stock at closing on a specific day divided by the stock's earnings for the previous 12 months. If the closing price for XYZ Corporation is $75 per share and the earnings reported for the previous 12 months are $5, then the P/E ratio is 15. A P/E ratio of 15 to 20 is fairly typical. A higher P/E ratio indicates that share prices are outstripping value; it indicates a perception that a company will grow rapidly in the future. *The Wall Street Journal, Investor's Daily,* and other financial periodicals include the figures for listed stocks in daily, weekly, and monthly reports. As prices change daily, so do the P/E ratios. Even if the price remains constant, the P/E ratio could change if the company reports lower or higher earnings than expected.

• Price/dividend ratio will ordinarily be a lower number than the P/E ratio, because few companies pay out all of their earnings as dividends. Ordinarily you must compute the price/dividend ratio by dividing the dividend paid by the closing price. An annual dividend of $2 per share amounts to a 4 percent yield if the closing price of the stock is $50.

• Investors place different values on various types of corporations' performance. The stock of a power company, for example, may be evaluated as an income producer, much like a bond. Utility companies typically pay out a substantial part of their earnings as dividends in order to attract new capital. As a result, income-oriented investors "buy an income stream" when they invest in utility or other high-dividend stocks. Growth stocks, on the other hand, offer investors the possibility that share prices will escalate to produce capital gains.

• Dividend action by the board of directors can influence a company's stock prices. If the dividend is increased, the stock appeals to income-oriented investors. The stock price rises for two reasons: The higher dividend is worth more, and a pattern of increasing dividends attracts long-term investors who may be retired and living off the income stream. Rising dividends tend to counter some of the effects of inflation. Some utility companies have a record of raising their dividends every year for 20, 25, 30, or more years, usually in the range of 3 percent to 6 percent each year.

Not all dividend actions are positive. A board may cut a dividend or eliminate it entirely if the company loses money on its operations. Losing an income stream will lead many investors to sell, causing the stock price to decline. Other shareholders may bail out of the stock because cutting or eliminating the dividend is an indication that the business is doing poorly. Very few people may be interested in buying the shares of a company that is experiencing difficulties and is forced, by a lack of profits and/or cash flow, to forego or reduce a dividend, but a lower price may attract certain buyers. Some stock buyers look for bargains—stocks whose prices may have been battered so heavily in an overreaction to bad earnings or dividend news that the stock is a buy at the lower price. This practice is sometimes referred to as bottom fishing.

• **Buy-back** programs result when a company declares its intention of buying back a substantial number of its shares or of investing some specific dollar figure in its own shares. A variety of situations may influence a company's decision to initiate a buy-back program:

1. A company may have accumulated a sizable pot of cash. After looking at several investment options, management and the board of directors may decide that buying back its own stock is a better investment than putting those dollars back into the business. If a company moves into the market and buys one million of its own shares, share prices may rise because the number of available shares declines. Or, the buy-back could have little or no effect. Generally, however, a buy-back program is perceived to be positive. When supply dwindles, prices tend to rise if buyers remain.

2. A company may offer a variety of stock participation plans for officers, managers, and employees. If the company's matching contribution to a tax-deferred compensation plan is paid in shares of the company's stock, it has to provide the stock from some source. The company could deliver treasury stock (shares once issued but bought back by the company), unissued shares, or shares bought in the open market. Many companies elect to buy shares on the open market to avoid diluting earnings if shares awarded in profit-sharing or deferred compensation plans enter the market. An employee might retire, for example, and take his deferred compensation in a lump sum. If that final payout includes several hundred shares of the company's stock and the employee sells it, the float of tradeable shares expands. As

the supply of shares increases, prices tend to drop. Companies therefore regularly buy shares in the market for various employee compensation incentives to keep the number of shares in the hands of the public relatively constant. The **float** of stock comprises those shares held mostly by individuals and some institutions that are traded or available for trading. Not all issued shares are in the float, as officers and a number of institutions hold shares for the long term. A thin market is one where the float is relatively small; a thin market leads to higher volatility.

3. Buy-outs, mergers, and leveraged buy-outs to take a publicly held company private, that is, buy all shares owned by shareholders, can run up the price of shares dramatically in the short term. A privately owned corporation, unlike a publicly owned corporation, need not publish reports of earnings or activities. In a regular buy-out, a company declares its wishes to buy all or some percentage of the outstanding shares of another company. One maneuver to accomplish this is a **tender offer;** that is, an offer to buy shares at a stated price is sent to every shareholder. To induce shareholders to tender (send in) their shares, the acquiring company may boost the price as much as 50 percent above the price shares have been trading at. Such an offer impacts the market immediately, and prices rise quickly, usually to a level slightly below the tender offer price. Some investors may elect to sell their shares on the open market immediately, rather than tender their shares. This may happen for several reasons: The tender offer may fail for any of many reasons, including a failure to raise the financing to buy all shares. Or a regulatory

body may indicate the buy-out is illegal; or, if the tender offer is for a specific number of shares, only a portion of each owner's shares will be accepted. Selling on the market assures that all shares will be sold, even if the price is a bit less than the tender offer and the seller pays a commission. Occasionally, a company's stock price may run up higher than the tender offer price; professionals may believe the tender offer will rise, to sweeten the offer. **Arbitrageurs** (those who buy and sell the same stocks) with deep pockets operate in this sort of market. One type of arbitrageur is a trader who plays the difference between the price he pays for stock and the price of the tender offer.

In a merger, an acquiring company may buy only the shares owned by one or several major shareholders. Having become a major shareholder, the buyer may then install his own board and vote to merge the two companies. Shareholder approval is required, but the promise of higher share prices may provide the incentive for approval.

In a leveraged buy-out, a company's managers borrow money to tender for outstanding shares using the assets of the company as collateral. Once the shares are bought, management takes the remaining shares off the market and declares the company to be closely held, or privately held.

If you own stock in a company that appears headed for some sort of takeover, you must follow the action closely. You may receive information from both sides if the takeover is hostile, that is, if the current management prefers to maintain control and defend against the takeover. You may be asked to tender (send in) your shares to the current managers or to the raider who

is attempting to take over. You might also choose to sell your shares in the market. If a tender offer for all shares proceeds—that is, the offer is agreed to by both companies—you must submit your shares if you expect to be paid. Otherwise, you may end up with orphan stock (stock for which no organized market exists). You might sell your shares later, but you would have to find a buyer yourself, as brokers would not handle it. Any dividends that might have been paid will stop. Attempting to hold out against a successful tender offer will probably cost you in the end.

Growth Stocks

Many stocks are classified by market watchers as growth issues. A company dedicated to growth reinvests profits or incurs expenses for increased research and development, sales expansion (such as adding more salespersons and advertising), and integration of manufacturing facilities. Expanding into an international program, for example, is one avenue for growth. Establishing such a sales office in Europe cuts into profits over the short term but it generates profits over the long term.

One of the classic growth companies has been the Minnesota Mining and Manufacturing Co., or 3M. A huge commitment to research and development delivers a continuing flow of new and innovative consumer and producer products to the market. As new products are developed, older and less-profitable products may be dropped, but overall the company continues to grow.

The stocks of some growth companies exhibit several characteristics. First, yields tend to be small, as profits may be limited and dividends slight because profits are reinvested. Second, stock prices for these companies may be far higher than current earnings would justify. Investors are "betting on the come," or **discounting** the future—that is, they are investing with the expectation that future earnings will increase the value of shares. While a P/E ratio may be high in a current market, expected increases in earnings could lower the P/E ratio in future quarters as the denominator of the fraction (earnings) rises.

Stock prices of some growth companies escalate at phenomenal rates. Microsoft Corporation produces MS-DOS (the operating system for IBM personal computers and clones), plus many other software programs, such as WORD, one of the most popular word-processing programs. On an initial public offering in 1986, Microsoft Corporation shares were priced at $21. Share prices subsequently climbed above $50 and shares then split two-for-one. Share prices continued to climb until they approached $80 on the split shares, equivalent to $160 on the original shares. Prices for shares outran earnings, but a P/E ratio of 37 was fairly typical during one period, indicating perceptions of fast future growth.

When biotechnology stocks hit the market in the 1980s, prices were bid up to astronomical levels with P/E ratios topping 100. Biotechnology was perceived to be a major growth area, and companies who got in on the ground floor were expected to be highly profitable in the future. Biotech companies did grow and some prospered, but share prices fell because profits did not keep pace with the introduction of marketable products.

Growth companies tend to plan for the long term of 10 to 20 years or more. Investors with a long-term perspective can prosper, if they have the necessary patience.

Precious Metals Stocks

Mining companies that produce gold, platinum, silver, and various exotic metals, such as rhodium, occupy another distinct niche in the market. Gold has been called the basic money—it is accepted all over the world—but its price and the price of gold mining company shares are among the most volatile in the market. Many gold mining companies operate in countries with huge mineral reserves: South Africa, Australia, Brazil, and Canada.

Trading the stocks of U.S. companies in countries outside the United States can be troublesome, as currency variations and different rules impinge on the exchange function. To minimize many of these problems, American Depositary Receipts were legalized for trading in the United States.

American Depositary Receipts

American Depositary Receipts **(ADRs)** are reminiscent of the gold certificates that were once issued with gold as collateral. Gold certificates were receipts for a deposit of gold held in a bank or by the government. The certificates were easier to trade than the metal itself but were considered as safe as gold because the metal backed up the receipts. Usually a holder of a gold certificate could exchange it for the actual gold.

An ADR is a similar receipt issued against company stock certificates kept in a bank. The bank buys shares in a company and deposits the certificates in its vault. It then issues ADRs on a one-for-one basis; that is, if the bank buys 1,000 shares, it issues 1,000 ADRs to be traded on an exchange or over-the-counter (OTC). The bank is the transfer agent. If a buyer turns around and sells a block of ADRs, the broker obtains the ADRs from the seller and sends them to the bank. The bank lists the new buyer as the holder of record and sends the buyer new ADRs. The underlying shares issued by the gold mining company do not leave the bank. Through the use of ADRs, buying and selling of the proxy (stand-in) shares occurs entirely within the United States.

When dividends, if any, are declared, the bank receives them as the owner of record of the underlying shares and distributes the cash to ADR holders according to how many shares they own.

Many investors may be trading ADRs without recognizing they do not hold the original shares. The trading of ADRs has the approval of the SEC, which monitors and controls the procedures. About 1,000 ADRs representing 1,000 different companies are actively traded in the United States today. The bank issuing the ADRs takes a small commission for handling the dividends and charges the standard fees for its actions as a transfer agent.

Stock Splits and Dividends

Sometimes a stock increases in price to a point where few investors can manage a round-lot order (a round lot is typically 100 shares). Exchanges of round lots simplify trading procedures and reduce costs. Transfers of smaller numbers of shares, known as odd lots, incur a penalty, typically ⅛- or ¼-point higher on the buy side and lower on the sell side, depending on the broker and the price for each share. When a stock becomes difficult to manage, the company's board of directors may authorize a **stock split.** In a two-for-one split, for example, one share of stock worth $100 will be split into two shares worth $50 each.

Why is the stock split useful? A stock split lowers the price of shares and facilitates trading. Buying a round lot of a stock priced at $100 per share calls for an investment of $10,000 plus commission. A buyer might want to invest only $5,000, but buying 50 shares would incur a penalty of ¼ point, or $.25 per share. Lower share prices encourage small investors to actively trade in a stock issue.

Boards of directors have varying philosophies regarding splits. Some companies like the prestige of a lofty share price. At one time IBM stock traded in the $400–$450 range. A stock split reduced the price to 75, from which it advanced to 129½. Other corporation boards may be less comfortable with a high stock price. Managers and directors may own shares they would like to sell from time to time, and the high price may inhibit buyers. Also, if secondary offerings (issues of new stock by the corporation or major stockholder, after an initial public offering) appear likely, a price in the $10–$30 range would make shares more marketable.

A stock split begins with a motion approved by the board of directors. The split is then announced for a specific date, known as the record date. A typical split is two new shares for one existing share, although splits of five-for-one, three-for-two, and other ratios are also fairly common. Suppose you owned 100 shares in XYZ Corporation and the company declared a two-for-one split to be effective July 1. Through June 30, shares would trade as usual, say at $100 per share for a total capital value of $10,000. On July 1 your shares are worth only $50 per share, but the company issues you another 100 shares. You now own 200 shares priced at $50 per share for a total capital value of $10,000. The capital value of your investment has not changed; you just have twice as many shares as before.

If XYZ Corporation had been paying $.50 per share quarterly (or $2 per share yearly) on the old shares, the new dividend would be $.25 per share quarterly (or $1 per share yearly). Often the board of directors will boost the dividend at the same time they split the stock. Instead of $.25, the new rate may be $.30 per share quarterly (or $1.20 per share yearly) for a 20 percent increase. A stock split typically increases the trading price for shares before the record date, particularly if the stock dividend increases. After the record date, prices may slip a bit but tend to recover over time.

Conversely, a company may call for a reverse stock split to boost the price. Many mainline brokerages will not handle stocks priced at less than $1 per share. These **penny stocks** are sometimes tainted by hyped-up sales methods and by the unsavory reputation of a few companies with low-priced shares. Many brokers believe they "smell up a portfolio." When a broker takes on a new client, he or she may immediately recommend selling shares in the penny stock range of under $1, $3, or $5, depending on the brokerage. Thus, when the price of a stock drops under $1, for example, the company's board may announce a reverse stock split. In the case of a $.50 stock, the reverse split may be a 1-for-10 deal. For every 10 existing shares, 1 new share, worth $5 at the outset, will be issued. Unfortunately, the forces that drove the share price down originally may continue or even accelerate a further decline of the new $5 shares. When there is a reverse stock split, the corporation's transfer agent calls in all of the old stock certificates and replaces them with new stock certificates.

Stock dividends are similar to small stock splits. A company may decide to reward its stockholders with some compensation but lacks the cash or profits to justify a cash dividend, so it issues a stock dividend. A typical stock dividend is 10 percent; that is, for every 10 shares of stock, the shareholder receives one additional share. The transfer agent distributes a proportional number of shares to stockholders on record as of a specific date. As in the case of stock splits, the additional number of shares does not affect the total capital value of your stock holding. Each share's cost basis is adjusted to account for the added shares.

Tracking Stocks

Stocks may be traded on various stock markets, over the counter or privately. Trading data from the NYSE, Amex, and National Association of Securities Dealers and Automated Quotation system

(NASDAQ) listings are reported each business day in *The Wall Street Journal* and *Investor's Daily*. Most metropolitan newspapers also report all Amex trades and many OTC transactions. NASDAQ listings include most, but not all, of the unlisted but publicly traded stock issues. Another substantial group of small corporations is traded off the pink sheets, daily quotes printed by the National Quotation Bureau.

You may check prices for stocks listed on one of the exchanges by referring to tables in *Investor's Daily*, *The Wall Street Journal*, and many newspapers. If your OTC stock is not one of the NASDAQ listings, you will need to call a broker for a quote. If your stock is listed only in the pink sheets, a broker may consult his daily copy for bid and asked prices. While many brokers subscribe to the pink sheets, not everyone has a current copy, so expect delays. For OTC stocks, whether listed on the NASDAQ system or in the pink sheets, the number of shares you intend to buy or sell may affect the price, as quotes are for 100 shares only.

Conclusion

Just as flowers trade in a flower market and fish in a fish market, stocks are the products bought and sold in the stock market. Stocks are shares of a corporation, and they come in a bewildering variety. Stocks also trade in various ways—on organized exchanges, such as the New York Stock Exchange, the world's largest, and over the counter.

A corporation issues shares to raise capital for operating and expanding its business. Selling shares to many individuals and institutions—such as pension plans, mutual funds, and bank trust departments—enables a corporation to collect huge amounts of capital from multiple sources. Owning shares in corporations enables individuals to build their own capital more quickly and to accumulate greater sums than in bank savings accounts or certificates of deposit. So a stock market benefits both issuers and buyers.

To become a savvy investor, you need to recognize the differences between the various types of stocks and how to evaluate the worth of the thousands of issues available. Knowing the basics is a must, even if you rely on others for investment advice. And keeping track of your investments calls for an understanding of how corporations distribute earnings to shareholders and the effects of a corporation's actions on the value of its shares as perceived by the market.

CHAPTER THREE

Debt Instruments

KEY TERMS FOR THIS CHAPTER

certificates of deposit	agency securities
compounding	mortgage bonds
T-bills	call provision
data entries	debentures
yield to maturity	sinking fund
flower bonds	municipals
zero coupon treasuries (zeros)	unit trusts
STRIPS	commercial paper

Debt instruments are essentially IOUs— somebody or some organization owes money to someone else. Debt instruments include certificates of deposit, treasury bills, an enormous variety of bonds and securities (both taxable and tax-free), commercial paper, and mutual funds holding any or all of these plus others. The key element common to all debt instruments is that they pay interest to the lender. When you purchase a bond, for example, you are making a loan of the money you paid to purchase it. When the bond matures, you will receive back the full amount you paid plus interest. It sounds simple, but rules, regulations, attempts at special marketing, and taxes add confusion and complexity.

Certificates of Deposit

Among the most common debt instruments are **certificates of deposit,** or CDs, issued by banks, savings and loan associations (S&Ls), and credit unions. (For convenience, let's call all three of the depository institutions banks.) A CD is a contract between you and a bank. The bank, S&L, or credit union agrees to pay you a specific rate of interest in exchange for your agreement not to withdraw the money. If you break the contract and withdraw your funds early, the institution exacts a penalty.

Advantages and Risks

Bank CDs are popular for two reasons.

1. They are nominally risk-free when insured by the Federal Deposit Insurance Corporation (FDIC) up to $100,000. In the wake of the S&L bailout, the Federal Savings and Loan Insurance Corporation (FSLIC) was merged into the FDIC to insure S&L deposits. (S&Ls typically offer higher interest rates than banks on CDs of comparable maturity.) Federally chartered credit unions may be insured by the National Credit Union Administration (NCUA).
2. CDs are readily available at your local bank. Convenience and the confidence of dealing with a real live person face to face are the reasons many savers invest in CDs, even when higher returns might be available elsewhere.

When you invest up to $100,000 in an insured CD, you are assured by the FDIC or NCUA that you will receive your interest when due and the return of your invested capital at maturity. You should be aware, however, that when the government takes over a failing S&L, the Resolution Trust Corporation (RTC) may not honor a higher-than-market rate originally offered by the failed S&L, though you will receive all of your principal up to $100,000. (The RTC is a new U.S. government organization charged with cleaning up the S&L mess.) All accounts under one name at one bank, S&L, or credit union will be aggregated when applying the $100,000 limit rule. For example, if you have a savings account balance of $5,000, a checking account balance of $500, and a CD for $100,000, the two small accounts totaling $5,500 will not be covered. If your balance is approaching the $100,000 limit, avoid allowing interest accretions to boost the balance beyond that limit. The RTC takes a tough stance. Where formerly the FDIC or FSLIC may have paid off accounts that exceeded the $100,000 limit in a takeover, the RTC will not pay in all cases. Transfer any excess interest to a different institution. Your spouse may protect up to $100,000 with accounts in his or her own name. If you want added protection, your best bet is to contact another bank or S&L rather than attempt to set up trust or joint accounts to increase coverage in your regular bank.

A different type of risk is interest rate risk, the risk related to inflation. Typically, interest includes an allowance for inflation, sometimes referred to as an inflation bias. When you loan $10,000 to a bank by purchasing a CD at $7\frac{1}{2}$ percent, for example, 5 percent of the interest, or $500, may be an inflation bias. The other $2\frac{1}{2}$ percent is the actual rental cost of the money. If you figure inflation at 5 percent a year, $10,500 should buy the same goods and services one year from now as $10,000 buys today. This amount of interest "keeps you whole"; that is, you suffer no loss of purchasing power during the year. But if inflation should accelerate and $11,000 is needed to buy the same level of goods and services one year later, you lose purchasing power—and that is one form of interest rate risk.

The remaining $2\frac{1}{2}$ percent rental fee you gain from loaning the bank your $10,000 will be subject to federal and state income taxes. At a marginal federal income tax rate of 28 percent (the top rate), you would be hit for $210, leaving you $40 spendable return—before any state income taxes. If you paid another 10 percent, or $75 in this example, for state income taxes, you could be a net loser of $35, assuming your estimate of the 5 percent inflation rate was correct. If you accept a low interest rate in exchange for principal security, you could be facing a guaranteed loss.

Calculating Returns on a CD

Computing interest rates is not so simple either. Begin with simple or bank interest. Simple interest is the money due to a lender for one year. For example, if you were to loan $1,000 to your bank for one year at 6 percent simple interest, at the end of the year the bank would pay you $1,060. But when you loan money to a bank by buying a CD, the bank computes the interest differently. Often the rate quoted, called the coupon rate, is based on a 360-day year. To compute daily interest, divide the coupon rate by 360 and multiply by the principal. For example, if you buy a CD for $1,000 at a coupon rate of 6 percent, the daily interest is .06 divided by 360 and multiplied by 1,000, or .16667 percent. If you multiply .16667 by 360, you get a total of $60 interest due for the 360-day year (.16667 × 360 = $60.00). But 360 days do not a whole year make. Multiplying the daily interest of .16667 by 365 yields $60.83, called the annual dollar interest. The equivalent simple interest dollar rate is $60.83, which, divided by $1,000, equals 6.083 percent.

So when the bank quotes a coupon or CD rate of 6 percent, the equivalent simple interest rate is 6.083 percent. You can convert the quoted coupon or CD rate to a simple interest rate by multiplying the CD rate by a constant of 1.0139. Using this constant, an 8.0 percent CD rate is the equivalent of 8.1112 percent simple interest rate.

A bond equivalent rate may be equally complex. Suppose your banker or broker quotes a CD on a bond equivalent basis instead of the coupon or CD rate. A debt instrument quoted on a bond equivalent basis uses a straight 360-day year. Following the example we used above, instead of receiving $60.83 in interest using the CD method, a CD paying on a bond equivalent basis earns only $60 interest, the same as simple interest for a 360-day banker's year. The difference between the CD rate and the bond equivalent rate is the interest you do not receive on the five-day difference, from 360 to 365 days. In the example, the difference is $.83, and you don't get it.

The message here is, be sure you truly understand the rate being quoted before you invest in a CD.

Compounding also affects returns. Compounding more often than once a year boosts the effective rate of return because interest is then being paid on interest, which is the essence of compounding. If your CD pays interest twice yearly, the interest earned after six months is added to the principal. Interest for the second six months is then earned on the original principal plus the first six months' interest. Interest may be compounded twice yearly, quarterly, monthly, or daily. The more frequent the compounding, the higher the effective interest rate. For example, if the simple rate of interest is 6 percent on an investment of $1,000, semiannual (twice yearly) compounding adds $.91 to the $60 of simple interest. Quarterly compounding adds $1.36, monthly compounding adds $1.68, and daily compounding adds $1.83. The effective interest rate (actual rate you receive) is then 6.18 percent for daily compounding. Sometimes banks or S&Ls will compound over 360 days but pay for 365 days to increase the effective rate further.

When you are evaluating rates, look for two factors: coupon or bond equivalent rate and compounding frequency. Both will affect how many dollars your CD earns. Another point to watch: If you invest in CDs for six months, a bank may quote an effective rate for the full year. Such a rate assumes that the coupon rate for a renewal of a second six-month period will be identical to the rate quoted for the first six months. In fact, rates seldom stand still for two successive six-month periods; thus, quoting an annual effective rate for six-month CDs is misleading.

Maturity (contract period of time) may also be important in your planning. Typically, CDs may be offered in three-month and six-month, one-, two-, three-, and five-year maturities. Usually the interest rate is higher for the longer periods. Long-term CDs gain the advantage of known interest rates plus frequent compounding. When interest rates are high, you can lock in a high rate for as far into the future as five years. When interest rates are low, a better strategy is to invest in short-term CDs, those of one year or less. When the CD matures, you might be able to reinvest the funds at a higher rate. Guessing the future direction of interest rates—a tricky task, at best—is the key to CD strategy.

Remember, however, that a CD is a contract with the bank. If you agree to leave your deposit in the CD with the bank until maturity, the bank agrees to pay a higher rate than it will for a straight savings or money market account (MMA) because it can loan out the money for longer periods with more confidence that it will not be needed to pay off deposits. The drawback with a CD is that you are not permitted to withdraw your money without penalty before maturity. Some banks permit the regular withdrawal of interest accumulations without penalty, but do not permit withdrawal of the principal. The amount of the penalty depends on which institution issues your CD and the maturity. Typically, a long-term maturity earns a higher CD interest rate, making the penalty for early withdrawal higher. For example, at age 59½, an IRA holder may be permitted to withdraw funds without penalty.

Other CD Options

Brokered CDs offer another choice. Instead of visiting your neighborhood bank, S&L, or credit union in person, you may invest in a CD with your broker. Several of the large brokerages search the market all over the United States to find the highest insured CD rates for various periods. You can get an idea of the various rates available by checking the "Banxquote" section in *The Wall Street Journal* each Friday. Typically, CDs from thrifts (mainly S&Ls but also some savings banks) offer higher rates than commercial banks. Thrifts in Texas, California, Massachusetts, and other states affected by the S&L crisis tend to take the lead in paying high interest rates on their CDs.

There are three possible advantages of buying CDs through your broker:

1. Higher effective rates. Be sure to ask about the factors affecting the rate of return at maturity.
2. No broker's fee. The institution offering the CD pays a finder's fee to the brokerage.
3. Minimum penalty if you need to withdraw funds early. Instead of the bank or S&L slapping you with a penalty, the broker returns your original investment plus most of the interest earned. The broker finds another buyer for the unexpired portion of the period. You do pay a small fee for this service, but it is usually less than the penalty you would have paid to the bank.

Zero coupon CDs (zero CDs) are a type of CD purchased through a broker. Zero simply means there is no interest paid directly on the CD—interest accumulates as an increase in redemption value. You may purchase a zero CD at a substantial discount from its maturity value. As time passes, interest accrues and compounds, amounting to the difference between your investment and the redemption value, though you actually receive no money. Like long-term CDs, the zero CD locks in a specific interest rate. You know the amount you will receive at maturity.

Zero CDs are often used to accumulate college funds because they produce a known total on a specific date. Be aware, however, that the Internal Revenue Service (IRS) levies a tax on the interest ac-cumulated each year even though you receive no money. You must pay the tax from other income. Zero CDs are particularly useful in Individual Retirement Account (IRA) plans because taxes on the earned, but unpaid, interest are deferred.

U.S. Treasury Securities

The Department of the Treasury issues two basic types of debt securities: bills and bonds.

U.S. Treasury Bills

U.S. Treasury bills, familiarly known as **T-bills,** are short-term debt instruments issued as discount securities; that is, they are sold for less than their face value. Three-, six-, and twelve-month maturities are available. T-bills for three- and six-month maturities are auctioned each Monday by the Federal Reserve System (popularly known as the Fed). When Monday is a holiday, the auction occurs the next day, on Tuesday. Auctions for 12-month T-bills are held every four weeks on a Thursday. T-bills are sold in minimum units of $10,000 (maturity value); they are sold at a discount and they pay no interest. Larger amounts can be bought with a combination of $10,000 and $15,000 T-bills. Buyers gain income from the difference between the original amount paid (discounted amount) and the maturity value. For example, if you bought a six-month $10,000 T-bill at auction for $9,400 and receive $10,000 after holding the T-bill for six months, the $600 difference is compensation for waiting. T-bills were formerly issued as certificates, but today T-bills are recorded as **data entries** in the Fed's computer. You receive a computer printout as confirmation.

Calculating Interest on T-bills

Complications involving how you figure the interest earned on T-bills arise from the discount method. If you buy a 12-month T-bill, figuring the simple annual interest rate is relatively easy. Simply figure the difference between the face value and the price paid, and divide by the price paid. For example, if you bought a one-year $10,000 T-bill for $9,200, the difference is $800. Dividing the $800 by $9,200 shows an 8.6957 percent rate. You actually invested only $9,200, and your return is based on your investment over a full year.

Calculating the simple annual interest rates on T-bills with less than one-year maturities gets more complicated. Using an example of a six-month T-bill that cost $9,400 discounted (with a $10,000 face value), the difference is $600 and the time is 182 days to maturity. Calculate the simple annual interest rate as follows:

$$\frac{\$600}{9,400} \div \frac{182}{365} = .0638 \div .4986 = .128 \text{ or } 12.8\%$$

The generic formula is:

$$\frac{\text{maturity value–price paid}}{\text{price paid}} \div \frac{t}{365} = \begin{array}{l}\text{simple annual} \\ \text{interest rate}\end{array}$$

where t = days to maturity. Note that as the discounted price drops, the simple annual interest rate rises.

Unfortunately, T-bill dealers, brokers, and buyers do not use the simple annual rate. They may use the discount rate or the bank equivalent rate.

Look first at the discount rate, which is the one you see reported most often in newspapers. Calculations are relatively simple, as the yield on a discount basis is the amount of the discount divided by 100. Amount of discount is the face, or maturity value, minus the price paid. On the $10,000 one-year T-bill, bought for $9,200, the discount is $800. Divided by 100, the discount rate is 8 percent on an annual basis. Compare this to the earlier simple annual rate of 8.7 percent. The discount rate quoted for T-bills will always be less than the simple annual interest rate and substantially understates the true rate.

Brokers and analysts use still a different rate when comparing T-bill rates with coupon securities, such as bonds. This rate is called the bond equivalent rate and is calculated below for a $10,000 six-month bond purchased for $9,400:

$$\text{BER} = \frac{365 \times .08}{360 - (.08 \times 182)} = \frac{29.20}{360 - 14.56}$$
$$= \frac{29.20}{345.44} = 0.0845 \text{ or } 8.45\%$$

The generic formula is:

$$\begin{array}{l}\text{Bond equivalent} \\ \text{rate (BER)}\end{array} = \frac{365 \times \text{discount rate}}{360 - (\text{discount rate} \times t)}$$

Buying U.S. T-bills

You buy T-bills at original issue one of several ways. Your bank or broker can buy your T-bills and will then charge a fee or commission. A typical fee is $25 for the purchase of one T-bill, $10,000 minimum. Brokers may also charge a percentage of the amount invested.

Buying T-bills directly from the Fed is fairly simple, and there is no service fee or commission. If there is a Federal Reserve Bank or branch nearby, visit the bank to ask for instructions on how to buy directly. If there is no Federal Reserve Bank or branch nearby, write to the Fed in your area for instructions on buying T-bills by mail. Your banker can provide you with the address of the Federal Reserve Bank that services your area.

Generally, you must file an application, or tender, before 1 P.M. Eastern time on Mondays (every fourth Thursday for one-year T-bills). Your certified check or a bank cashier's check for the full maturity value of the T-bill must accompany your application. The following Thursday the Fed will return the difference between the price you paid and the face amount, usually by a direct deposit to your checking account. At maturity, the Fed deposits the face amount electronically into your checking account unless you elect to roll over the principal into a new T-bill. You must notify the Fed before your existing T-bills mature if you elect to roll over the principal.

Individuals buying less than $200,000 in T-bills submit noncompetitive bids. Individuals and institutions planning to buy more than $200,000 worth of T-bills must submit a competitive bid. Only the highest bids are accepted by the U.S. Treasury. Small buyers agree to accept the average of the competitive bids as the price for their T-bills. All noncompetitive bids are totaled, and the total dollar amount is set aside for small investors first before any competitive bids are accepted.

An active secondary market permits you to sell T-bills before maturity for ready liquidity. This over-the-counter (OTC) market is operated by about 35 to 40 dealers in treasury securities. Rates vary daily according to the overall level of interest rates and supply and demand for T-bills among investors. Thus, if you bought a six-month T-bill and need cash after holding it for a month, you can sell it through your broker, who will charge a commission.

If you decide to sell your T-bill before it matures, you must convert the data entry into a saleable entry by asking the Fed for the negotiable security on paper. Ask your broker for details on how to do this, as you will be selling your T-bill through the broker.

Advantages of T-bills

T-bills are recognized as the least risky investment you can make for several reasons:

1. T-bills are direct obligations of the U.S. Treasury.
2. Interest rate risk, or the possibility that the capital value of a security will gain or lose based on the fluctuations of interest rates, is minimal due to the short maturities of T-bills.
3. A huge and active secondary market exists for T-bills. You may sell T-bills any day the markets are open to gain quick liquidity.

Many active traders use T-bills as a backup fund. A stock trader who believes the market is headed down, for example, may "go to cash"; that is, sell the stock and immediately invest the proceeds in T-bills as a safe haven. By doing this, the trader's capital is protected and it earns a T-bill rate. Other traders may put the cash proceeds from a stock, bond, or mutual fund sale into a money market mutual fund.

Finally, the interest payable on T-bills (and treasury notes and bonds) is free of state taxes. For investors in those states with relatively high state income taxes, this benefit raises after-tax rates.

U.S. Treasury Notes and Bonds

Treasury notes and bonds are more traditional instruments called coupon securities. The term originates from the former practice of issuing bearer bonds with coupons attached, which were clipped and forwarded to the treasury when interest was due. T-bonds are now issued as registered certificates with the buyer's name and taxpayer identification number printed on the certificate. T-notes and T-bonds are also issued in data entry (or book entry) form in the name of the buyer—ownership records are kept by computer, and buyers receive a confirmation of their ownership. Interest checks are mailed semiannually (twice yearly) to registered owners or transferred electronically to the owner's bank account. Notes or bonds in data entry form may be converted to certificates for sale in the aftermarket; that is, the active market for notes and bonds after original issue but before maturity.

T-notes and T-bonds are similar instruments, differing only in maturity. T-notes are issued with maturities ranging from 2 years to 10 years. T-bond maturities range from 10 years to 30 years. T-bills fill in the short maturities end of the treasury securities market. The U.S. Treasury sells negotiable (saleable) T-notes and T-bonds regularly, usually each quarter, to finance the federal deficit and to pay off maturing notes and bonds.

Buying U.S. Treasury Notes and Bonds

Treasury notes and bonds may be bought directly from Federal Reserve banks in a manner similar to T-bills. Most of the T-notes and T-bonds are sold at auction to dealers who bid for them at prices they expect will yield a profit when they resell them to individuals and/or various institutions, including foreign buyers.

T-notes and T-bonds are issued in denominations of $1,000, $5,000, $10,000, $100,000, and $1,000,000, except for notes with maturities of less than four years, which are issued in a minimum denomination of $5,000.

If you wish to buy T-notes or T-bonds at original issue from the Fed, contact the bank or branch in your area for details on the procedure. The U.S. Treasury regularly updates a flyer, PD 800-A, that provides current information on how to buy treasury notes and bonds directly and the location of Federal Reserve banks and branches. (See Resources for the address to write to for this flyer.) You must still contact the Fed in your area for tender (application) forms and specific instructions.

The sale of notes and bonds follows a general schedule. (Specific dates for sale are released to newspapers 10 days to 2 weeks in advance.)

- Two-year T-notes are issued at the end of each month.
- Four-year and five-year T-notes are issued every three months in March, June, September, and December.
- Seven-year T-notes and 20-year bonds are issued in January, April, July, and October.
- During the weeks that include the 15th day of February, May, August, and November, the Treasury usually issues 3-year T-notes, 10-year T-notes, and 30-year T-bonds. These three releases are generally referred to as the Treasury's quarterly refundings. A sizable portion of the proceeds from quarterly refundings are used to pay off maturing T-notes and T-bonds in a rollover of the debt, called refunding or refinancing.

As stated previously, most T-notes and T-bonds are sold at auction similar to the way T-bills are sold, but there are some differences. The auction may be either on a yield basis or a price basis. A yield basis means that the competitive bidding depends on the yield investors are willing to accept on the security. For example, an investor who bids 9.82 percent yield is willing to accept an annual yield of 9.82 percent, and the T-note or T-bond is priced accordingly. Reports sometimes indicate, "Bonds were priced to yield 9.82 percent," or some other figure. Auctions on a price basis call for competitive bids for a specific dollar figure, a $10,000 bond priced at $9,750, for example. In either case, investors do not know the exact interest rate

until after results of the auction are announced.

Most individual investors submit non-competitive bids without specifying a yield or a price. Instead they agree to accept the average yield and equivalent price determined from the average of the competitive bids, similar to the procedure for T-bills. If securities are to be sold at less than their par (maturity) value as a result of the auction, investors receive a discount—the difference between the selling price and the par value. If, however, the T-note or T-bond sells for more than the par value, the investor must pay a premium—the difference between the selling price and par value.

Original issue treasury notes and bonds may also be purchased from commercial banks and brokers, who will probably add a fee.

Treasury notes and bonds trade actively on secondary markets. Many of the issues are listed in financial papers. Prices are noted with one digit omitted plus 32nds of a point or as a decimal. As interest rates have become more volatile, changes in the prices of T-bonds have begun to offer opportunities for capital gains similar to those for stocks.

Notes and bonds have two yields.

1. Current yield is the relationship on a given day between the annual interest payable on a bond and its price. A bond paying $100 interest each year may sell at $1,000 if the general level of interest rates is 10 percent. Or a bond paying $80 current interest may sell for $800. The dollars of interest paid yearly on a bond do not change, but the interest rate those dollars represent may and

usually does change regularly, as the price paid for the bond varies. To obtain the current yield, simply divide the annual interest by the amount you paid for the bond, including commissions if any.

2. **Yield to maturity** (YTM) is the interest rate a bondholder can expect over the life of a bond if he holds it to maturity and collects the face value of the bond. If you bought a $10,000 T-bond for $8,000 with a coupon rate of 8 percent, the $80 interest would be equal to a 10 percent current rate ($80 divided by $800). If the bond was due to mature in 10 years, the YTM would be higher than the current rate because you would receive $10,000 at maturity, a $2,000 gain over your purchase price of $8,000.

For a quick approximation of the YTM, divide the gain between price and maturity value by the number of years to maturity and add the yearly increment to the interest in dollars. The total dollar value is then figured as a percentage of the purchase price. For example, on the $10,000 bond purchased for $8,000, the $2,000 gain over 10 years results in $200 appreciation each year on a straight-line basis. Adding the $200 to the $800 of interest results in $1,000 or a YTM of 12.5 percent based on the purchase price of $8,000.

However, YTM is not a straight-line function, as compound interest affects the annual amount of gain. You will need a calculator capable of handling compound interest to figure a true YTM, or you can ask your broker to look it up in his yield tables. The YTM for the $1,000 bond purchased at a dis-count at $800 with a maturity of exactly 10 years from the purchase date is 11.40 percent. The smaller figure for the true YTM compared to the straight-line amortization results from the compound interest payments on interest. The YTM for listed bonds is included in most media reports.

Other Characteristics of U.S. Treasury Notes and Bonds

One of the givens on Wall Street is the relationship between interest rates and bond prices. The rule is, as interest rates rise, bond prices fall; as interest rates fall, bond prices rise. This inverse relationship is best explained with an example. Suppose you bought a long-term bond paying 8 percent interest several years ago. A $1,000 bond would thus pay $80 each year. However, times change and interest rates for government securities rise to 10 percent. You decide to sell your bond, but no investor will pay $1,000 for a bond that pays only $80 per year when he can buy one that pays $100 per year. If you wish to sell your 8 percent bond, you need to price it to yield 10 percent. You must drop your price to $800; the $80-per-year interest now equals 10 percent ($80 divided by $800). The reverse occurs if interest rates drop; that is, the price of the bond rises, possibly to a premium over par (maturity value); hence the inverse relationship between bond prices and yields.

Treasury notes are not callable (redeemed by the government prior to stated maturity date). Treasury bonds may be called, but usually not until five years before maturity. The effect of a call provision is to create two YTM figures. The first YTM is figured to the stated maturity. The second YTM is calculated to the call date. U.S. Treasury securities, however, are seldom called.

Flower Bonds

Flower bonds are special issues of treasury bonds that came on the market between 1953 and 1963. These issues are accepted at full par value in the payment of federal estate taxes (hence the name, with its association to funerals). Only the issues noted in Table 3A qualify for the special rules in payment of estate taxes. Note that the coupon rates vary from 3 percent to $4\frac{1}{8}$ percent. As a result of their low interest rates, flower bonds typically sell at discounts but at higher prices than overall interest rates would indicate because of their value in paying estate taxes. No additional flower bonds are being issued, and when those eligible for paying estate taxes are tendered, they are accepted and retired.

Several conditions apply to the use of flower bonds for the payment of estate taxes.

1. The bonds must be owned by the decedent at his or her death.
2. The par value plus accrued interest of the flower bonds tendered may not exceed the amount of the federal estate taxes.
3. The executor or administrator of the decedent's estate must submit the flower bonds to the Division of Securities of the Department of the Treasury at least three weeks prior to the date

TABLE 3A	FLOWER BONDS
Coupon Rate	Maturity
$4\frac{1}{4}$%	August 15, 1987–92
4	February 15, 1988–93
$4\frac{1}{4}$	May 15, 1989–94
3	February 15, 1995
$3\frac{1}{2}$	November 15, 1998

they are to be used for the payment of estate taxes.

Since there is little income produced by these low-interest bonds, flower bonds are not usually added to a person's portfolio until a short time before his or her expected demise.

Zero Coupon Treasuries and STRIPS

Zero coupon treasuries (zeros) are not issued by the U.S. Treasury. Instead, major brokerages buy long-term treasury bonds and strip away the future income payments from the underlying bonds. Individuals wanting regular interest buy the strips. Others looking for long-term gain buy the underlying securities, or zeros, at low prices. As the bonds approach maturity, values increase because the bond will be paid off at par (maturity) for a long-term capital gain. Yearly value accretions are taxed as income. These derivative securities are sometimes given creative titles, such as CATS (Certificates of Accrual on Treasury Securities) and TIGRs (Treasury Investment Growth Receipts).

Two years after the brokerages first offered stripped coupon bonds, the U.S. Treasury announced a similar program,

Separate Trading of Registered Interest and Principal of Securities (**STRIPS**). The STRIPS program permits others to separate the bonds from the interest—the treasury does not do it directly. The securities are direct obligations of the U.S. government and are issued in data entry form. STRIPS were first offered in 1985. Now the term zero coupon treasuries applies to STRIPS as well as CATS and TIGRs. Quotations of stripped securities are reported daily in *The Wall Street Journal*.

Price volatility for the stripped securities is far greater than for treasury notes or bonds. While the security of principal and interest is assured, interest rate risks are magnified. Zeros are also available in the form of mutual funds.

U.S. Savings Bonds

The U.S. Treasury also sells U.S. savings bonds. Savings bonds are not negotiable and prices do not change. You may buy savings bonds at local banks, S&Ls, Federal Reserve banks and branches, through payroll deduction where you work, and directly from the Department of the Treasury. (See Resources for the ordering address.) At the end of March 1990, the public held $119.88 billion of savings bonds, up 7 percent over the previous 12 months. Savings bonds are issued in two series: Series EE and Series HH.

Series EE Savings Bonds

Series EE savings bonds (EE-bonds) are available in small face amounts of $50,

$75, $100, $200, $500, $1,000, $5,000, and $10,000. Prices are half of the maturity values and EE-bonds double in value in 12 years at the minimum rate of 6 percent. Individuals may purchase a maximum of $15,000 ($30,000 face amount) worth of EE-bonds each year. Interest rates vary every six months with rates changing each May and November. The market interest rates are based on 85 percent of the rates being paid on treasury securities with five-year maturities during the period immediately before rates change. A minimum rate of 6 percent applies if the calculated market rate should drop below that level. Owners of EE-bonds must hold them for a minimum of five years to earn the market rates. Otherwise, short-term rates are less and depend on how long the owner holds the bonds before redeeming them. Purchases are limited to $15,000 annually.

EE-bonds function like zeros. Interest may accumulate tax-deferred until the bonds are redeemed or they mature without extension. Maturities on newly issued EE-bonds are being routinely extended to a uniform 30 years. Maturities for some earlier E- or EE-bonds were extended to 40 years. (E-bonds differ from EE-bonds in the way they pay interest and are no longer being issued.)

Interest accrues on EE-bonds by increasing redemption value every six months. Since the redemption value remains constant for six months until it jumps again, you should plan redemptions for the first part of the month that values increase. If you are buying EE-bonds, plan to buy them near the end of any month: Since they earn interest as if you had bought them earlier, you gain a full month's interest. You may check maturity values for

E- and EE-bonds by asking at your bank or by writing for a table of redemption values from the Bureau of the Public Debt (see U.S. Treasury in Resources for the address).

EE-bonds offer three major advantages for small investors.

1. You may buy EE-bonds with no cost or commission, and there is no cost at redemption.
2. Federal taxes may be deferred until redemption (unlike other zeros), or you may pay taxes on each year's increase in redemption value. If you elect to pay federal taxes on each year's added redemption value annually, all of the final redemption value except for the final year's interest will be free of taxes.
3. Interest on EE-bonds is free of all state and local taxes.

Since January 1, 1990, EE-bonds have included a new feature. All accrued interest on EE-bonds used to pay for the education of children will be excluded from the federal tax liabilities of parents. To qualify for this exclusion, EE-bond proceeds (principal and interest) must be used to pay tuition and eligible expenses (such as lab fees and books for the taxpayer, taxpayer's spouse, or taxpayer's dependents) at qualified educational institutions. Only EE-bonds bought after December 31, 1989, qualify. Payments for eligible expenses must be paid directly to the educational institution.

Only EE-bonds issued to a person who is at least 24 years old before the bonds are issued qualify for the excludable interest. If you are a grandparent and want to help fund your grandchildren's educa-

tion, you cannot buy the EE-bonds directly; you must give the money to your son or daughter. They can then buy the EE-bonds in their names for their children's education.

The excludable interest benefit phases out for parents with modified adjusted gross incomes over $60,000 when filing jointly or $40,000 for single filers. Married persons filing separately are not eligible regardless of income. Phase-out limits are adjusted for inflation. Above the $60,000 limit, benefits are phased out in proportion to the amount up to $90,000 adjusted gross income (AGI) when none of the interest is excludable. For a couple with AGI of $75,000, half of the interest would be excludable when used to pay eligible educational expenses.

If the amount of the redemption of EE-bonds exceeds the amount paid for eligible educational expenses, the amount of excludable interest will be reduced by a pro rata amount. For example, if bond proceeds equal $10,000, divided into $5,000 of principal and $5,000 of interest, and qualified educational expenses total $8,000, the taxpayer would only be able to exclude 80 percent of the interest earned, or $4,000 for this example.

Accumulating income from older EE-bonds for children's education calls for a different strategy. Older EE-bonds may be owned by the minors with a parent or grandparent as beneficiary. Interest can be deferred to avoid possible income tax at the parents' marginal rate until a child reaches 14. After age 14, a child pays tax on earnings at his or her own rate, beginning at 15 percent after exemptions and deductions. EE-bonds could then be redeemed, taxes paid on the accrued earnings, and the after-tax remainder invested at a higher earnings rate to accumulate funds for college.

Series HH Savings Bonds

Series HH savings bonds (HH-bonds) are no longer available for sale. You may acquire them only by exchanging mature EE-bonds for an equivalent value of HH-bonds. Exchanging EE-bonds for HH-bonds defers the income tax on the interest accrued on the EE-bonds during their lifetime until the HH-bonds are redeemed or mature without extension.

HH-bonds pay semiannual interest at a flat rate of 6 percent. Interest is taxable at the federal level but not at the state or local levels. HH-bonds normally mature in 10 years but are being routinely extended to a maximum of 20 years.

Government Agency Securities

Government **agency securities** and debt instruments are issued by government agencies other than the U.S. Treasury. Here is a look at some of the agencies issuing popular securities.

The Government National Mortgage Association (GNMA) assembles and guarantees GNMA (also known as Ginnie Mae) certificates—$25,000 pieces of a pool of mortgages. Only Federal Home Administration-insured and Veterans Administration-guaranteed mortgages are included in the mortgage pool. Interest paid on the mortgages is passed through to certificate holders in proportion to their holdings.

Ginnie Mae certificates are backed by the "full faith and credit of the U.S. Government"; that is, the federal government guarantees the timely payment of both interest and principal. Ginnie Mae certificates are highly prized as income producers, because they yield about 1 percent to $1\frac{1}{2}$ percent more interest than treasury bonds. Interest paid on Ginnie Maes is not exempt from state and local taxes.

Two problems affect Ginnie Mae certificates. First, the minimum price on original issue is high—$25,000 with $5,000 additional increments. Expected maturity is 30 years, but early payoff of the underlying mortgages trims the term to about 13–14 years on average. When traded on the secondary market through brokers, partially paid Ginnie Maes may be bought for $10,000 to $20,000, and the broker collects a commission for making the trade.

Second, when a mortgagee within the pool pays off the principal of the mortgage loan, the principal is distributed as a return of capital to Ginnie Mae certificate holders in proportion to their holdings. Having to reinvest the capital received irregularly and in odd amounts can be a nuisance if you want to avoid spending capital.

A popular solution to both problems is to buy Ginnie Mae securities through a mutual fund, preferably a no-load (no commission) fund for minimum cost. Ginnie Mae funds buy the certificates and offer fund buyers smaller pieces, usually an initial minimum of $1,000 with additional amounts as low as $10 in some cases. Further, when portions of the principal are returned, the mutual fund manager reinvests the capital in more certificates. Although the Ginnie Mae certificates held by a mutual fund are guaranteed, the fund shares do not carry a guarantee.

Other government agency securities include:

• Federal Home Loan Mortgage Corporation (FHLMC), popularly known as Freddie Mac, is a corporation that is wholly owned by the 12 Federal Reserve banks. Participation certificates issued by Freddie Mac are similar to the Ginnie Mae certificates except that they are guaranteed by Freddie Mac rather than the U.S. government or the Federal Reserve banks. As a result, Freddie Mac pass-through certificates return a slightly higher rate than Ginnie Maes.

• Federal National Mortgage Association (FNMA), popularly known as Fannie Mae, also issues pass-through securities similar to the Freddie Mac securities. Although Fannie Mae guarantees the timely payment of interest and principal, the pass-through securities are not guaranteed by the U.S. government, and the securities yield a higher return than Ginnie Maes even though Congress is likely to stand behind the certificates.

• Tennessee Valley Authority (TVA) is owned by the U.S. government and issues bonds in increments of $1,000 in data entry form to support the development of the Tennessee valley and adjacent areas. Bonds are not guaranteed by the U.S. government.

• Student Loan Marketing Association (SLMA), familiarly known as Sallie Mae, borrows money by selling bonds with a minimum initial denomination of $10,000 and additional amounts in $5,000 increments. SLMA bonds are not guaranteed by the U.S. government or by states.

• Resolution Refunding Corporation (REFCORP) was started in 1989 to provide more funds for the bailout of failed S&Ls. REFCORP raises funds from the sale of bonds for use by the RTC. Interest is not guaranteed by the U.S. government and is taxable at the federal level.

Corporate Debt Securities

Corporations issue bonds in many varieties. Corporations do not issue short-term bills but may call their long-term debts either notes or bonds, with bonds issued for the longest terms. Corporate bonds may resemble government bonds, but they also differ in many ways. Here is an overview of the major types of corporate bonds.

Collateralized Bonds

First **mortgage bonds** are a form of collateralized bond backed by a lien on property (a plant and/or equipment). If you buy a corporate mortgage bond and the company goes bankrupt, you have a secured lien; that is, you hold a security interest in the property. If the plant or equipment is sold, your security must be satisfied, which usually means you get your entire principal or some portion of your principal back. First mortgage bonds may be issued in series, with each series identified by the interest rate. For example, XYZ Corporation first mortgage bonds, $9\frac{1}{2}$ percent Series due September 30, 2010 indicates the name of the corporation, bond collateral, percentage rate, and the date of maturity.

Only a small percentage of the corporate

bonds issued is listed or reported in financial newspapers. As with government bonds, the security value (bond price) will vary up or down in accordance with the general movement of interest rates. As interest rates rise, the prices of bonds decline and vice versa. Security, or the risk associated with the bonds of a specific corporation, are rated by private agencies (see page 63).

Maturities may vary from 100 years for some early railroad bonds to the current, typical short maturity of 10–15 years. Interest rate volatility induces corporate issuers to shorten maturities to avoid surprises down the line.

Another safeguard for issuers, and a possible hazard for bond buyers, is the **call provision** incorporated into most corporate bonds. A call may occur when, at the issuer's option, the company elects to call in the bonds. To call an issue or part of an issue, the company must usually pay a penalty to the bondholder. A typical penalty might be one year's interest plus the full face value of the bond. The amount of the penalty may decline as the bond nears maturity. Any call provisions are detailed in the indenture, the document that defines the terms and conditions affecting a specific issue of bonds, and are usually noted on the bond itself. Typically, corporate bonds may not be callable during the first 5, 10, or some other number of years.

Why would a company call bonds? It might wish to reduce interest rates. For example, if a company issued bonds during the high interest periods of 1980–1982, rates could be in the 16 percent to 20 percent range. If the bonds were callable after 10 years, the company treasurer could look forward to refinancing those high-interest

bonds. The company issues new bonds with lower interest rates, in the range of 10 percent to 12 percent, and uses the proceeds to call and pay off the earlier bonds.

As a buyer, you should be aware of any call provisions that could affect bonds you buy. Ask your broker about calls before buying, and check your bonds when you receive them. While you may not be able to avoid buying bonds with call provisions, you can avoid bonds with near-term call dates, particularly if you wish to lock in a high rate during a credit crunch.

A specialized form of collateralized bonds is the equipment trust certificate. Railroads, and now airlines, use trust certificates to finance the purchase of equipment—locomotives and cars for a railroad and airplanes for airlines. Instead of paying directly for major pieces of equipment, a railroad may, for example, set up a trust with financing from a bank or individual borrowers. The trust raises the money and buys rolling stock (cars and locomotives) for a railroad that acquires the equipment on lease. The railroad makes regular payments to the trust, which in turn passes the payments through to certificate holders. Should the railroad default on its payments, the trust could foreclose on the equipment. Locomotives, rail cars, and airplanes are sufficiently standard that they could be resold. This flexibility reduces the risks associated with the loan, and interest rates tend to be lower than on noncollateralized bonds.

Debentures

Debentures are bonds that are not collateralized; that is, they are not backed by a lien on property. Debentures are issued with only the backing of the good faith and credit of the corporation. In the hierarchy of debt repayments, debentures rank behind mortgage-backed bonds.

Bonds that are not backed with liens on specific property have added risks and increased interest rates. However, many large corporations issue debentures, and they are accepted by bond buyers. You need not avoid debentures; just be aware that they are different from mortgage-backed bonds. Debentures may also be issued with call provisions.

Even lower on the hierarchy of debt repayments than regular debenture bonds are subordinated debenture bonds. Just as the name implies, subordinated debentures rank below regular debentures and, therefore, are more risky. When you consider bonds of any kind, equate risk with interest rate—high risk, high interest.

Junk Bonds

So-called junk bonds have been very much in the news in recent years. During the 1980s these bonds were issued in huge quantities, often in the billions of dollars, to finance takeovers and buy-outs. The junk terminology refers to the less-than-premium quality ratings of these bonds—a term preferred by brokers is the euphemism high yield bonds.

One of the problems junk bonds introduce is the downgrading of prior investment grade issues from the same company. For example, Company A took over Company B; both are major corporations with excellent credit ratings. The massive borrowing with junk bonds to finance the take-

over, however, reduced the credit rating of Company A bonds. As a result of the perceived downgrading of quality, prices of all Company B bonds dropped by about 20 percent at one time.

Prices for junk bonds may drop sharply at times, as they did during late 1989 and 1990. Major corporations financed by junk bonds went into default because cash flow from operations would not cover the high interest costs of the junk bonds. Drexel Burnham Lambert, Inc., the major proponent of junk bonds, went into bankruptcy and disappeared. Michael Milken, the junk bond king, admitted guilt in several actions and went to jail. Investors who bought the high-yield bonds, including pension funds and insurance companies, suffered major losses. S&Ls that bought junk bonds to improve their investment yields failed when the value of the junk bonds in their portfolios plummeted, contributing to the S&L bailout debacle.

If you want to dabble in high-risk junk bonds, consider buying shares of high-yield (junk) bond mutual funds to gain professional management and wide diversification. Even if some issues in a fund's portfolio default, earnings may not be significantly affected. However, diversification alone will not protect you against a broadly declining market or the aftershock of event risk, that is, the possibility of a decline in the bonds' value as a result of a catastrophic event.

Convertible Bonds

Convertible bonds include what is sometimes called an equity kicker. To improve the marketability of its bonds, a corporation may include a provision for convertibility of bonds to the company's stock. Convertible bonds work much like convertible preferred stock. If the company prospers and common stock prices rise dramatically, bonds may be converted to stock for an immediate profit.

Convertible bonds are hybrid securities: They act like bonds to provide a floor of value as interest payments generate income, and they may act like stock when the price of a company's stock approaches the point where conversion of the bonds would generate a profit. Investors may buy bonds with the idea of converting them at a profit when and if the company's stock rises.

Unfortunately, convertible bonds may also pay lower interest rates than similar bonds and dawdle for years at a price below a profitable conversion price for the stock. You pay a premium of sorts when you buy a convertible bond; either the interest payout is low or the price of the bond is high for value received.

Trading Corporate Bonds

Bond operations begin with a purchase. Since most corporate bonds are issued at a par value of $1,000, a broker may offer you five bonds, for a total value of $5,000. A round lot of bonds is 100, and investors in these large quantities are generally institutions, but odd-lot bond dealers have expanded the market beyond institutions to individuals who may buy 1, 5, or 25 bonds. Buying fewer than five bonds is uneconomic because of three costs on a round-trip—a buying commission, the spread between bid and asked prices, and a selling commission. For small bond purchases, bond mutual funds usually offer a better alternative. Buying bonds through a no-load bond fund avoids the commissions, and buy-and-sell transactions occur at the same net asset value (NAV), which is the value of the shares in the fund. (See Chapter 4 for a discussion of mutual funds.)

Bonds typically trade according to their YTM, the interest rate that is a common denominator for all issues. For maturities in the far future, current yield (dollars of interest divided by price) correlates closely with YTM. As bonds approach maturity, the YTM dictates and controls interest rates, as the bonds will be paid off at maturity by the issuing company. A bond typically sells at either a discount or a premium based on the interest rate. If general interest rates are higher than the bond rate, the price will be discounted. When the bond's interest rate is higher than general levels, the bond will sell at a premium. There may be no practical discount limit, but a call provision may limit how much of a premium investors are willing to pay.

Bonds are traded OTC except for a few listed issues. Price quotations are hard to come by except from a broker—another reason for small investors to invest in bonds through mutual funds. You can check the action on bond funds every day in *The Wall Street Journal*, *Investor's Daily*, and most large metropolitan newspapers. The bond quotes you see drop one of the zeros; thus, a bond quoted at 88½ is actually priced at $885.

Bonds may be paid off in different ways. In the early call the full price of bonds plus a possible penalty is paid before normal maturity. Term bonds are those where the full face value of the bond is paid at the maturity date.

Another way to pay off bonds calls for a **sinking fund,** a device for accumulating cash each year. Old sinking funds collected cash or cash equivalents in a fund and paid off the bonds at maturity; but some cash-hungry companies spent the cash instead of segregating it. Now, most sinking fund bond issues call for redemption of some percentage of the bonds issued each year using the sinking fund cash to pay off the bonds. Some sinking fund plans will pay off some bonds but still leave a large chunk to be paid at maturity; these are called balloon sinking fund plans.

There are two types of sinking fund systems. One system for selecting bonds to be redeemed each year with sinking fund cash is by lottery according to serial numbers. Owners picked by lot must turn in their bonds for redemption, as interest stops at the redemption date. Another system is for the company to buy the bonds in the open market, paying for them with sinking fund cash.

Obviously, the price of the bonds shortly before the specified redemption date dictates which method is used. If the bonds are selling at a discount, the company spends less cash to buy the required number of bonds in the market. If bonds are selling at or above par, the trustee, acting for the company, will select bonds randomly for redemption. Those whose bonds are selected may not be too happy to give up bonds that are selling at a premium in the market or are paying higher interest than they can expect from reinvesting the cash they receive from the redeemed bonds. The random selection of bonds for

sinking fund redemption is one risk to be considered when buying the bonds.

The bond issue may also be paid off over a span of years by issuing serial bonds scheduled for redemption on specific dates. An investor can select which bonds he prefers according to maturity. Usually, interest rates differ for the various maturities in a serial bond issue, with the shorter maturities earning lower interest rates.

Municipal Bonds

The last major class of bonds is issued by states and local taxing authorities, such as schools, water and sewer systems, port authority, and toll bridge authority. All of these are known generically as **municipals,** or muni-bonds. There are more than a million different issues of muni-bonds in the market, most of them small and sold locally. Muni-bonds generate less income for investors than taxable treasury or corporate bonds for one important reason— their interest is forever free of federal income tax liability.

Unless specifically exempted, muni-bond interest may be taxed at the state level. Usually, a state with an income tax will exempt interest on its bonds for residents of that state. Residents of other states buying the same issue would be taxed by the state where they reside. For example, if you live in California and buy an issue of California muni-bonds, you will pay no state tax (assuming the issue is exempt from state taxes, which is usually the case) and no federal tax. These are known as double tax-frees. However, if you live in Oregon and buy the California muni-bond, you would be liable for State of Oregon income tax on the California muni-bond's interest. If you live in New York City and buy a local muni-bond, it could be free of city, state, and federal income tax. Such bonds are called triple tax-frees.

Recently, the tax-free benefit on state and local muni-bonds was modified by Congress. Now, two classes of muni-bonds may be available where you live. One class comprises bonds issued to finance essential services, such as the construction of roads and bridges, schools, and similar activities. The interest on these muni-bonds is exempt from federal income tax for everyone. A second class comprises muni-bonds issued to provide low-interest loans to a business as an inducement to locate in a community or to help first-time homeowners with lower mortgage loan rates. These so-called nonessential muni-bonds pay a slightly higher interest rate than muni-bonds issued for essential services. However, they also generate preferential income that may affect a high-income taxpayer's alternative minimum tax (AMT) computations. Taxpayers with large amounts of preferential income, such as nonessential muni-bonds, depreciation write-off, and similar deductions, must calculate a possible minimum tax and pay it or the normal tax, whichever is higher. If you are susceptible to the AMT, you should probably avoid that class of muni-bonds.

Your tax bracket should dictate whether you invest in tax-free muni-bonds or regular taxable bonds. The key is after-tax income. Table 3B shows the equivalent interest rates for the three current federal tax rates. You can also figure the equivalent value yourself with a simple calculation. To find the taxable equivalent of tax-free interest, divide the tax-free rate by 1 less your marginal tax rate. For example, suppose a tax-free bond yields 7 percent interest and your marginal tax rate is 28 percent. To find the taxable equivalent, subtract .28 from 1 to get .72; then divide 7 by .72 for a taxable equivalent rate of 9.722 percent. That is, a taxable bond yielding 9.722 percent leaves you with the same after-tax, or spendable, income as a tax-free bond yielding an even 7 percent.

TABLE 3B		EXEMPT VERSUS TAXABLE INCOME					
				TO EQUAL A TAX-FREE YIELD OF			
TAXABLE INCOME, 1991*		Tax Bracket	5%	6%	7%	8%
Joint Return	Single Return		TAXABLE INVESTMENT WOULD HAVE TO EARN			
$0–$34,000	$0–$20,350	15%	5.88%	7.06%	8.24%	9.41%
$34,000–$83,150	$20,350–$49,300	28%	6.94%	8.33%	9.72%	11.11%
$83,150	$49,300	31%	7.25%	8.70%	10.14%	11.59%

*Net after deductions and exemptions.

Going the other way is even simpler. To find the tax-free equivalent of a taxable bond rate, multiply the taxable rate by 1 less your marginal rate. For example, to find the tax-free equivalent of a taxable bond yielding 9 percent, with a marginal tax rate of 28 percent, subtract .28 from 1 to get .72; multiply 9 by .72 for an equivalent rate of 6.48 percent.

Muni-bonds may carry a bond rating (for risk and quality) similar to those for corporate bonds if the issue is large and expected to be sold nationally. Small issues for local improvement districts, a single school building, library, or other need for limited funds will not be rated. Even if a bond issue is not rated, you may gauge the risk by noting what kind of a bond it is. (For a more detailed explanation of bond ratings, see p. 63.)

Here are the most important classes of muni-bonds:

1. General obligation (GO) bonds carry the obligation of the issuing organization and its taxing authority to pay interest and principal. GOs are the highest quality bonds issued by a state or municipality.
2. Limited or special tax bonds are backed by the revenues expected to be collected from taxes on cigarettes, gasoline, gambling, race-course betting, or other special activities. No other income from taxation is available to pay principal or interest. Thus, risks may be higher, and the bonds will likely yield a higher return.
3. Revenue bonds are issued to finance a tunnel, bridge, hospital, or other facility from which revenue is expected. That revenue, usually from tolls, is pledged to pay principal and interest. If revenue falls short of projections, muni-bondholders may wait longer for their payoff than expected.
4. Insured muni-bonds typically carry little risk but also yield lower returns. Muni-bonds may be insured by one of several private insuring organizations. Insurance may be of limited value because only muni-bonds with little risk will be insured. Also, insured bond issuers must pay a fee to the insuring organization that reduces the payout to investors.

Most buyers of individual muni-bonds plan to hold them to maturity, so secondary markets for muni-bonds are spotty at best. Selling muni-bonds on the secondary market typically costs more than selling corporate bonds, because fewer buyers are around and even fewer may be familiar with the bonds you wish to sell. As a result, commissions are higher to compensate brokers for the extra effort they must make to acquaint possible buyers with the muni-bonds they have for sale. Spreads, the difference between bid and asked prices, are wider also, because the cost of taking bonds into a dealer's inventory is higher and the bonds may stay there longer.

Institutions are the big buyers of tax-free muni-bonds. **Unit trusts** (UT) and tax-free mutual funds are also big buyers, reselling their shares to individuals. In most cases you are better off buying units in a trust or shares of a mutual fund than buying individual muni-bonds, due to the poor secondary market for muni-bonds.

Unit trusts are aggregations of many issues of muni-bonds purchased by a brokerage. A typical unit trust may comprise $100 million in muni-bonds with a wide diversification of location and risk. The brokers then sell units priced at $1,000 for a proportional piece of the total trust. As compensation the brokerage charges a commission in the range of 4 percent to 4½ percent. The trustee manages the trust but does no trading; the trustee only collects interest payments and forwards the tax-free interest along to unitholders. As the muni-bonds in the trust mature and are paid off, unitholders receive part of their original investment capital back until all bonds in the trust are paid and the trust dissolves. Since little management is required other than forwarding interest payments, trust expenses tend to be low, on the order of ¼ of 1 percent of the trust assets per year.

Mutual funds collect money invested and buy a diversified portfolio of muni-bonds. Interest is passed through to investors free of taxes. A few mutual funds operate as single state funds to provide that state's investors with double tax-free income—free of both state and federal income tax. Managers of tax-free mutual funds buy and sell securities, to maximize returns, and reinvest any capital realized from the payoff of mature muni-bonds. The NAV is the price you pay per share for no-load (no commission) funds or the price you pay plus commission. The NAV of major tax-free funds appears daily in the financial pages of newspapers. Expenses charged for the operation of a tax-free mutual fund will be higher than the minimal expenses for a unit trust, mainly because the portfolio is actively managed, that is, securities are evaluated, bought, and sold for the portfolio to maximize performance.

Bond Ratings

Bond ratings for risk and quality are the key to investing in bonds. Three private organizations, Standard & Poor's, Moody's, and Fitch, rate major issues of bonds sold nationally (Table 3C). The ratings relieve bond buyers of the onerous task of checking repayment provisions and finances of the issuing corporations or municipal authorities. The companies issuing bonds pay the rating organizations for their work, even if the rating for a particular company is less than favorable. Ratings depend on analyses of the issuer's ability to make interest payments on time and to pay the bond principal.

A company is rated as part of an industry that is also rated. A strong company in a weak industry could be downgraded, for example. The company's balance sheet is critical, as the percentage of debt in the company's capital structure may affect its ability to pay. Past and future cash flow may be calculated or estimated to compute the coverage or the ratio of cash flow to interest payments. Ratings involve more than accounting calculations, as considerable experience and judgment are applied. Rating systems vary somewhat between the different agencies. Comparable letter ratings are noted in Table 3C.

Each of the rating organizations publishes monthly updates, since a company's bonds may be downgraded if its financial picture worsens. Make sure you know the rating of any bonds you buy individually or through the portfolio of a bond mutual fund.

Classification	Moody's[1]	Standard & Poor's[2]	Fitch[3]
TABLE 3C　BOND RATING SYSTEMS			
Highest investment grade	Aaa	AAA	AAA
High-quality investment grade	Aa	AA	AA
Less than investment grade but with favorable attributes	A	A	A
Adequate but with some susceptibility to adverse conditions	Baa	BBB	BBB
Speculative (possible junk category)	Ba	BB	BB
High risk	B	B	B
Poor quality, possibly in default	Caa	CCC	CCC
Likely to default or defaulted	Ca	CC	CC
Default-lowest rating	C		
-interest not being paid		C	C
-valued mainly for liquidation or reorganization of company		D	DDD

[1] Moody Investors Services, Inc.
[2] Standard & Poor's Corporation
[3] Fitch Investors Services, Inc.

Commercial Paper

Millions of dollars in **commercial paper** enable corporations and other big players to borrow money from banks, mutual funds, and other institutions, including insurance companies. Essentially, commercial paper is an IOU—an unsecured promissory note with a fixed maturity. For example, XYZ Corporation offers $1 million of its "paper" to a money market mutual fund. The paper is a certificate backed only by the creditworthiness of XYZ Corporation. Commercial paper is typically a discount security similar to T-bills except for the possible risk of default since the issuer is a private firm rather than the U.S. Treasury. The difference between the discount issue price and the face value at ma-

turity represents the yield. Commercial paper maturities tend to be short, usually between 30 and 90 days.

The same rating services that rate corporate bonds rate commercial paper for risk, but they use different notations. Paper may be rated A-1 or P-1 (equivalent to the AAA bond rating), possibly with a + to indicate a firm's creditworthiness. A-3 or P-3 rates are the lowest. Few private investors buy commercial paper because of its high minimum investment, often of $100,000 or $250,000. A few brokerages may buy a collection of small denomination notes for resale to major investors. Money market mutual funds are big buyers of commercial paper; individuals may participate in the market by buying shares of the money market funds.

Money Market Mutual Funds

Key players in the nonstock investment arena are the more than 600 money market mutual funds (MMFs). Total assets exceed $500 billion, and millions of investors are involved. MMFs invest in T-bills, commercial paper, and similar short-maturity instruments, generically known as money market instruments. MMFs maintain a constant share value at $1 per share; yields vary daily and range close to or slightly above T-bill rates.

Since their inception in 1972, MMFs have revolutionized the financial market by offering small investors a chance to earn money market interest with minimal investments, usually $1,000, although a few MMFs accept smaller initial deposits.

MMFs are not insured, but no investor has lost any part of his investment.

Conclusion

The term fixed income securities is a misnomer in today's volatile and flexible markets. Few investments outside of insured CDs and EE-bonds guarantee avoiding any loss of capital. Bonds of all kinds vary in price and current yields based on initial prices move up or down every day.

Generally, CDs and bonds offer less risk than stocks but also yield less over typical market cycle periods. Individual investors need not be totally sophisticated to benefit from bonds and mutual funds that invest in debt securities.

CHAPTER FOUR

Mutual Funds: The People's Market

KEY TERMS FOR THIS CHAPTER

program trading	open-end funds
insider trading	closed-end funds
net asset value (NAV)	prospectus
money market instruments	load
average maturity	12b–1 fees
sector funds	contingent redemption

Look at the stock market today:

- Institutions execute 80 percent to 90 percent of the trades on the New York Stock Exchange (NYSE). Individuals play a minor role.
- Program traders send prices up or down with computer-driven, breath-taking speed to generate volatility that can be scary—and costly.
- Global markets are so closely interlinked that a sneeze in Tokyo can send a chill over Wall Street.

The big boys play hardball, sometimes with savage intensity, and can intimidate small, amateur investors who lack the ex-

pertise and savvy of the pros. **Program trading** engages big investors who buy or sell groups of stocks against futures contracts that involve hundreds of millions of dollars. **Insider trading** earns an immediate advantage for pros close to the market who have access to information not available to the public. Numerous subtle developments in the exchange of securities have turned the market of stocks into a quagmire that can easily trap unwary, small investors as prices move up and down with sickening speed.

The answer for many small investors can be found in the truism, "If you can't beat 'em, join 'em." If the institutional elephants are trampling individual mice, and you are one of the mice, then join up with an institution. The easiest, quickest, least costly way to "join 'em" is to buy shares in a mutual fund. These gargantuan money managers compete on equal terms with giant pension and endowment funds, megamillion-dollar managed portfolios, and arbitrageurs. Mutual funds require understanding on your part before you make an investment.

Mutual Funds—What Are They?

Mutual funds are organized and chartered as corporations. As such, they sell shares for cash, often in small amounts. Typically, $1,000 is the minimum initial investment required to buy mutual fund shares. Some funds permit initial investments of any amount, although an investment of $.10 might be rejected.

Suppose you invest $1,000 in XYZ Diversified Fund. Your money buys a number of full and fractional shares. How many shares your dollars buy depends on the **net asset value (NAV)** or price of the shares at the close of business on the day the mutual fund manager receives your cash. For simplicity, let's say the NAV is $10 per share. Your $1,000 initial investment would then buy 100 shares.

XYZ Diversified Fund combines your $1,000 cash with other shareholders' investments to form a capital pool. The fund managers buy shares in operating companies that they believe will fulfill the objectives of the fund. At the end of every business day, the managers compute the NAV of XYZ's shares by totaling the closing market price for all shares in XYZ's portfolio, adding in any cash in the fund's bank accounts, and subtracting daily expenses and management fees. The managers then come up with a new total asset valuation. When the managers divide the total assets by the number of shares outstanding, the result is the NAV per share. If the prices of the operating companies decline, then your NAV could drop below the initial $10 per share rate. If prices rise, then the NAV climbs above the $10 per share rate.

Mutual funds claim a huge piece of the total investment pie. At the beginning of 1980 564 mutual funds controlled about $100 billion of assets. Over the decade of the 1980s the mutual fund industry grew 10-fold to become one of the really big players on Wall Street. By the beginning of 1990 more than 3,000 mutual funds controlled over $1 trillion of assets. Through mutual funds, individuals gain the benefit of playing in the big league even though their investment may be as little as $10.

As they grew in size and clout during the 1980s, mutual funds splintered into many different categories, trying to earn profits from different niches in the economy. See the box for major categories of mutual funds with representative funds in each category.

Mutual funds may invest in almost any security you can buy or sell on your own. XYZ Bond Fund, for example, may invest shareholders' cash in U.S. Treasury bonds or notes. Another bond fund may reach for higher returns by buying the high-yield (or junk) bonds issued by investment bankers to finance the leveraged buy-outs of major corporations. Other mutual funds may in-

---

MUTUAL FUND CATEGORIES
(with examples)

Aggressive Growth (Most Speculative)
- Benham Gold Equity (NL)
- Columbia Special (NL)
- Dreyfus New Leaders (NL)
- Janus Venture (NL)
- Magellan (LL)
- Value Line Leveraged Growth (NL)
- Vanguard Explorer (NL)

Growth (Speculative)
- Acorn (NL)
- AARP Capital Growth (NL)
- Fidelity Value (NL)
- Founders Special (NL)
- Gabelli Growth (NL)
- Ivy International (NL)
- T. Rowe Price New Era (NL)
- Twentieth Century Heritage (NL)

Conservative Growth (High Quality)
- Babson Value (NL)
- Fidelity Fund (NL)
- Janus Fund (NL)
- Neuberger-Berman Partners (NL)
- Nicholas (NL)
- Safeco Equity (NL)
- Scudder International (NL)
- Vanguard Windsor II (NL)

All-Season, Balanced, or Total Return
- Dodge Cox Balanced (NL)
- Fidelity Equity-Income (LL)
- Lindner Dividend (NL)
- Safeco Income (NL)

- United Services Income (NL)
- Vanguard Wellesley (NL)

Asset Allocation
- Blanchard Strategic Growth (LL)
- Permanent Portfolio (LL)
- USAA Cornerstone (NL)
- Vanguard Asset Allocation (NL)

Income (Corporate Bonds + High-dividend Stocks)
- Axe-Houghton Income (NL)
- AARP General Bond (NL)
- Dreyfus A Bonds (NL)
- Fidelity High Income (NL)
- Royce Income Series (NL)
- Vanguard FIS Short Term (NL)

Income (Government)
- Benham GNMA (NL)
- Benham Zero Target (NL)
- Bull & Bear Government Securities (NL)
- Fidelity Mortgage Securities (NL)
- Neuberger-Berman Money Market (NL)

Tax-exempt Income
- AARP Tax-Free Bond (NL)
- California Tax-Free Income (NL)
- Fidelity High Yield (NL)
- T. Rowe Price Tax Free (NL)

Money Market
- All major fund families

Tax-Free Money Market
- All major fund families

NL = No-load
LL = Low-load

---

vest in foreign countries, gold or other precious metals, drug companies, or housing stocks. Only the imagination and creativity of mutual fund managers limit invest-ment objectives. Three large subcategories of mutual funds are important: money market funds, tax-free mutual funds, and sector funds.

Money Market Funds

Money market funds (MMFs) invest shareholders' cash in **money market instruments.** Bank or thrift certificates of deposit (CDs), treasury bills (T-bills), commercial paper, and similar short-term IOUs are known in the trade as money market instruments. More than 600 MMFs now control more than $500 billion. Both the number of funds and total assets are growing. MMFs were invented in 1972 to offer small investors a chance to earn the same high-interest rates as large depositors. At that time interest rates available on savings accounts at banks and savings and loan associations (S&Ls) were controlled by the Federal Reserve Board (the Fed). Since 1972 MMFs have revolutionized banking and money systems in the United States.

MMFs are not insured. Even so, they are closely regulated by the Securities and Exchange Commission (SEC), and no investor in a MMF has ever lost so much as a nickel.

MMFs maintain a constant NAV, usually $1 per share. Funds maintain the constant $1 per share by keeping maturities short to avoid interest rate risk. Managers turn over their funds often, buying short-term securities that may mature in 10 days and reinvesting the cash in new short-term securities. Although the capital value of shares remains constant, interest rates change daily. The SEC requires that interest rates be stated as a seven-day average.

Average maturities may range from 20 days to 60 or 70 days. When interest rates appear to be heading higher, fund managers will shorten maturities; for example, they will buy CDs and other money market instruments due to be repaid in 21 days rather than 28 days. This tactic enables the manager to regain control of the money and reinvest it sooner at what he perceives will be a higher interest rate. If the manager believes interest rates are headed lower, he will invest in securities with longer maturities to lock in higher rates for longer periods. One useful clue to the possible direction of short-term interest rates is the consensus view of MMF managers as expressed by the **average maturity** of all MMFs by Donoghue's *Money Fund Report* (see Chart 4A for a sample average over a 13-week period).

MMFs offer a place to park savings with quick access (liquidity). You can access a checking account at your bank around the corner by writing a check—MMFs offer similar check-writing convenience. MMFs pay higher interest rates than banks, however, typically $1\frac{1}{2}$ percent to 2 percent higher. Thus, you gain the liquidity of check writing along with more income from your money.

Check writing can also offer instant access to money you have invested in other types of mutual funds within a family of funds. For example, suppose you own shares in XYZ Diversified Fund, which invests in the common stocks of a number of different companies. Ordinarily you would need to write a letter to the fund requesting the manager to sell a specific number of your shares and send you the cash. This operation could take 10–14 days. But if you maintain a MMF in the same family as the XYZ Diversified Fund, you can simply call the manager on a toll-free number and transfer money from the

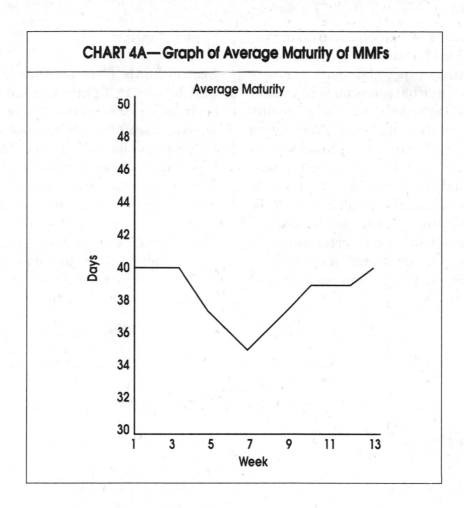

CHART 4A—Graph of Average Maturity of MMFs

Average Maturity

XYZ Diversified Fund to the fund family's MMF. Then, write a check on the MMF. Total time—10 minutes or less.

MMFs serve as a safe haven for your cash if you engage in market timing, a system to reduce risk by getting in and out of the market at suitable times. Some market timing systems call for switching out of a stock fund, for example, into a MMF if the market appears to be heading down. Instead of losing capital value as the stock mutual fund's NAV declines, your money remains safely parked in the fund family's

MMF. There it retains its constant NAV of $1 per share and earns daily interest. When the overall market and your stock mutual fund reverse and begin moving up again, switch your money out of the MMF back into the stock fund. You can make these switches by telephone, usually at no cost.

Tax-free Mutual Funds

Tax-free mutual funds (TFMFs) invest in municipal bonds (muni-bonds) issued by state and local governments and taxing authorities. (See Chapter 3 for a review of the tax-free status of these bonds.)

Numerous mutual funds buy only muni-bonds, and the federal tax code permits those funds to pass the interest through to investors free of taxes in the same way as if they had bought the individual bonds. Some mutual funds invest only in bonds issued by a single state, such as New York or California, to gain the double tax-free (no state or federal tax) interest available to residents of that state. Since income from TFMFs escapes tax, interest rates are lower.

Sector Funds

Sector funds form another large group that invests in tightly focused industries or industry subgroups. These funds are known as sector funds because they invest in specific sectors of industry. Because they lack broad diversification, sector funds tend to be more volatile and risky than most other diversified stock mutual funds.

Two large groups of sector funds were offered by Fidelity and Vanguard in 1991. The list below gives some examples of sector funds. While the degree of concentration within a single industry exhibited by

TWO GROUPS OF SECTOR FUNDS

Fidelity Select Portfolios
Air Transportation
American Gold
Automation & Machinery
Automotive
Biotechnology
Broadcast & Media
Brokerage & Investment Mgmt.
Capital Goods
Chemicals
Computers
Defense & Aerospace
Electric Utilities
Electronics
Energy
Financial Services
Food & Agriculture
Health
Housing
Industrial Materials
Leisure

Life Insurance
Medical
Paper & Forest Products
Precious Metals & Minerals
Property & Casualty
Regional Banks
Restaurant Industry
Retailing
Savings & Loan
Software & Computer Services
Technology
Telecommunications
Transportation
Utilities
Vanguard Specialized Portfolios
Energy
Gold & Precious Metals
Health Care
Service Economy
Technology

these two sector funds was relatively new when they introduced it, gold, energy, chemical, and similar funds have concentrated attention on a narrow part of the market for many years.

Open- and Closed-end Funds

Two distinctly different forms of mutual funds operate in today's markets: open-end funds and closed-end funds.

Open-end Funds

The most common form of mutual funds are the **open-end funds,** so-called because their number of shares is open ended. Open-end ABC Fund, for example, stands ready to sell more shares or redeem shares from current owners on any business day. Continued new money flowing into the fund expands the number of shares. As money flows in and shares increase, total assets rise to keep the NAV relatively constant over a short term. Market action and the adeptness of ABC Fund's manager may cause the NAV to rise. Or, despite the best efforts of the manager, market action may cause the NAV to decline. Remember, the NAV is calculated at the end of every business day and seldom remains constant.

Shares in an open-end fund trade only at the fund's office, and only the fund manager can issue new shares or redeem shares owned by investors. Shares are tracked almost exclusively by computer entry, with each new purchase or redemption being acknowledged by a computer-generated confirmation, rather than a certificate, which serves as evidence of ownership. Issuance of certificates complicates trading and is discouraged.

When you buy shares in an open-end fund, the price is the NAV computed at the end of the day. If you send $1,000 to ABC Fund, for example, and it arrives (by mail or wire transfer) on a Tuesday before 4 P.M. Eastern time, your investment is translated into shares at the price computed at the end of that Tuesday. Some mutual funds may set earlier deadlines for money to be invested at that day's closing NAV. If the NAV at the end of Tuesday is $7.31 per share, your $1,000 buys 136.799 shares if the fund is a no-load (no commission) fund, or 125.171 shares if ABC Fund carries an $8\frac{1}{2}$ percent load (commission). If you own shares in no-load ABC Fund and submit a request to redeem $1,000 that arrives in good order as described below on Tuesday, the manager will reduce the fund's holdings and your account by 136.799 shares and send you the cash within seven days. No-load buy/redeem prices are the same, but the load fund's redemption (bid) price is the actual NAV without a load. Thus, the number of open-end fund shares may be, and usually is, different every day.

Mutual funds require that instructions to redeem shares arrive in good order at the manager's office. (A typical request for redemption is shown in the box on page 72.) Even though you bought shares in a mutual fund through a broker, you must write a letter to the fund to redeem shares; the broker cannot do it for you. A broker may, as a convenience, generate the letter, but you must sign it and your signature must be guaranteed. Authorized officers of commercial banks and member firms of

---

SAMPLE REDEMPTION LETTER

Date

0000 Mutual Fund
Address
City, State, Zip

Gentlemen:

   Please redeem _____ shares* of 0000 Mutual Fund. My account number is_____. Please send proceeds to the following address (state your full address) as soon as possible.

Sincerely,

Your Name

Signature guarantee _____
Authorized Signature

---

* If you wish to redeem all shares in your account, write:
Please redeem all shares of 0000 Mutual Fund.

   Some funds may accept a redemption request under some dollar limit without a signature guarantee. To avoid possible problems, it is safer to get a guarantee. Authorized officers of commercial banks and member firms of the New York Stock Exchange can guarantee signatures. Notarized signatures are not acceptable.

---

the New York Stock Exchange (NYSE) can guarantee signatures (notarized signatures are not acceptable). Some funds may accept a redemption request under some dollar limit without a signature guarantee, but to avoid problems, it is safer to get a guarantee. A letter that does not comply with these requirements will not arrive in good order. These requirements are stiff, but they are there for your protection.

Closed-end Funds

Closed-end funds, although treated as mutual funds, operate differently from open-end funds. First, the number of shares in a closed-end fund remains con- stant. When the fund opens for business, it offers a specific number of shares, say 10 million, through an underwriter. Once shares are sold under an initial offering, they trade on one of the stock exchanges or over-the-counter (OTC).

Second, the price of shares depends on supply and demand. The NAV is computed daily, as with open-end funds, but the ac- tual share trade price may be, and usually is, considerably different from the NAV on the trade date. Shares in a closed-end fund trade just like the shares of other corpo- rations on an exchange or OTC. If the trade price is less than the NAV, the fund's shares sell at a discount. If the trade price of shares exceeds the NAV, the shares are said to be trading at a premium. Most closed-end funds typically trade at a discount from the NAV. Since shares of closed-end funds trade on an exchange or OTC, the price for each trade may be fixed at any time during the day—it is not dependent on the value of the NAV at the time of the trade or at the end of the day.

Third, shares in closed-end funds trade through brokers. Expect to pay a commission on each trade either buying or selling. There is no such thing as a no-load or load closed-end fund.

Daily reports on open-end mutual funds appear in *The Wall Street Journal, Investor's Daily*, and most metropolitan newspapers. Reports on closed-end stock, bond, single-country funds (as the name implies, they invest only in one country), and special funds appear every Monday in *The Wall Street Journal* to reflect closing prices for the previous Friday (see Table 4A for a sample report).

One note of caution: Avoid buying shares of a closed-end fund at the initial offering. Initial shares are sold without a commission; however, a concession to the broker directly from the fund managers reduces the value of the shares by about 7 percent to 7½ percent below the initial offering price. This means there may be shares and/or cash in a closed-end fund's portfolio worth only $.93 for every dollar in share value offered initially. Wait for a few days, weeks, or even months before buying shares in a new closed-end fund. During the first week or two, the underwriters and broker network usually maintain a firm price while all shares are being placed (sold). After that, the issue is turned loose to find its own level of value. Typically, closed-end shares drop about 20 percent from their offering price within a few months. There are exceptions, of course; nothing is fixed in the market.

The Prospectus

Your key source of information regarding a mutual fund is the **prospectus,** a pub-

TABLE 4A	PUBLICLY TRADED FUNDS			
NAV & Discounts: Closed-end Funds				
Fund Name	Where Traded*	NAV**	Closing Price	Percent–Discount + Premium***
Aberc. Ltd.	NYSE	17.70	15¾	− 11.02
Biminik Est.	Amex	9.51	12⅛	+ 27.50
Gorge Mtn.	OTC	14.63	11⅝	− 20.54
Kotona Ptn.	OTC	16.04	14¼	− 11.52
Minima PLC	NYSE	15.54	11¾	− 24.39
Notes: NAV as reported by fund—unaudited. Closing prices Friday.				

* Exchange or OTC where fund trades
** Net asset value

$$*** \text{Discount + Premium} = \frac{\text{(Closing Price–NAV)}}{\text{NAV}}$$

lication produced by the fund to describe its objectives and operations. The SEC requires every open-end mutual fund to send you a copy of the prospectus before or co-incident with your purchase of shares. If you buy shares from a broker, he or she must supply a prospectus to you. For your own protection and to avoid misunder-standings, insist on receiving a prospectus before buying mutual fund shares and read it carefully.

Admittedly a prospectus is dry reading, but it supplies you with valuable infor-mation. While the SEC can require a mu-tual fund to send you a prospectus, it can-not, unfortunately, require you to read it. Two parts are especially vital: the sum-mary of fees and expenses and the sum-mary of important information. Read these brief sections even if you choose not to read the full document.

The summary of fees and expenses (see box on page 75) notes all commissions, re-demption fees, exchange fees, and any other transaction fees, plus annual oper-ating expenses. Projections of these costs and expenses over 1, 3, 5, and 10 years, based on a 5 percent annual return and a redemption at the end of each period, per-mit comparisons between funds.

Two categories of expenses are incurred by all mutual funds. Expenses are de-ducted from income earned by the secu-rities held in a fund's portfolio.

The first category of expenses includes the necessary operating expenses—trans-fer agent fees, legal fees, and custodian bank fees. The expense ratio relates op-erating expenses to the fund's assets. Small funds typically report higher expense ra-tios because they spread expenses over fewer shares. Specialty funds, such as gold

and international funds, may also incur higher-than-average expenses—managers must travel more widely because infor-mation about foreign companies is not as readily available as information about companies in the United States. Probably the lowest expense ratio in the industry was the .21 percent charged by Vanguard's 500 Index Trust in 1989.

The second category of expenses in-cludes management fees for a fund's ad-visers. Management fees cover the salaries of clerks and telephone operators, printing costs, and the myriad costs of running a business. Earning the management fee is the primary reason mutual funds exist. Load and no-load funds operate in much the same manner; low-load (low-commis-sion) mutual funds subtract a portion of your investment as a commission to pay for marketing expenses. The main source of income for all funds is the management fee.

Look for the management fee in the pro-spectus. Fees typically range from $\frac{1}{2}$ per-cent to 1 percent and drop on a sliding scale as the fund's assets grow.

A combined rate of expenses plus man-agement fee of around $1\frac{1}{2}$ percent is fairly typical, but the range is wide. One of the myths of Wall Street is that no-load funds charge higher management fees than load funds. Actually, all funds (except low-load) operate as no-load funds since load funds do not participate in the commissions charged by brokers.

The prospectus' summary of important information is usually on the cover or the first text page. Look for a statement of the fund's objectives and the managers' plans for achieving them. A growth fund, for ex-ample, may include a statement similar

Examples of Expenses and Fee Schedules for a No-load Fund (Generic Income Fund) and a Fund with a Contingent Redemption Fee (Precious Metals Fund).

GENERIC INCOME FUND

The following table illustrates all expenses and fees that a shareholder of the Fund will incur. The expenses and fees set forth below are for the 1991 fiscal year.

FUND EXPENSES

Shareholder Transaction Expenses		Annual Fund Operating Expenses	
Sales Charge on Purchases	None	Management Expenses	0.13%
Sales Charge on Reinvested Dividends	None	Investment Advisory Fees	0.15
		Shareholder Accounting Costs	0.15
Redemption Fees	None	12b-1 Fees	None
Exchange Fees	None	Distribution Costs	0.04
		Other Expenses	0.04
		Total Fund Operating Expenses	**0.51%**

The purpose of this table is to help you understand the various costs and expenses that you would bear directly or indirectly as an investor in the Fund.

The following example illustrates the expenses that you would incur on a $1,000 investment over various periods, assuming (1) a 5% annual rate of return and (2) redemption at the end of each period. The Fund charges no redemption fees of any kind.

1 year	3 years	5 years	10 years
$5	$16	$29	$64

FEE TABLE
Precious Metals Fund

The purpose of the fee table is to assist investors in understanding the costs and expenses that you would bear directly or indirectly as an investor in the Fund. For more complete descriptions of the various costs and expenses, see following sections of this prospectus.

Shareholder Transaction Expenses		Annual Fund Operating Expenses (as a percentage of average net assets)	
Contingent Deferred Sales Charge (as a percentage of the lesser of total cost or net asset value of shares redeemed)	4.00%	Management Fee	0.58%
		12b-1 Fee	0.53%
		Other Expenses	0.67%
Exchange Fee (per exchange)	$5.00	**Total Fund Operating Expenses**	**1.78%**

Example

You would pay the following expenses on a $1000 investment, assuming (1) 5% annual return and (2) redemption at the end of each period:

1 Year	3 Years	5 Years	10 Years
$57	$73	$91	$199

to: "The (fund) is a no-load mutual fund with the primary objective of long-term growth of capital with secondary objectives of regular income and preservation of capital. The (fund) invests primarily in common stocks." An income stock fund may state: "The investment objective is current income with the prospect of increasing dividend income and the potential for capital appreciation. The (fund) invests primarily in higher than average dividend-paying common stocks of well-established large companies." The prospectus for an aggressive mutual fund may include statements of policy such as: "The (fund) may borrow money from banks to purchase or carry securities. This use of leverage must be considered a speculative investment activity." Some aggressive funds may also state that it is their intention to buy or sell options and/or futures to hedge positions or to gain more income. These statements indicate a higher level of risk associated with owning the fund's shares.

Portfolio holdings may not be listed in a prospectus. Attempts to lighten the reading load and to state information in common English have led to shorter prospectuses. If you request it, a fund will send you an expanded version listing its holdings as of a specific date. More useful information on the makeup of a fund's portfolio can be found in a recent annual or quarterly report of the fund's activities. The fund will gladly send you a copy of its most recent report for your study; just ask.

Other important information is contained in the prospectus: initial purchase minimums, repurchase minimums, how to redeem shares, whether check writing is permitted, and restrictions (if any) on car-rying out these transactions by telephone or in writing. Read the prospectus and understand your proposed investment. The SEC's disclosure requirements are intended to help you become a more knowledgeable investor.

Loads, No-loads, and Low-loads

Open-end mutual funds attract buyers for their shares by one of three methods: load funds, no-load funds, and low-load funds.

1. **Load** funds sell shares through brokers who earn a commission on each sale. In the jargon of Wall Street the commission is known as a load, from the dictionary definition of load as "a burden." The maximum commission allowed by the SEC is $8\frac{1}{2}$ percent of the money invested. A dwindling number of stock and specialty funds charge the maximum $8\frac{1}{2}$ percent load due to growing competition from no-load mutual funds. At the $8\frac{1}{2}$ percent rate, for every $10,000 you invest with a broker to buy shares in a load fund, $850 stays with the broker and the brokerage firm as a front-end commission; $9,150 buys shares in the load fund picked for you by the broker. The front-end commission is the full charge for a round-trip; you would pay nothing more to redeem shares at a later date. Note that no part of the commission or load goes to the mutual fund itself. The load is an incentive for the broker to market the fund's shares.

Load percentages typically vary from 0 for money market mutual funds to 4 percent to 4½ percent for bond funds and 5 percent to 8½ percent for stock and specialty funds, such as gold and international funds. The commission rate drops as the amount of money invested increases. For a sale of $1 million, for example, the commission may drop to as little as 1 percent. Your broker sells shares to you based on his analysis of your investment objectives, risk tolerance, and your other holdings. The broker takes no active role in managing the portfolio of the mutual fund; he is strictly a salesperson.

2. No-load funds sell shares directly to individual investors. They spend part of their earnings or assets to advertise in newspapers, such as *The Wall Street Journal*, in magazines, such as *Forbes* or *Money*, and by direct mail to shareholders or lists of potential investors. Instead of 91½ percent of your investment buying shares, as in the case of some load funds, all of your investment—100 percent—buys shares in a no-load fund. All of your money goes to work for you. No-load fund families offer an exciting variety of funds from which to choose. Since their growth, or even their existence, depends on service to individuals, no-load funds offer ready advice by telephone or mail.

Investing in a no-load fund is easy: You simply call or write the fund for an application and return it with your check in the envelope provided. A few of the large no-load fund families maintain sales offices in major cities for face-to-face service. Load funds continue to dominate in number, but nearly 1,200 no-loads offer enough variety to satisfy almost every investment objective.

3. Low-load funds sell shares directly to investors in the same way as no-loads, but they charge a 1 percent to 4 percent commission or load. This low commission flows directly to the mutual fund to pay marketing costs, such as advertising and promotion.

Read the prospectus from a mutual fund you may be considering to look for a possible front-end load or other charge and the range of other costs. These costs were once considered hidden, buried in the back pages of a prospectus. Recently the SEC forced funds to disclose fees and charges in a simple and consistent manner.

Fees and Charges

The 12b-1 Fee

Probably the most misunderstood allowable mutual fund fee is the one known as the **12b-1 fee.** The number refers to the section of SEC regulations that permits open-end mutual funds to charge up to 1½ percent of a fund's assets for marketing and distribution each year. Note that 12b-1 fees are not charged against a fund's earnings or new money being invested. The charge is against assets. If a fund's assets total $100 million and management charges a 1 percent 12b-1 fee, the fund's asset base declines by $1 million, thus depleting the assets available for investing. If a fund's asset base declines, shareholders can expect earnings to decline because less money is being invested in the market. Once started, 12b-1 fees continue year after year.

Not all mutual funds levy 12b-1 fees. Newsletters and the daily reports of open-end mutual fund performance carry a notation for those mutual funds that charge 12b-1 fees. However, to find the exact percentage, you may need to consult the prospectus. Some mutual funds that charge front-end loads also levy 12b-1 fees—a double charge for marketing and distribution. The 12b-1 fees are more common among no-load funds, as managers tap the fund's assets for cash to bolster marketing efforts.

The Contingent Redemption Charge

The **contingent redemption** charge, or contingent deferred sales charge (CDSC), may reduce the amount you receive if you elect to cash out of some funds. A few mutual funds market their shares through brokers on a so-called no-load basis. When you buy shares in these funds from a broker, you pay no commission. All of your investment funds go to work for you, as in the case of a true no-load fund. There is a hitch, however. The broker actually earns a concession, or sales fee, from the mutual fund manager equal to about 4 percent of your investment—less if your investment is relatively large, over $100,000 for example. When you decide to redeem shares, you will find that a deferred sales charge, a fee contingent on how long your investment stayed in the fund, reduces the amount you receive. A typical CDSC may be 6 percent if you redeem shares within the first 12 months, 5 percent during the second 12 months, and so on with a 1 percent reduction each additional year. After six years you may redeem all shares with no redemption fee.

The rationale for the CDSC is that the fund needs time for your cash to earn a return that recoups the concession paid to the broker. If you redeem shares before the fund has earned back the broker's fee, you pay the redemption charge. Some brokers may not explain the contingent redemption fee clearly, opting to emphasize the no-load feature instead. Check the prospectus for details regarding a possible contingent redemption fee.

Noncontingent Redemption Charges

Noncontingent redemption charges may be levied for a no-load fund. A redemption fee may apply for a specific period of time or forever. A redemption fee fixed as a percentage of the NAV at redemption can be particularly onerous after several years. As the fund's NAV expands, so does the size of the redemption fee. Some noncontingent redemption fees may be stated in dollars alone or in combination with a percentage fee. Check the prospectus for details regarding possible noncontingent redemption charges.

Many fixed redemption fees are designed to discourage frequent or abusive switching. If you pay a redemption fee every time you move out of a stock or bond fund into the safety of a money market mutual fund, you may switch less frequently.

Evaluating Mutual Funds

To discourage misleading representations and the abuse of the no-load designation, the SEC now requires that daily reports of mutual fund performance figures in *The Wall Street Journal* and the financial sections of major newspapers carry notations that disclose the necessary information. (See Table 4B.)

Newsletters and financial magazines compare the performance of mutual funds regularly. Grouping funds by category helps to reduce the confusion when comparing performance. Results reported by a gold fund, for example, would not be consistent with reports from a money market fund. Aggressive stock funds are typically compared with each other, and so on. Not so apparent is the comparison of results for load versus no-load or low-load funds.

A comparison of the returns from a load fund to a no-load fund is distorted if the load is not factored in. For example, suppose Fund A (a load stock fund that exacts an 8½ percent load) and Fund B (a no-load fund) each report a 10 percent total return for the year. If you were to amortize the load over only one year, return from Fund A would drop to 1½ percent (10 percent less 8½ percent load) to compare with a 10 percent return from Fund B, a true no-load fund. Spreading the load over 8½ years would drop the load charge to 1 percent for each year. Fund A's return would then drop to 9 percent (10 percent reported return less 1 percent for the year's amor-

TABLE 4B			**MUTUAL FUND: EXAMPLE OF A DAILY REPORT**				
Fund Family	NAV[1]	Offer[2]	NAV Change[3]	Fund Family	NAV	Offer	NAV Change
Addode[4]				*CTCSP*			
Ag Gro[5] p[6]	11.59	12.67	–.02	BTL f	14.60	NL	+.01
Grow f[7]	14.65	16.01	–.06	BGro f	13.20	NL	–.07
Eq-Inc.	11.24	11.89	+.11	CEqui f	9.89	NL	–.13
InterB p	9.16	9.80	–.13	Inc-C f	16.19	NL	–.11
Xbpr p	20.76	22.69	–.03	*FLSIP*			
				Accen t[10]	14.66	NL	—
BXTPR				Qtr t	11.33	NL	–.03
AsAll r[8]	15.88	NL[9]	–.03	*MHDOP*			
Grow r	13.61	NL	–.09	Sht-TmB	22.24	24.31	+.09
Equity r	21.39	NL	–.06	Gr-Inc	16.79	18.35	—
Income r	11.33	NL	+.11	Eqty-Gro	14.26	15.58	+.03
All-S	8.40	NL	+.08				

[1] Net asset value—at close of business previous market day. May also be labeled Bid or Sell.
[2] Offering price, or Buy or Asked. Difference between offer & NAV is load or sales charge.
[3] Change in NAV from previous day's NAV.
[4] Name of fund family.
[5] Abbreviated name of fund within family.
[6] Small p following abbreviated fund name indicates fund charge, a 12b-1 fee for marketing against assets.
[7] Small f following abbreviated fund name indicates previous day's data instead of current day's figures.
[8] Small r following abbreviated fund name indicates fund may charge a contingent deferred sales charge (CDSC) or a redemption fee. A CDSC may apply if shares are sold within a limited period. A redemption fee applies any time.
[9] Fund charges no front-end sales charge. Offer price is same as NAV.
[10] Small t following abbreviated fund name indicates both a contingent deferred sales charge and 12b.1 fee apply.

tized load) and compare more favorably with the 10 percent return from Fund B. Many investors forget to take into account how a front-end commission impacts earnings and total return.

Mutual Fund Registration

Before a mutual fund can legally sell shares anywhere in the United States it must first meet the regulations of the SEC. The prospectus that accompanies offers to sell shares in the fund must also be approved by the SEC. The primary focus of the SEC is to make sure the prospectus discloses all the facts an astute investor needs to make a prudent investment decision.

Most states also regulate the sale of securities, including mutual funds, to its citizens. State securities commissions came into being originally under blue sky laws. (The term derives from the objective of preventing the sale of securities with little substance other than the blue sky overhead.) Registration is relatively routine, but the process does involve fees from mutual funds, both initially and annually. Most large funds are licensed to sell shares in all states. Smaller funds may elect not to incur the expense of registering in some states. For instance, a fund may believe the amount of business it could expect to do in a state would not pay back the costs of registration. Thus, if you live in one of the thinly populated states, such as Idaho or Montana, you will likely have fewer registered mutual funds to choose from than if you live in New York or California.

Although it is not illegal to own shares in a fund that is unregistered in your state, a fund will not send you an application nor will a broker offer to sell you shares in a fund that is not registered where you live. So what can you do if you are living in a state where a particular fund is not registered but you would like to buy shares in that fund? You can apply from an address in a state where the fund is registered, possibly the address of a relative or friend. Mutual funds prefer not to engage in such subterfuges, however, so your best bet is to look for a similar fund that is registered in your state.

Mutual Funds as Limited Partnerships

While most mutual funds are organized and function as corporations, a few funds are organized as limited partnerships. Partnerships include general and limited partners. Individual investors are limited partners and have no liability beyond their cost of buying shares. General partners are responsible for managing the fund and assume unlimited liability.

For all practical purposes an investor will not be affected by the different status except for taxation. As one of the limited partners, an investor receives full distributions before taxes at the fund level and reports income on his personal income tax return.

Income and Capital Gains Taxation

All mutual funds report net income after expenses, including any taxes paid. As long as a mutual fund distributes 98 percent of its income and 98 percent of any realized capital gains to shareholders, the fund pays no taxes on the income. What you see is what you get.

Mutual funds report net income, short-term capital gains, and long-term capital gains each year. Before January 31, mutual funds are required to send Form 1099-DIV reports to the Internal Revenue Service (IRS) and to shareholders. Use these reports when calculating your income tax liabilities. If a fund incurs a net capital loss from transactions, you may not use it to offset capital gains from other sources. The fund carries any internal losses forward to offset capital gains in a later year.

Yield and Total Return

Dividends paid by a fund to shareholders are the yield. Yield is particularly important when comparing the performance of MMFs. A MMF may compute dividends daily, then compound earnings daily and post them monthly by sending you a confirmation of reinvested dividends. A stock mutual fund may report dividends only once a year. Yield resembles your earnings on a bank savings account where the value of your capital does not change.

Total return includes yield plus capital gains realized from internal transactions by the fund and the difference, if any, in the NAV of shares. A long-term bond fund may, for example, yield 10 percent, or $2 per share, for the year at the same time that the NAV declines from $20 to $18 per share. The total return would be 0—10 percent yield is offset by a 10 percent decline in the NAV. If the fund reported capital losses on any transactions, the loss would not be reported. If the reverse market ac-

tion causes the bond fund's NAV to rise $2, to $22 per share, then total return could reach 25 percent for the year—10 percent yield, 10 percent increase in NAV, plus 5 percent realized capital gain. Astute investors use total return when comparing performance of mutual funds.

Timing Mutual Fund Investments

Stock and bond mutual funds typically distribute yearly dividends and realized capital gains at or near year's end. MMFs declare dividends more often. Since SEC regulations require mutual funds to distribute up to 98 percent of their earnings each year to avoid paying a corporation tax, final annual figures are not known until the books close on December 31. Dividends paid or capital gains distributed shortly after January 1 of the following year are considered by the IRS to be taxable for the previous year that ended December 31.

While these mechanics of operation are commonly known, investors may trip over a small problem—investing too soon before a dividend or gain distribution date. Suppose you invest $1,000 in shares of CDE Fund that are priced at $10 per share on December 15. On December 20, CDE Fund declares a $1 dividend and the NAV drops to $9 per share. You appear to lose nothing because you now have $1 in dividends plus shares in CDE Fund worth $9 per share—the same $10 you invested. However, all dividends (except those from tax-free funds) are taxable. If your marginal tax bracket is 28 percent, your $1 dividend is actually worth $.72.

Avoid putting new money in stock or bond mutual funds within a few weeks or months of the date when distributions are expected. Not all funds distribute dividends and gains at or near year's end. The fund's prospectus or a newsletter that reports on many funds can alert you to the date a mutual fund distributed dividends or gains the previous year, and you can use that information to time your investments. While you await a propitious time for investment, park your cash in a MMF where it will not lose capital while it earns daily interest.

Conclusion

Mutual funds offer small investors the opportunity to build a portfolio of assets at minimum risk and minimum cost for these reasons:

• A major risk involved with investing in individual issues (stocks or bonds) is the possibility of picking a security that fails to perform as anticipated, that is, a bum stock. This is stock risk, and the time-honored method of dealing with stock risk is diversification, owning a number of different stocks or bonds. If one stock or bond fails to perform, the effect on the overall portfolio is minimal. Buying shares in a mutual fund affords instant diversification, as the fund owns shares or bonds from many different companies, and each mutual fund share represents a slice of ownership in all securities owned by the fund.

• Sharing expenses with thousands or millions of other shareholders through a mutual fund reduces investment costs. If investors stick with no-load mutual funds, the dollar costs of buying and selling shares is zero, but these investors must act on their own to pick the fund(s) and send their money to the fund managers, thereby increasing their expenditure of time. Small amounts may be added to mutual fund accounts for little or no cost to permit regular investments.

Mutual funds have become the small investor's choice, particularly for people who can make their own investment decisions.

CHAPTER FIVE

Commodities

KEY TERMS FOR THIS CHAPTER

spot market	marked to market
futures	clearing corporation
hedging	tick
contract	price limit
lay off risk	long
speculators	short
leverage	open outcry
margin	spread trading
position	

The trading of commodities, the basic raw materials that go into the products we use in everyday life, is a fast-paced, active part of Wall Street carried on mainly by professionals. Individuals play, but only a few survive. Commodities can range from gold to rapeseed to pork bellies and include cotton for clothing and packaging, oil for many different uses, tallow for soap, and other products. Commodities trade, sometimes wildly, on specialized exchanges in the United States and around the world.

Trading commodities affects each one of us every day, because the prices determined in the trading pits affect our cost of living. The world price for oil determines how much we pay for gasoline at the pump. The price of corn affects how much we pay for bacon and breakfast cereals at the supermarket. Even more than stocks of U.S. corporations or bonds issued by the U.S. Treasury, commodities are traded on a worldwide market. The price for one ounce of gold may be quoted on the Commodity Exchange (COMEX) in New York, but every buyer and seller on the floor keeps an eye on prices in London, Geneva, and Hong Kong. There are no isolated commodity markets.

Commodities affect everyone. You can benefit from knowing how markets work whether you invest or sit on the sidelines.

The Spot Market

When a miller enters the market and buys 5,000 bushels of wheat to be processed into flour, he buys on the cash market or **spot market,** so-called because the transaction is settled on the spot. In other words, the miller contracts for delivery of 5,000 bushels of wheat at today's price.

How much does the miller pay for his wheat? The price depends on how much wheat is available (supply) and how much the miller and all the other users of wheat want to buy (demand). These factors change minute by minute according to the weather, politics, currency exchange values, and an almost limitless number of other variables. Prices represent the sum total of all opinions on both sides of transactions. Spot prices at the market's close are reported daily in the financial press.

Commodity exchanges deal in wholesale quantities, but their prices affect retail prices directly, as in the case of eggs, or indirectly, as in the case of a raw material such as rubber for tires.

Although a huge volume of business transpires on the cash markets, these transactions have little appeal to speculators and hedgers. The real action is in the commodity futures markets.

The Futures Market

The **futures** market involves trading for commodities to be delivered at some future date for a specific price determined today. Futures trading benefits both sellers and buyers but in different ways. Trading in commodity futures began as an effort to reduce the buyer's risk of raw material price fluctuations through a process known as **hedging.** The flour miller who buys the 5,000 bushels of wheat and pays the spot price knows immediately how much his raw material costs. He does not know how much he will be paying for wheat three months down the road even though he may have quoted a price for flour to be delivered to a baker at that time. If he contracts to deliver so many hundred-pound sacks of flour six months later at a price fixed today, he could lose heavily if the price of wheat rises sharply in the interim. Or, he could gain a huge profit if the price of wheat drops and his price quotation for flour remains firm.

Flour millers prefer not to engage in the business of guessing what might happen to the price of wheat. They are in the business of producing flour. So they hedge. The miller buys a specified amount, known as a **contract**—in this case 5,000 bushels of wheat to be delivered in six months. At the delivery date the miller enters the spot market and buys another 5,000 bushels of wheat. He also sells a contract to close out his buy position in the futures market, in effect, canceling out his original buy contract. If the spot price for the wheat is higher than he expected, he loses on the grain he buys—he pays more for it than he anticipated. But he profits from an equal rise in the value of the contract he bought six months previously. The value of the first contract rises because the price of wheat rises. Thus, he breaks even on the cost of the wheat he needs to produce flour. (See box on page 85 for calculations of how hedging works to minimize the effect of fluctuating raw materials prices on the

EXAMPLE OF HEDGING THE COST OF WHEAT

A miller contracts with a baker to supply flour from 5,000 bushels of wheat to be delivered in six months. Miller bases price on wheat at $3.50/bushel. To hedge, he buys a futures contract at $3.50/bushel. Six months later futures price has risen to $3.75/bushel, and cash wheat is $3.65/bushel.

	Cash Transaction	Futures Transaction
Date—buy futures contract		$3.50/bushel
Date + 6 months—buy cash wheat	$3.65/bushel	
Date + 6 months—sell futures contract		$3.75/bushel
Futures profit ($.25 × 5,000)		$1,250.00
Cash price paid (expected @ $3.50)	$17,500.00	
Cost of unhedged wheat ($3.65 × 5,000)	$18,250.00	
Loss on cash purchase	($750.00)	
Total gain from hedging ($1,250 − $750)		$500.00
Commissions on two contracts		($120.00)
Net gain		$380.00

final cost of a product, flour in this example.)

Growers also use futures to hedge and reduce their risks. A farmer may sell his wheat three, six, or more months ahead of harvest. When he sees a future price that he likes, he can lock in a profit by agreeing to sell his crop at the future price after harvest. He gives up the prospect of selling at an even higher price than the current quoted price for future delivery, but he gains the security of knowing that his wheat will bring a known price—and a known profit.

Producers and growers hedge to **lay off risk;** that is, transfer the risk of fluctuating raw materials prices to **speculators.** Commodities markets bring hedger and speculator together. Each has different goals.

Hedgers are conservative. They wish to avoid risk by minimizing the effect of changing prices on their activity, whether it is making something out of a raw ma-

terial or selling a crop they have grown and harvested.

Speculators are deliberate risk-takers. They are the high flyers who hope to earn big profits from a minimum investment, and they accept greater risks than any other group of players on Wall Street. Speculators trade in commodities strictly for the profit and for the **leverage** they gain in the market. Margin, or leverage, is the key to high profits, and it works like this: If you agree to a contract for some commodity at $10,000 and pay $500 for the right to take that position, the $500 is the **margin,** a proportional portion of the contract's value paid by both the buyer and seller of a contract to guarantee the contract will be fulfilled. (Buying or selling a contract means you have taken and hold a **position** in the market.)

Margin leads to the high profit possibilities for commodities traders, a process known as leverage. To continue with the example used above, if you put up 5 percent on margin to control a $10,000 contract, you speculate with $500. If the price of the contract increases to $11,000, your profit is $1,000 and your gain is 200 percent over your margin, less commissions. If the price of the contract declines to $9,000, you have lost your original investment of $500 plus an additional $500.

In commodities trading the value of every margin account or position is **marked to market** at the end of each trading day; that is, all losses and gains are updated by an independent **clearing corporation** which revalues each contract to the closing price. If the margin coverage has declined, the speculator is called upon to put up more margin, that is, to deposit more cash to maintain his position. If the market moves quickly during the day, the margin call may come earlier than the end of trading for the day. A quick telephone call from the broker may require the speculator to transfer cash immediately, or the contract will be sold before its value declines below the margin. The speculator

may lose most of his money—this is the risk of speculating in the commodities market. Under erratic and volatile trading he could lose more than his original margin.

Commodities Trading

Contracts

Commodities are traded as contracts. A contract involves some specific wholesale quantity unique to each commodity. For example, a contract for wheat is 5,000 bushels. The complete contract specifications for wheat futures traded on the Chicago Board of Trade (CBOT) are noted in the box below. Here are explanations of some of the wheat contract terms:

• Grades are specified as No. 2 Soft Red wheat or other alternatives. Quality specifications are detailed and specific for each grade of wheat to assure both buyers and sellers they are contracting for a stan-

WHEAT FUTURES CONTRACT SPECIFICATIONS	
Trading Unit	5,000 bushels
Deliverable Grade	No. 2 Soft Red, No. 2 Hard Red Winter, No. 2 Dark Northern Spring, No. 1 Northern Spring at par, and substitutions at differentials established by the exchange
Price Quotation	Cents and ¼ cents per bushel
Tick	¼ cent per bushel ($12.50 per contract)
Daily Price Limit	$.20 per bushel ($1,000 per contract) above or below the previous day's settlement price. Variations for spot month.
Contract Months	March, May, July, September, & December
Contract Year	Starts in July; ends in May
Last Trading Day	7th business day before last business day of delivery month
Last Delivery Day	Last business day of delivery month
Ticker Symbol	W

dardized product; that is, a known product. If the wheat that is actually delivered fails to make the grade (samples are tested to assure the wheat delivered meets specifications), price differentials adjust for quality. If a shipment fails to meet specs, the price will be lower than par, the price noted in the contract.

• Prices are quoted in increments as small as ¼ cent per bushel.

• **Tick** is the minimum difference permitted between a bid to buy or an offer to sell and the last (previous) price. If the previous price was $3.52 per bushel, the next price would have to be at least $3.52 and ¼ or $3.51 and ¾. A trade at a higher price is called an uptick, and a trade at a lower price is called a downtick.

• The daily **price limit** is $.20 per bushel. Daily limit is one of the rules that can trip up speculators. If the price of a contract moves up $.20 per bushel, trading at a higher price stops. Trading has reached its daily limit. If you are trying to buy wheat futures, you are locked out because no higher prices will be accepted and no one will sell for less that day. If you own a contract and the price declines the daily limit, you can't get out of your position. Sometimes, the price declines the daily limit for several days and speculators are trapped—they are unable to sell out their position and are required to add to their margin. A market that rises or falls the daily limit presents real hazards for the speculator who fails to track his positions regularly, sometimes on a minute-by-minute basis.

• Other wheat futures contract specifications noted in Table 5A are important to traders but of less general interest.

Other commodities have their own specifications. A contract for sugar is 112,000 pounds, for example. (See Table 5A for a

TABLE 5A	SELECTED SPECIFICATIONS FOR COMMODITIES				
Product	Trading Unit	Deliverable Grades	Price Quotation	Tick	Daily Price Limit
Corn	5,000 bushels	#2 yellow at par	¢ & ¼¢/bushel	¼¢/bushel	10¢
Soybean meal	100 tons	44% min. protein	$ & ¢/ton	10¢/ton	$10/ton
Kilo gold	1 kg (32.15 troy oz.)	Bar gold, 999 fine	$ & ¢/troy oz.	10¢/troy oz.	$50/troy oz.
Pork bellies	44,000 lbs.	USDA inspected 14–16 or 16–18 lb. pork bellies	$/100 lbs.	25¢/lb.	2¢/lb.
Random length lumber	150,000 board ft. (MBF)	2 × 45 in. random length at spec.	$/MBF	10¢/MBF	$5/MBF
Cotton	50,000 lbs. (approx. 100 bales)	Strict low middling 1⅛ in. U.S. white cotton	¢ & ¹⁄₁₀₀¢/lb.	¹⁄₁₀₀¢/lb.	2¢/lb.
Frozen orange juice	15,000 lbs.	Orange juice solids (3% more or less)	¢ & ¹⁄₁₀₀¢/lb.	⁵⁄₁₀₀¢/lb.	5¢/lb.
Coffee	37,500 lbs. (approx. 250 bags)	Washed arabica coffee (tested for grade & flavor)	⁵⁄₁₀₀¢/lb.		6¢/lb.

listing of selected commodities and their specifications.) In addition to the amount of product specified, a contract includes the names of the buyers and sellers, a date in the future for delivery, and the price. Contracts are legally binding agreements between a buyer and seller assured by the margin deposits of both.

Market Activity

The following information about the commodities market is presented for the purpose of general appraisal only. Commodities trading is highly risky and is engaged in primarily by professionals, most of whom spend all their time pursuing profits. If you want to invest in commodities, you need a specialized broker with a separate commodities trading license, one who understands and deals in commodities regularly. You will need to establish a margin account and agree to a separate commodities trading account. Your deposit into the margin account is a good faith deposit that also protects the brokerage firm against losses. The firm operates your account with your money except for any cash borrowed in your margin account. The amount of the margin account and your limit on borrowing will be part of your agreement and will vary from broker to broker. You will be charged interest on money you borrow from the brokerage firm at a rate known as the broker loan rate. No part of the following is intended to encourage you to trade commodities.

To begin trading commodities, you enter an order with your broker either as a buyer or seller. If you intend to buy one contract of wheat, for example, for delivery at some specified future date, you go **long;** that is, you take a position as a buyer. In commodities trading, many traders go **short;** that is, they sell contracts with the expectation of closing them out at lower prices before delivery of wheat or other commodity. A trader who sells wheat short at $3.50 per bushel will profit if he buys a closing contract for $3.30 per bushel. For each contract you commit to, you pay into your commodity trading account an initial margin. If you buy two contracts for wheat, using the numbers from our earlier example, you would put up $1,000, as each contract requires a margin of $500.

Your broker telephones his representative on the trading floor of the CBOT or other commodities market. Batteries of telephones line the trading floor to transmit buy and sell orders and confirmations of those orders when executed. A clerk, called a runner, time-stamps the order and physically carries the order to a broker in the pit.

The trading pit is an octagonally shaped series of stepped ramps that permit each broker to see all the other brokers. If you have seen a trading pit either from the observation window of the visitors gallery or on television, the action appears to be totally chaotic, with traders' arms extended as they shout almost continuously, offering to buy or sell in a system called **open outcry.** Yet, chaotic as it appears, the functions of the traders are actually well organized and highly efficient.

The pit trader who receives your order searches by eye and voice contact for an

Figure 5A   Hand Signals

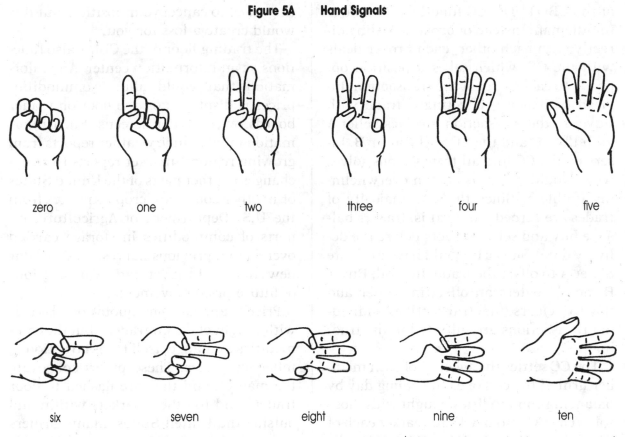

| zero | one | two | three | four | five |

| six | seven | eight | nine | ten |

Hand signals are used to confirm voice bids in the open outcry system. A bid of $3.21 would be signaled by a sequence of hand signals for the numbers 3, 2, and 1.

offsetting offer at a mutually agreeable price. Verbal agreements are then confirmed with hand signals (see Figure 5A). Hand signals assure accuracy, as voice contact is difficult in the hubbub of the pit. Each hand signal represents a specific number that communicates the number of contracts and the price, and traders abbreviate totals to speed up the process. For example, an order for wheat at $3.50 per bushel might call for a five and a zero, with the understanding that these cents figures relate to the dollar price. The pit trader writes on his ticket the number of contracts, delivery month, price, the number of the clearing firm represented by the pit trader who is the principal for the opposing trade, initials of the pit trader, and a notation of the time. Follow-up paperwork documents the transaction for both seller and buyer. A messenger picks up the information and phones your broker to confirm the trade's execution. Typically, the entire process—from the time you enter an order with your broker to the time you receive verbal confirmation of the trade—takes about two minutes.

All of the tickets documenting orders for completed trades go to one of the 145 member firms of the Clearing Corporation (CC) of the CBOT. The CC functions as a huge middleman. Instead of brokers dealing directly with each other, each broker deals with the CC, which takes a position opposite to each party of the transaction. Instead of Seller A effecting a trade with Buyer B, the transaction involves Seller A with the CC and the CC with Buyer B. Inserting the CC into all transactions solves what would otherwise be an overwhelming problem. Since the vast majority of trades are zeroed out (that is, traders balance buy and sell contracts before the delivery date), Buyer B would have to locate Seller A to offset the trade. Instead, Buyer B merely enters an offsetting order and the CC clears the transaction. Individual transactions are initiated in the trading pit.

The CC settles the account of each member firm at the end of each trading day by balancing commodities bought with those sold. The CC also marks to market each of the outstanding positions at the end of the day. Marking to market means that each contract is revalued to the closing price. If the price of wheat went up two cents, then all contracts for wheat are revalued upward by two cents. The CC collects from those traders who have lost during the day and credits the accounts of those traders who gained. Thus, on the opening of the market the next day, all accounts are cleared and trading begins afresh. The CC maintains tight control over margins as prices fluctuate and makes sure enough money remains on hand at all times to assure that contracts will be settled. If your trade shows a decline in price, your broker may phone you, asking you to put up more margin. Instead of putting up more cash, you have the option of entering an offsetting trade to cancel your position, but this would create a loss for you.

The trading floor of the CBOT also functions as an information center. Any information that could affect commodities prices is displayed on the floor on reader boards or computer screens. Such information may include weather reports from growing regions, market reports from exchanges in other parts of the United States or in other countries, crop estimates from the U.S. Department of Agriculture, reports of commodities in storage carried over from a previous harvest, and similar news that could affect traders' perceptions of future price movements.

Prices appear on quotation boards within sight of the pit traders, but the commodities exchange itself takes no action to influence prices. These prices constitute the market, and they are flashed to floor traders and to other markets within and outside the United States. Many farmers receive price quotations via radio or on computer screen via modem from price quotation services. Newspapers report price quotations daily.

Risks of Commodities Trading

Conventional thinking has long indicated that about 95 percent of all commodities traders lose all or a large part of their initial capital. According to a study of futures trading accounts by Allegiance Financial in 1990, a discount commodities broker and a division of Kemper Clearing Corporation, the average futures trading account lasted only 11 months, mainly because less than a third of the accounts actually made money.

Theoretically, the commodities trading market represents a zero-sum game—for every dollar gained a dollar is lost. Winners can come out with a profit of $1 only if a loser sustains a $1 loss. But, in fact, commissions on both sides of each transaction turn commodities into a negative-sum game—winners win by the amount losers lose plus commissions.

Commissions are not cheap. Full-service brokers may charge $50–$60 for each round-trip trade; that is, a buy and a follow-up sell, or a short sale followed by an offsetting buy. Round-trip trades are typical because nearly all trades are offset to avoid the problems of actually delivering 5,000 bushels of wheat or other commodity. A full-service broker can help a new investor get started by offering advice, expertise, and education. Investors pay for this coddling and support with higher commissions.

Discount brokers may charge $20–$35 for each contract on a round-trip. Thus, to reduce the amount of money taken from the pool by commissions, traders actively seek out discount brokers to handle trades. Once an investor attains a level of know-how that permits him to make his own decisions, the savings on as few as 10 round-trip trades a year could amount to $6,000, according to the Allegiance study.

Other statistics that came out of the Allegiance study indicate that only 4 percent of the players earned profits of $10,000 or more a year. Nearly 25 percent of the players reported losses that exceeded $10,000 for the year. Overall, about 29 percent of the accounts studied were profitable, but many of the profits were minuscule.

Active participants in commodities trading have developed a number of strategies for reducing risks while at the same time reducing potential profits. Instead of going for broke with naked positions, these strategies may benefit from various moves of commodities according to time or difference in contract terms.

Strategies to Reduce Risks

Spread trading, also known as a straddle, attempts to take advantage of different markets or different products. Spread trading calls for buying one contract and simultaneously selling another contract related to the first. You might, for example, buy one wheat contract (5,000 bushels) for September at $3.58 per bushel and sell a December wheat contract for $3.61. The difference is the spread. Several weeks later the price for September wheat has risen to $3.64 and December wheat has risen to $3.64. This strategy is known as a time spread. An immediate sale nets a gain of $.06 per bushel on the September contract and a loss of $.03 per bushel on the December contract for an overall profit of $.03 per bushel, or $150 on one contract, less commissions. In a spread a trader usually wins on one contract and loses on the other. The speculator profits when the amount gained on the win exceeds the loss plus commissions.

Intercommodity spreads involve simultaneously buying a contract for one grain, wheat for example, while selling a contract for a different grain, such as corn. The trader attempts to profit from different price movements of the different grains. In an intercommodity spread, an additional element of buying and selling contracts due to expire at different delivery times may add a further element of protection against loss.

Conclusion

Commodities trading is an integral part of the overall market, but it offers few op-portunities for the casual or part-time investor. You should know about the operations if you maintain an interest in Wall Street activities, but proceed with extreme caution before becoming actively involved in commodities trading.

CHAPTER SIX

Financial Futures

KEY TERMS FOR THIS CHAPTER

diversification

negative correlation

inverse relationship

commodity pool

hard currency

Eurodollar market

convertible

soft currency

open interest

float

European Currency Unit

stock index futures

proxy

entry price

Futures trading in currencies, indexes, and financial instruments is closely related to commodities futures trading. Substitute treasury note futures for wheat futures, and only the details change. Indexes of stocks, bonds, and international currencies become the commodities traded in the financial futures markets. Commodities trading occurs worldwide, but the trading of financial futures, such as U.S. Treasury notes and bonds, began around 1970 and continues at an increasing tempo, primarily in the United States, as the variety of contracts grows and the volume of trading expands.

Although a financial futures contract may be based on a stock index, which measures the movement of the stock market rather than wheat or other commodity, the basic reason for trading remains the same—the control and management of risks through hedging. Conservative investors and fund managers hedge their portfolios by laying off (transferring) a portion of the risk from market fluctuations to speculators willing to accept risks in their search for profits. The common interests of both hedgers and speculators allow the financial futures markets to function.

Knowledgeable investors consider participation in the futures market a risk-reducing form of **diversification.** Pension fund managers have studied the **negative**

correlation between financial futures and stock values for years; that is, when stock prices decline, certain financial futures rise and vice versa. This **inverse relationship,** similar to the inverse relationship between bond prices and interest rates, helps managers of diversified portfolios with futures to increase long-term earnings. Individual investors may participate in futures trading activity through a **commodity pool,** in which a number of individuals pool their cash and a manager invests the money for the benefit of the pool participants.

Despite the many similarities, a number of substantial differences exist between the commodities and financial futures markets.

Currency Futures

Currencies from around the world, but principally those so-called **hard currency** (currencies which are readily convertible into other currencies), change in value relative to each other continuously, sometimes by substantial percentages over short periods. A U.S. dollar may be worth 140 Japanese yen one day, and a week later it may be worth only 131 yen. Similar differences occur between the U.S. dollar, Canadian dollar, German deutsche mark, English pound, Swiss and French francs, and lesser currencies used in transacting the world's commerce. While many variables affect the relative prices of the world's currencies, the principal driving force remains supply and demand.

As the United States ran negative trade balances for years, many U.S. dollars ended up in foreign hands. A major factor contributing to the huge supply of dollars outside the United States is that all countries pay for Middle East oil in dollars. As a result of this flow of dollars, an entirely new market, called the **Eurodollar market,** developed outside the United States, with dollars as the medium. Billions of dollars are now traded on that market without ever getting back to the United States.

The overhang of supply—that is, the sheer volume of U.S. dollars held in various banks, investment companies, and individual accounts outside the United States—depressed the price of dollars relative to most other world currencies in the early 1990s. During the 1980s, the English pound rose in value relative to the U.S. dollar from just over parity, about $1.07 for each pound, to a ratio of about $2.00 for each pound. In trading terms, it took about two U.S. dollars to buy one English pound. When the Japanese yen was trading at a ratio of about 120 yen to $1, assets in the United States were relatively cheap in terms of the yen, and the Japanese became huge buyers of U.S. real estate and other assets. These and other transactions in turn affect the relative value of U.S. dollars and other world currencies. The differences and the perceived future differences come together in the currency futures markets in the United States and overseas.

Hedging, the same process employed by commodities users and growers to control material costs, is a major force in international currency trading. The technique of hedging affords a means of controlling risk, even though, unlike a commodity, currency is never consumed.

Suppose a machinery manufacturer in the United States sells a major piece of factory equipment, such as a punch press, to a company in France with the price fixed in francs. Delivery is scheduled for six months following placement of the order. During that period the relationship between French francs and U.S. dollars could change dramatically. If the value of the franc declined, the manufacturer would receive fewer dollars than he anticipated. Thus, he would lose part or all of his expected profit.

To protect his profit from the fluctuations of **currency exchange values,** the manufacturer could buy a franc futures contract at the time he sells the punch press. At delivery he cashes the futures contract. If the franc's value declined relative to the dollar in the interim, he would lose on the contract for the punch press but gain on the futures contract to break even on the currency transactions. This leaves his dollar profit from the building and sale of the punch press intact. He has avoided the risk of a currency loss by paying a relatively minor commission and depositing margin to buy the franc contract.

The Chicago Mercantile Exchange (known as the Chicago Merc) offers both futures and options (see Chapter 7) for the major currencies of the world—British pound, Canadian dollar, Japanese yen, Swiss franc, German deutsche mark, Australian dollar, and French franc. These currencies represent the major **convertible,** or hard, currencies. Many of the world's currencies are **soft currencies,** meaning they are not readily convertible to other currencies. The Russian ruble, for example, is a major currency, but it cannot be converted readily into pounds, dollars, or francs. Russia earns hard currency from the sale of gold and petroleum that is paid for in dollars or one of the other convertible currencies.

Daily currency quotations are reported in *The Wall Street Journal* and other newspapers worldwide. **Open interest,** which is also reported, is the total number of futures contracts traded that have not yet been liquidated by an offsetting futures transaction. The change from the previous day's close is also reported to indicate the direction of the price movement during that trading session.

Each of the currency contracts traded on the Chicago Merc is defined by specifications that include size, tick, and characteristics similar to the specifications for grains and other commodities. Contract specifications for major currencies are detailed in Table 6A.

TABLE 6A	SELECTED SPECIFICATIONS FOR CURRENCY FUTURES			
Currency	Trading Unit	Price Quote	Tick	Daily Price Limit
Australian Dollars (AD)	$100,000 AD	US$ per AD	.0001 (1 Point)	150 Points
British Pound (BP)	62,500 BP	US$ per BP	.0002 (2 Points)	400 Points
Deutsche mark (DM)	125,000 DM	US$ per DM	.0001 (1 Point)	150 Points
Japanese Yen (JY)	12,500,000 JY	US$ per JY	.000001 (1 Point)	150 Points
Swiss Franc (SF)	125,000 SF	US$ per SF	.0001 (1 Point)	150 Points

International currency futures may also include groups of currencies from more than one country rather than a single country's currency. The United States Dollar Index (USDX) futures and options are traded on FINEX, a Division of the New York Cotton Exchange (NYCE). The USDX parallels the Federal Reserve Board's trade-weighted dollar index and is updated 24 hours each day from foreign exchange quotes by hundreds of banks worldwide. The USDX represents the value of 10 major world currencies relative to the index base in March 1973, when the world adopted plans to allow their currencies to **float** or change value relative to each other. Since 1973 when it began at 100.00 the USDX has varied from a high of 164.72 in February 1985 to a low of 82.07 in October 1978. Component currencies in the USDX are the German deutsche mark, Japanese yen, French franc, Belgian franc, Swiss franc, English pound, Canadian dollar, Italian lira, Netherlands guilder, and Swedish krona. Each country's currency is weighted according to its volume of trading, with the German deutsche mark making up 20.8 percent of the value, the Japanese yen 13.6 percent, and the English pound 11.9 percent. The remaining percentages are spread among the other seven currencies.

FINEX also trades **European Currency Unit** (ECU) futures. The ECU includes all 12 of the European community currencies weighted according to their volume of commerce. Again Germany dominates with 30.1 percent of the ECU value. ECU futures permit U.S. companies doing business with several European countries to hedge their positions.

Trading of currency contracts follows a similar route to the pattern for commodities, which was explained in Chapter 5.

Financial Futures

Stock index and interest rate futures are used as a mechanism for controlling risks by the owners of large portfolios of stock, including many mutual funds, pension funds, and major money managers. A portfolio manager may own many shares in the companies that are part of the Standard & Poor's 500 Index, for example. To avoid a major loss in share values, such as the one that occurred in October 1987, the manager may sell Standard & Poor's (S&P) futures contracts. If the value of the stocks in his portfolio declines, he loses there but compensates for portfolio losses with profits realized at the closing of his index futures contract. The cost of risk protection, a form of insurance, is the commission on the index future plus commitment of the margin.

As in other futures markets, speculators operate in the financial futures markets to accept the risks others are trying to avoid. Speculators attempt to earn huge profits from small investments through the use of margin.

Two basic types of financial futures are traded on the Chicago Merc, the Chicago Board of Trade (CBOT), the New York Stock Exchange (NYSE), the American Stock Exchange (Amex), and regional exchanges. They are stock index futures and interest rate futures.

Stock Index Futures

Many different indexes measure movements of the stock market in general as well as specialized segments of the stock markets. The index of stock market movement itself is the investment vehicle (security) and futures contracts reflect a dollar multiple of index values, such as $100 times the index.

Stock index futures permit a cash settlement at the close. Instead of closing out a position (offsetting a long futures position with a short futures position or vice versa), the holder of an index futures contract may take the value of the contract, not the index itself, in cash, depending on which option yields the most cash. The money comes from adjustments in the margin position of contract holders at the close (see the box below for an example of a cash settlement for an index futures con-

tract). There are several stock index futures contracts.

● The Standard & Poor's 500 Index (S&P 500), one of the most popular stock index futures contracts, is based on 500 stocks traded on the NYSE, Amex, and National Association of Securities Dealers and Automated Quotation (NASDAQ). The S&P 500 futures contract trades on the Chicago Merc. Because of its wide diversification, its pattern of movement is similar to that of the market, and the S&P 500 is often considered a **proxy,** or stand-in, for the market itself. The market value of the 500 stocks in the S&P 500 is equal to about 75 percent to 80 percent of the value of all stocks listed on the NYSE. Within the S&P 500, 80 percent of the companies are industrials, 8 percent are utilities, 4 percent are transportation, and 10 percent are financial institutions. (See Chapter 9 for more on the S&P 500.)

EXAMPLE OF A CASH SETTLEMENT USING STANDARD & POOR'S 500 INDEX

Strategy—Investor expects market to rise
   Buys one S&P 500 futures contract—Strike price** $350.00
      Margin—$11,000 Initial
              $ 5,000 Maintenance (minimum)
      Premium—$1,000
      S&P 500 closes at $348—Out-of-money***
      Entry price = $348.00
   35 days later—Closes account for cash
      S&P 500 closes at $356.25
      Contract value at close (356.25 × 500)   178,125.60
      Strike price (350.00 × 500)   175,000.00
                            Gross profit   3,125.00
                            Cost of premium   (1,000.00)
                            Net profit* $2,125.00

*Does not include commission on futures contract or interest on margin.
**Price per unit at which holder of an option may purchase or sell the underlying security.
***Strike price is higher than the underlying index value for a call or less than index value for put.

One S&P 500 futures contract is valued at $500 times the index value. For example, if the S&P 500 future is quoted at 300, the value of one S&P 500 contract would be $500 times 300, or $150,000. S&P 500 futures contracts move in .05 index point ticks; that is, the minimum price movement is $25 (.05 times $500). A typical margin for one S&P 500 contract might be $10,000, with a maintenance margin level of $6,000.

Futures traders may go either long or short, depending on their perception of the market. A trader buying a long futures contract expects the market to rise. At some future time the trader hopes to close out his position at a higher price and pocket a profit. A trader selling short a futures contract expects the market to decline. He expects to buy back the S&P 500 futures contract later at a lower price and pocket the difference. Since the S&P 500 tracks the overall stock market so closely, speculators may effectively buy the market by investing in S&P 500 futures contracts. Instead of tracking individual stocks, S&P 500 traders track the overall market.

To participate in the S&P 500 futures market, you would first need to set up a trading account with a broker, one who specializes in financial futures. You must deposit cash or cash-equivalent securities, such as U.S. Treasury bills (T-bills), in the account as margin, a good-faith deposit guaranteeing performance. Most traders elect to deposit readily marketable securities such as T-bills, because they continue to earn interest. Cash on deposit does not earn interest.

The price at the time you buy or sell a contract is known as the **entry price.** At the end of the day, the contract will be marked to market; that is, it will be adjusted to the closing price of the S&P 500. Your profit or loss will be the difference between your entry price and the closing price each day. If the S&P 500 continues to rise from your entry price, you may withdraw cash from the trading account. However, if the index declines and the value of the contract falls below the margin maintenance level, your broker will call for more margin. You must either deposit more cash in your trading account or liquidate your position at a loss.

Contracts are limited to quarters ending in March, June, September, and December. The last day of trading is the Thursday before the third Friday of each contract month, and settlement is at the opening on Friday. Contracts expiring at the close of the trading quarter may be paid off in cash at the special opening quotation on the Friday after the last day of trading or rolled over into a new contract at the investor's option.

• Value Line Index includes about 1,650 stocks. The index is price weighted—a $1 change in the price of the stock of a major corporation, say a rise from $80 to $81, will have the same influence on the Value Line Index as a $1 change in the price of the stock of a smaller corporation, from $9 to $10. The index is maintained by the Value Line Investment Services and is calculated with a geometric average (see page 143 for an explanation of geometric average).

Futures contracts based on the Value Line Index are traded on the Kansas City Board of Trade (KCBT). The value of the Value Line Index futures contract is $500 times the value of the index. Futures contracts expire quarterly on the Thursday before the third Friday of the contract month, such as March for the first quarter. Cash settlements are available.

A mini-S&P 100 futures contract is also traded on the KCBT. The S&P 100 futures contract is priced at $100 times the index.

• Major Market Index (MMI) is another price-weighted index of 20 major corporation stocks. The MMI futures contract is traded on the CBOT and is priced at $250 times the index quote.

• New York Stock Exchange Composite Index Futures (NYSE CIF) contracts are traded on the New York Futures Exchange (NYFE). NYSE CIF contracts are priced at $500 times the index. Contracts for each of four months are traded, concurrently with contract months ending in March, June, September, and December. The last day of trading is the Thursday preceding the third Friday of the contract month. Settlement is in cash based on the third Friday's opening price of all stocks listed in the NYSE CIF.

• Commodities Research Bureau (CRB) index futures are traded on the NYFE. The CRB index tracks the prices of a group of commodities and is closely followed as an indicator of inflationary trends. The CRB index futures contract is priced at $250 times the index quote. The CRB index futures contracts mature on the third business day of the contract month. Contract months are March, May, July, September, and December, with three months traded at all times. Settlement at contract maturity is by cash payment.

See Chapter 9 for more information on how these indexes are constructed.

Interest Rate Futures

Interest rate futures (or interest rate index futures) such as T-bill interest rates, municipal bond index, treasury bonds, mortgage-backed futures, and others, trade on different exchanges.

The T-bill futures contract was initiated by the International Monetary Market (IMM), a division of the Chicago Merc, in 1976 as a means of hedging interest rate risks. The 91-day T-bill futures contract offers traders an opportunity to buy or sell for future delivery a T-bill with 91 days to maturity and a face value of $1 million. The basis for trading is an index that is calculated by subtracting the interest rate from 100. For example, if an interest rate is 9 percent, then the index would be 91 (100 less 9). If interest rates climb, the price of the T-bill futures contract falls and vice versa.

Prices for T-bills and T-bill futures contracts tend to move together during the bills' early period, but they come closer together in value as the T-bills near maturity. On the futures' closing date, the futures contract becomes a cash position and prices of the T-bills and the contract are identical. During the interim, changes in the T-bill futures contract reflect market interest rate changes and the increasing value of the underlying T-bill as it accrues interest. Although T-bills are auctioned weekly for the U.S. Treasury by the Federal Reserve System, the futures contracts mature in the contract months of March, June, September, and December. The delivery date is three successive business days beginning the day after the last day of trading for a specific maturity. Fortunately, brokers dealing with interest rate futures publish a calendar with last trading and delivery dates clearly marked. The overwhelming majority of futures contract traders offset their positions to simplify the transactions rather than take delivery of the underlying T-bills, although delivery is possible. T-bill futures contracts may run as long as two years to maturity to provide a longer period for hedging.

T-bill futures are also traded on the MidAmerica Commodity Exchange (MidAm), which is associated with the CBOT. The MidAm trades in smaller contracts, and its T-bill futures contract trading unit is $500,000 face value of T-bills with 90 days to maturity. Prices of the MidAm futures contracts are determined by auction based on an index created by subtracting the T-bill interest rate from 100. Rather than deliver actual T-bills at settlement, the MidAm T-bill futures contract provides for a cash settlement if offsetting trades have not been initiated.

U.S. Treasury Bond Futures

U.S. Treasury bond (T-bond) futures contracts are traded on FINEX, a division of the NYCE, in conjunction with the NYFE. T-bond futures contracts tend to be more complex than the T-bill contracts because bonds of varied maturities and coupon rates may be included. Basically, the T-bond futures contract traded on FINEX is for $100,000 face value of the bonds with at least 15 years to maturity (or, if callable, with 15-year call protection) and adjusted to a nominal 8 percent coupon. (A call provision permits the U.S. Treasury to call in bonds after the call date, which is noted

as part of the bond's specifications.) Prices on the bonds are used to adjust them to the nominal 8 percent interest rate. Contract months are March, June, September, and December. Settlement is a complex process involving the Federal Reserve data entry system and a pricing dependent on the actual maturities of bonds to be delivered. Most bond futures contracts are closed out prior to delivery.

U.S. Treasury bond futures contracts traded on the MidAm are smaller than those traded on FINEX—the trading unit is $50,000 of face value bonds. Other specifications, 15 years to maturity or call date and interest rate adjusted to 8 percent, are similar to specifications for the FINEX contract. The last trading day for the MidAm bond futures contract is the business day prior to the last seven business days of the delivery month, and the delivery day is the last business day of the delivery month.

Eurodollar Deposit Futures

Eurodollar deposit (U.S. dollars deposited in non-U.S. banks) futures contracts began trading on the International Monetary Exchange in 1981. The contract is for three months with a face value of $1 million. Contracts mature in March, June, September, and December. The last day of trading is the second London business day prior to the third Wednesday of the delivery month. Since Eurodollar deposits cannot be delivered, cash settlements are available unless contracts are offset. Eurodollar futures contracts also trade on the Singapore International Monetary Exchange, permitting trading 24 hours a day.

Conclusion

The information offered here about futures trading and contracts aims to acquaint you with the overall market—it is not meant to encourage you to become a trader in futures contracts. If you should see references to closing prices or changes of significant magnitude in these futures contracts, you will understand what these contracts and their objectives are. Futures contracts serve a special need for major corporations needing to hedge the costs of money. Risks assumed by speculators who take the opposite side of hedging contracts are enormous. Engaging in futures contracts transactions is, and should continue to be, limited to professionals who understand the risks and have the resources to withstand losses from time to time.

CHAPTER SEVEN

Options

KEY TERMS FOR THIS CHAPTER

call option	*naked call*
underlying stock	*put options*
premium	*out-of-the-money*
contracts	*in-the-money*
strike prices, exercise prices	*intrinsic value*
index option	*time value*
option	*settled*
call writer	*multiplier*

Options offer a chance to improve your odds of winning when you invest. When you buy stock, you have one chance in three of winning: you win if the stock advances in price. You neither gain nor lose if the stock price fails to move. You lose if the stock moves down.

If you write (sell) a **call option,** your odds of winning rise to two in three. You win if the price of the **underlying stock** moves up. You also win if the stock's price doesn't change, because you retain the **premium.** You could lose if the stock's price falls below the level of protection afforded by the call option. (These terms will become familiar as you study this chapter.)

Options are well named, because they provide you with numerous alternatives to protect your investments from market risks, to increase income from a stock portfolio, to help you buy stocks at lower prices, to position your portfolio to benefit from a major market move in either direction, or to allow you to participate in the market with much less cash. All of this flexibility comes with new risks—and a price. Investing with options offers you opportunities with less risk than venturing into the commodities and futures markets. One benefit of an option over a commodities or futures contract is the absence of margin calls on the buy side of options transactions. Once you buy an option contract, that's it.

The options market is an entirely different market from stocks, bonds, commodities, or futures. Options have traded over-the-counter (OTC) in the United States for more than 100 years and trace their origin back to the Greeks. The opening of listed options offered by the Chicago Board Options Exchange (CBOE) in April 1973 changed the market forever. Options were standardized into **contracts** for 100 shares of an underlying stock with fixed expiration dates and **strike prices** (the price at which you call or put shares), also called **exercise prices,** set at regular intervals. These features made options more tradeable. A clearinghouse, similar to those used in commodities and futures, assured completion of contracts and improved liquidity for participants. Demand for options grew amazingly fast and in 1991 averaged between 60 million and 70 million stock contracts annually on the CBOE. **Index options** add a similar volume. The New York Futures Exchange (NYFE), Chicago Mercantile Exchange (Chicago Merc), Philadelphia Stock Exchange (PHLX), and others added their own options to further increase the volume of options listed and traded. Although numerous exchanges list options, contracts are available only for stocks of a limited number of corporations. Option contracts tend to be available only on the stocks of major corporations to assure a wide interest among investors.

Options—What Are They?

An **option** is a contract that gives the owner the right, but not the obligation, to buy or sell shares of an underlying stock at a specified price on or before a specified date. American- and European-style options differ in terms of when they can be exercised. American-style options may be exercised, or closed out, at any time prior to the expiration date and are almost exclusively available in the United States. A European option can only be closed out on the expiration date, and a few European-style options are available in the United States as well. The PHLX offers limited European-style options.

Options on stock indexes and futures are similar to options on stocks. Two types of options are available—calls and puts.

Call Options

Call options give the owner (buyer) the right to buy shares of an underlying security at a specified price within the time limits of the contract. For example, if you were to buy a call option on IBM stock, the underlying security, you might buy one with a strike price of $105, $110, $115, $120, or $125. The strike price, also called the exercise price, is the specified share price at which you could buy shares of IBM stock from the seller of the call option. Note that strike prices vary in increments of $5 for the underlying stock. Strike price increments are $2.50 when the underlying stock price is $25 or less and $10 if the underlying stock price is $200 or more.

The specified date is the call expiration date, which might be one month, two months, three months, or up to nine months into the future. Expiration date for a specific month is the Saturday following the third Friday of the month, although options actually expire at the close of trading on the Friday. (Saturday allows back office personnel to correct errors and assure that all trades are completed.) To exercise an option, you must notify your broker in advance by filing an exercise notice. Advance notice rules vary by broker, so check with your broker for his deadlines for filing an exercise notice.

Suppose the day's close for IBM is $122 per share and you were to buy a call at $125 per share to expire eight months ahead. You might have to pay a premium of $300 for the right to buy 100 shares of IBM at $125 per share. (A quote in a newspaper would be shortened from $300 to $3, but each call contract is for 100 shares of the underlying stock, hence the $300 premium.) When you buy a call contract, you are, in effect, betting the market will rise. However, IBM stock, for this example, would have to rise to $128 per share before the expiration date for you to break even on the deal. You have bought control of 100 shares of IBM stock that was worth $12,200 ($122 per share times 100 shares) on the day you bought the option for $300. If the price of IBM fails to reach $125 per share, you would allow the option to expire without any further action, because it is worthless; you could enter the market and buy shares of IBM for less. When that happens—and it happens much of the time— you lose your premium. If the price of IBM rises to $126.50 per share, or some other

price between $125 and $128, you could exercise the option—call up 100 shares and immediately resell the shares in the market to gain, in this case, $150 ($1.50 per share for 100 shares). Given your $300 premium, you would still lose $150 on the two transactions (buying the option and selling the called stock), but at least you would retrieve some of the premium.

These figures do not include the cost of the three commissions: the cost of buying the call, the cost of buying the stock from the seller, and the cost of selling the stock in the market. Ordinarily, the stock must rise by at least the value of the premium to warrant calling the stock and reselling. To avoid paying two additional commissions, most options players sell a call to close out their existing buy contract when the difference yields a profit or recoups part of the premium. The single commission for the closing option costs less and simplifies the closing compared to calling and immediately reselling the shares of stock.

If your IBM stock reaches $128 per share, you recoup your investment in the option, except for commissions. If the same IBM stock reaches $131 per share, you have doubled your original investment of $300, again without considering commissions. Leverage (that is, the opportunity to double, triple, or gain multiples of the original option premium) is the honey that attracts the option buyer bees. Buying calls is a highly speculative strategy, since only about 5 percent to 10 percent of the calls prove to be profitable. Call buyers take a position in the market when they believe the market is due to rise, but their investment is a fraction of what it would cost to pay full price for shares or to buy shares on margin. When call buyers guess right, options can make substantial profits.

On the other side of the transaction, the call seller (also known as the **call writer**) stands to benefit if the stock remains near the $122 price or if it falls no lower than $119 ($122 less the call premium of $3 per share). If the price of IBM stock fails to rise to a profitable level by the call expiration date, the option expires worthless and the call seller pockets the premium.

Selling calls against a holding of underlying stocks affords portfolio managers and individuals the opportunity to increase income from stocks. When you sell a call option, the premium becomes extra income and you still own the stock, unless the price rises to the exercise price and is called away; when the stock is, you give it up at the agreed strike price. When you sell a call, you give up the right to a large increase in the price of the underlying stock for the period up to the expiration date. Nevertheless, major money managers and institutional portfolio strategists sell calls on stocks in their portfolios routinely to increase income. Selling calls is considered a conservative strategy.

Writing (selling) calls normally requires that you own the shares of the underlying stock. If you sell a call without owning the shares, you are selling a **naked call.** Brokers will require you to put up enough cash to cover a possible loss, much the same as margin. Similar precautions protect the broker if you sell puts.

Options trade on an exchange floor in an auction market to bring buyers and sellers together. If you wish to buy or sell an option, you contact your broker. The broker notifies his representative in the pit and a trade is effected. Your order is confirmed and a computer confirmation follows. The process is quick and efficient. Prices of options are determined by supply and demand in the auction pit.

Put Options

Put options give the owner the right, but not the obligation, to sell shares of an underlying security at the strike price on or before the expiration date. When you buy a put, you are buying the right to sell 100 shares of the underlying stock at the strike price to the seller of the put, regardless of what happens to the stock price. The term originates from the action to "put" the stock to the seller. For example, if you buy an IBM put with a strike price of $125 per share, with the price trading at $127 per share, you can sell 100 shares at $125 per share at any time up to the expiration of the put. If the price drops to $115 per share and you sell 100 shares, you earn a profit of $1,000 less the cost of the put and the commission. If IBM stock rises above $125 per share by the end of the option period, the put expires worthless. Strategy calls for buying a put if you expect the price of the underlying stock to decline. If you sell a put, you agree to buy the shares put to you at the strike price. You would sell a put if you expected the market to remain flat or fall.

If you expected the entire market to decline, you would likely buy a put on one of the stock indexes instead of individual stocks. You take similar steps in buying or selling a put as in buying or selling a call, working through a broker.

You should be aware of one major difference between calls and puts. If you sell a call, the most you can lose is your underlying stock when it is called away at the strike price. If you buy a call, the most you can lose is your premium when the call expires worthless. If you buy a put, allowing you to put shares to the seller, the most you can lose is your premium if the stock fails to drop. However, if you sell a put, there is no limitation on how much you can lose. When you agree to buy 100 shares of XYZ Corporation at $50 per share, you enter an open-end agreement. If the price should drop to $20 per share, you must still buy the shares at $50 per share. Selling puts is the riskiest maneuver in options trading. It was for this reason that call options were offered for several years before put options became available.

Pricing Options

Factors affecting the premium value of options are the price of the underlying stock, time to expiration, volatility of the underlying stock's price, cash dividends (if any), and interest rates. Premiums are paid when the buyer agrees to a contract with the broker.

The main factor in determining the option premium is the price of the underlying stock. Option premiums change minute by minute as the underlying stock's price changes and other factors impact the option buyers' and sellers' perceptions of what might happen. If the strike price of a call option is above the price of the underlying stock, the option is said to be **out-of-the-money.** That is, the call buyer acquires the option to buy stock at a price higher than it is currently trading. The opposite is true for puts. An out-of-the-money put is one where the strike price is lower than the price at which the stock is trading. If IBM is trading at $127 per share and the put is at $125, the put is out-of-the-money.

If the strike price for a call is lower than the trading price of the underlying stock, the option is said to be **in-the-money.** If the buyer had bought a call at the exercise price of $120 per share on stock priced that day at $122 per share, he would have an immediate profit on the sale if he were to exercise the call. However, he pays a price for an in-the-money option in the form of a higher premium. Continuing the example, when the premium to buy a call option at the strike price of $125 per share with IBM selling at $122 per share was $3, the premium for an option with the strike price of $120 might have been $6.50. The difference between the strike price for an in-the-money option and the market price of the stock is called the **intrinsic value** of the option ($122 minus $120, for this example). Out-of-the-money options have no intrinsic value. Similar values in reverse apply to put options.

The expiration date also affects the premium value of an option by introducing a **time value** to the option contract. As the expiration date approaches, the value of the contract and its premium tend to drop, as long as the price of the underlying stock does not change dramatically, because less time is available for the stock's price to rise. An in-the-money premium relates time value to intrinsic value: A premium's time value is the amount by which the premium exceeds the option's intrinsic value. That is, time value equals premium minus intrinsic value. Continuing the example used above, the time value component of the in-the-money premium of $6.50 for IBM is $6.50 less $2.00, or $4.50.

The price of an option's premium also relates directly to the volatility of the underlying stock. Some stocks move slowly, even ponderously, while others move up and down frequently and, occasionally, by large amounts. Stocks perceived to be highly volatile attract high option premiums because the stock could move into an in-the-money position within the period prior to expiration.

Cash dividends are another factor in premium value: They continue to be paid to the underlying stock owner. Dividends affect the market price of the underlying stock, however, and the underlying stock price affects option premiums. If a stock splits or a stock dividend is distributed, options are adjusted to account for the changes.

Interest rates influence option premiums by their effect on the prices of underlying stocks and by increasing or decreasing the cost of money tied up in option contracts. Typically, higher interest rates tend to reduce both call and put premiums, as these premiums pay no interest.

Option Trading Strategies

Costs for commissions and transaction expenses, interest on margin accounts, and taxes will affect the profitability of any option strategy. (They are omitted in the following examples to simplify the figures and to emphasize the strategies.) Using a discount broker will reduce commissions, but you must be a knowledgeable investor. Until you understand the market, you will do better with a broker who specializes in options and who will take the time to explain what is happening. If you are brave enough to enter the game, engage in small single trades at first to "taste the action." Don't engage in multiple transactions until you have taken time to learn the system.

Buying a Call to Benefit from Stock Rise

Buying a call when you believe a stock is about to rise puts you into position to participate in a stock price move without buying the shares outright.

Suppose you buy a call option on Stock A with a strike price of $60 per share when the price is $59 per share (see box on page 108). The call option contract gives you the right, but not the obligation, to buy 100 shares at $60 any time before the August expiration (third Friday). It is June and a summer rally could easily push the price of Stock A well above $60. Your premium is $3 ($300 for the 100-share contract). During the period prior to expiration, Stock A's price rises from $59 to $65 per share, and the premium rises to $5. Your option is now in-the-money and you have two alternatives:

1. You can call the stock and buy the 100 shares for $6,000 and simultaneously sell them for $6,500 for a gross profit of $200 ($500 profit on the sale less $300 for the call premium).
2. You can sell a call option at $5 and receive $500. Deduct the original $300 cost to buy the call and your gross profit is $200.

BUY A CALL ON STOCK A EXPECTING SHARES TO RISE			
Buy a call on Stock A—strike price = $60			
Stock A rises to $65 & premium rises to $5		**Stock A falls to $55 & premium falls to ⅝ ($0.625)**	
Alternative #1		Alternative #1	
Exercise call & buy		Sell option before	
stock	−$6,000.00	expiration	+$62.50
Sell stock	+ 6,500.00	Premium	(300.00)
Gross profit	500.00	Net loss	($237.50)
Premium	(300.00)		
Net profit	$200.00		
Alternative #2		Alternative #2	
Sell option @ $5	500.00	Option worthless	
Premium	(300.00)	at expiration	$0.00
Net profit	$200.00	Premium	(300.00)
		Net loss	($300.00)

Either way your profit is 67 percent on your $300 original investment. If you had bought 100 shares of Stock A at $59 per share and sold them at $65 per share, your profit would have been $600 but only a return of 10 percent on an investment of $6,000 ($60 per share times 100 shares).

If, instead of rising as you expected, Stock A falls to $55 per share, the option premium falls to ⅝ or $0.625. If you act before expiration, because you believe the price will continue falling, you can salvage $62.50 by selling a call. Your loss is $237.50. If you wait until the expiration date, your option to buy Stock A is out-of-the-money and becomes worthless. You lose your entire $300.

Buying a Call to Lock in a Stock Price

If you believe Stock B will rise, but you don't have enough cash to buy the shares outright at the moment, buying a call can lock in a current price for as long as nine months. Let's say you expect to retrieve enough cash from another investment to buy shares of Stock B in about seven months. You buy a call at $60 per share when Stock B is trading at $59 per share to lock in the $60 price. The premium for this out-of-the-money call is $4 ($400 for a 100-share contract). One month before expiration, Stock B has risen to $70 per share, and you now have the cash to buy the shares at the option price of $60 per share. Your total cost is $6,400—$6,000 for the stock and $400 for the option. If you had waited, your costs would be $7,000. Your gain on the option strategy is $600.

Of course, Stock B could drop in price. You could lose up to the total $400 premium, or you might sell an option at a fraction of the cost to recoup a part of the premium. Calculations would be similar to those in the box above.

Hedging a Short Sale to Reduce Potential Loss

Suppose you sell Stock C short expecting a decline in price. You can limit your risk by simultaneously buying a call. Stock C is selling at $50 per share when you sell it short by borrowing shares from your broker. (In a short sale, you expect to replace the borrowed shares later at a lower price and profit from the difference.) The price of Stock C could rise, so you buy a call option at $50 per share on Stock C at a premium of $5.50 ($550 for 100 shares). If the price of Stock C should rise to $65 per share, you could exercise your option to buy 100 shares of Stock C at $50 to replace the stock you borrowed. Your gain on the stock you buy with the option partially or totally offsets the loss on your short sale. However, until you actually exercise the option, your broker could call for more margin to cover your short-sale position; buying the call option does not protect you against margin calls.

If Stock C falls to $35 as you expected, your call option expires worthless, because it is out-of-the-money. When you buy in the stock to replace the shares previously borrowed (that is, enter a buy order with your broker for 100 shares of Stock C), your gross profit is $1,500 ($50 minus $35 times 100 shares) less the $550 you paid for the option, for a net of $950. (See the box below for details of the profits and losses of both actions.)

Strategies for Put Options

Similar strategies in reverse are possible with put options. You buy puts if you expect the market value of a stock to decline.

HEDGING A SHORT SALE

Stock C Rises

Buy a call option on Stock C (Strike price = $50)	
Premium $5.50	($550)
Sell 100 shares @ $50 short	5,000
Instead of falling in price, as expected, Stock C rises to $65	
Exercise option and buy 100 shares @ $50 to replace borrowed shares	(5,000)
Net loss with option	(550)
Without option	
Sell 100 shares @ $50 short	5,000
Later, buy stock @ $65 to replace borrowed shares	(6,500)
Net loss without option	(1,500)

Stock C Falls

Buy a call option on Stock C	
Premium	($550)
Sell 100 shares @ $50 short	5,000
Buy 100 shares @ $35 to replace borrowed shares	(3,500)
Net profit	$950

Commissions on option transactions and cost of margin on short sale not included.

If the stock declines, your put allows you to sell 100 shares to the seller at the strike price and you profit from the decline less the premium of your put. If the stock rises instead, your put is out-of-the-money and expires worthless.

You can lock in a profit on a long portfolio by buying a put. Suppose your stock has already run up in price and you wish to protect that profit. You buy a put at or near the stock's current price. If the stock should decline, you profit from the put and lose on the stock. Your cost for this protection is the price you pay for the put. This strategy can be rewarding if the stock moves up. You have protected your stock position against loss without affecting its upside potential for the relatively small price paid for the put option.

Numerous strategies are constantly being developed by investors and brokers to take advantage of the leverage opportunities available with options. See Resources for books detailing various option strategies.

Options on Stock Indexes

Like options on stocks, options on stock index futures, commodities futures contracts, and financial futures, convey the right, but not the obligation, to buy or sell a contract for the underlying security. Option buyers pay a premium and option sellers collect a premium that is determined in an auction market by supply and demand. Transactions are similar in almost every way to the options market for calls or puts on stocks, except for delivery. If the underlying security is a stock index futures

contract, then the option buyer or seller may, at his choosing, exercise the option any time prior to the expiration date or allow the option to expire worthless if it is out-of-the-money. Options on indexes, commodities, and financial futures are **settled** in cash or by closing out the option and taking the difference in cash.

Here is a look at the various stock indexes on which futures options can be traded.

Standard & Poor's 100 Index futures option. The CBOE began trading options on the Standard & Poor's 100 Index (S&P 100) futures in 1983. Options on futures of an index differ little in concept from options on stocks, but they do differ substantially in the details. Option on the S&P 100 (ticker symbol OEX) is the most popular option traded on the CBOE and the most actively traded of all listed options.

The trading unit, or contract value, for an option on S&P 100 futures is the value of the S&P 100 times 100, the index **multiplier.** For example, if the S&P 100 is trading at 250, then the value of the S&P 100 futures option is $25,000 ($250 times 100). The CBOE controls the option contract strike prices at $5 or $5 times multiplier of 100 ($500) increments and may open new options at higher or lower strike prices if the S&P 100 approaches the limits of existing options. Options on the S&P 100 futures expire monthly in the four nearby months (the current month plus three following months), on the third Friday of the expiration month.

Premiums are quoted in dollars and fractions per unit. Each point represents $100, and the minimum fraction by which a quote may change is $1/16$, when prices are less than $3, and $1/8$, when prices are higher than $3. For example, a premium of 2 $\frac{3}{16}$ represents $218.75 ($200 plus the decimal equivalent of $\frac{3}{16}$, or $18.75). Index values are continually updated throughout the trading session.

Standard & Poor's 500 Index futures option. The Standard & Poor's 500 Index (S&P 500) futures option is another popular stock index option traded on the CBOE. The multiplier is $500 times the value of the index. There is a cash settlement at expiration if not closed out earlier. Trading and strategies for the S&P 500 futures option are similar to those for the S&P 100 option. Table 7A indicates how the S&P 500 futures options are reported in financial newspapers. The numbers in each of the call and put columns are the prices of a contract at each strike price. For example, a May call for a strike price of 230 (S&P 500) would cost $12.50, or $1,250 for a contract.

Value Line Index futures options. These are traded on the Kansas City Board of Trade (KCBT). The multiplier is $500 times the value of the index, and options are settled in cash. The underlying security is the price-weighted Value Line Index of about 1,650 stocks.

Major Market Index (MMI) options. These are traded on the American Stock Exchange (Amex). The MMI is a price-weighted index of 20 blue-chip stocks constructed to simulate the Dow Jones Industrial Average. The multiplier is $100 times the value of the MMI.

New York Stock Exchange (NYSE) Composite Index options. These are traded on the NYFE. The underlying security is a capitalization-weighted index of all of the approximately 1,700 stocks traded on the NYSE. NYSE Composite Index options are available on a minimum of nine strike prices set at increments of two points, for example, 142, 144, 146, etc. The NYSE Composite Index option is a popular hedging mechanism for the major market as it represents the full range of stocks traded on the NYSE.

Other Stock Index options. In addition

Strike Price	Calls			Puts		
	Apr[1]	May	Jun	Apr	May	Jun
225	11.90	14.80	17.90	2.40	6.10	9.00
230	9.70	12.50	15.40	4.70	7.80	11.10
235	8.00	11.10	14.10	8.10	12.20	15.60
240	6.20	8.40	11.80	11.30	15.10	[2]
245	3.90	6.10	9.70	9.10	[2]	[2]
250	2.10	4.40	7.40	[2]	[2]	[2]

TABLE 7A   REPORTS ON S&P 500 FUTURES OPTIONS

Closing prices
Open interest[3] (0000) calls, (0000) puts

[1] Expiration months for options
[2] No bids available
[3] Number of buyer and seller contracts remaining open (unsettled) at day's end

to these major stock index options, a number of other stock index options are traded on various exchanges. Among these options are:

Amex Computer Technology Index options

Amex Institutional Index options

Amex International Market Index options

Amex Oil Index option

PHLX Gold/Silver Index option

PHLX National Over-the-Counter Index option

PHLX Utility Index option

Pacific Stock Exchange (PSE) Financial News Composite Index.

Stock Index Option Strategies

An example of how an investor in options on the S&P 100 futures might profit from an anticipated rise in the stock market is detailed in the box below. The investor buys a call option on the S&P 100 futures option for a premium of $1,000 and a strike price of 230 on a December option. On October 7, the S&P 100 closes at 235.79. The premium from an auction is a call price of 10×100, for a dollar value of $1,000. By November 7, the OEX has risen to a closing value of 252.79 and the investor elects to exercise the option for a cash settlement. The gross settlement is $2,279, representing the difference between the strike price of 230 and the closing on November 7 of 252.79 times the multiplier. Out of the gross settlement the investor deducts the cost of the call premium, $1,000, and nets a profit of $1,279. (For clarity, none of these figures include commissions.)

Other strategies for using options on stock indexes include

• hedging portfolios of stocks to avoid major losses if the market declines,

• protecting individual stocks from market risk in case the stock or market declines, and

• preserving capital without giving up opportunity for a market increase. This last strategy calls for investing a portion of one's capital in treasury bills or money market mutual funds. The remaining capital is used to buy index call options in anticipation of a market rise.

S&P 100 OPTION STRATEGY WHEN MARKET EXPECTED TO RISE

Market Rises		Market Falls	
Strike price = 230		Strike price = 230	
Current S&P 100 @ 235.79		Current S&P 100 @ 235.79	
Premium	($1,000)	Premium	($1,000)
S&P 100 rises to 252.79		S&P 100 falls to 232.60	
Gross settlement		Gross settlement	
([252.79 − 230] × 100)	2,279	([232.60 − 230] × 100)	260
Net profit	$1,279	Net loss	($740)

Commission on option not included.

Options on Commodities

Trading options on commodities futures resembles the trading of options on stocks except for the definition of the underlying security. An option on a commodity is based on a futures contract for that commodity. For example, a futures contract for wheat is for 5,000 bushels, and an option on that futures contract will be based on a variety of wheat futures prices at intervals of $.10. Prices for commodities futures are reported without a decimal (for example, as 250 indicating a price of $2.50 per bushel) with minimum ticks of $\frac{1}{8}$ cents. An increase of $\frac{1}{8}$ would be reported as 250 $\frac{1}{8}$. Thus, a range of strike prices for options on wheat futures contracts could be 240, 250, and 260. Options on commodities futures contracts may have daily limits to correspond with daily limits on the underlying futures contract. In the case of the option on wheat futures, the daily limit is $.20.

Both calls and puts on commodities futures trade for the same purposes as calls and puts on stocks—to control risks. Conservative investors use options for hedging and speculators use options to gain profits from leverage by assuming the risks hedgers are transferring. Options on commodities futures trade on the Chicago Board of Trade (CBOT) and other exchanges. Settlement of commodities options transfers the underlying futures contract to the option holder at expiration, just as stock is delivered to a call option holder when the option is in-the-money. An offsetting option can also be bought or sold to cancel the position for an overall profit or loss. If the option is out-of-the-money, it expires worthless, similar to other options that fail.

Options on the Commodities Research Bureau (CRB) index futures contract are traded on the NYFE. Originally, the CRB futures contract was equal to $500 times the CRB index, but in 1990 the multiplier was changed to $250. Both puts and calls are traded with ticks of .05, equal to $12.50. There are no price limits on the CRB option. Settlement results in the holder receiving either a long or short CRB futures contract: A long call receives a long futures contract when exercised; a put receives a short futures contract when exercised. Both the long and short futures contracts will be at the strike price of the options and may be settled immediately, similar to the way a call option holder may call stock and immediately sell it. All in-the-money options are automatically exercised at expiration, which is the third business day of the expiration month (March, May, June, September, or December).

Options on Financial Futures

Among the popular options on financial futures are the options on short-term and long-term interest rate futures. The short-term option on interest rate futures is based on U.S. Treasury bills (T-bills); the long-term option is based on U.S. Treasury notes and bonds. Buying put or call options on interest rate futures enables an investor to invest in where he believes interest rates are headed. Two major factors affect interest rate movements:

1. The condition of the economy exerts a major effect—the demand for money in

an expanding economy tends to raise interest rates. The reverse occurs in a downtrending economy, where supply exceeds demand and rates fall.

2. The Federal Reserve Board (the Fed) varies the money supply in the partial exercise of its role in maintaining a sound economy. The Fed may increase the money supply (see Chapter 14) in an effort to force interest rates lower as a means of boosting the economy; or the Fed may restrain the money supply to control inflation. Obviously, these interventions by the Fed affect interest rates.

At any one time there are about as many investors who believe interest rates are due to rise as there are investors who believe interest rates are due to fall. These differences in opinions fuel the market for interest rate futures contracts and options on interest rate futures contracts. Options on interest rate futures contracts are used by financial managers to hedge large positions in bonds or other fixed-income investments to minimize major losses if the market moves against them. These markets are highly specialized and involve options on futures contracts with face values of $1–$5 million. For these reasons, options on financial futures contracts are of little interest to individual investors.

The following information is offered for general information purposes only. If you should want to learn more about the transactions, contact the exchange involved. (See Resources for a listing of exchanges and their addresses.)

Calls and puts on three-month T-bills are traded on the Chicago Merc. The trading unit is a contract for $1 million face value of T-bills.

Calls and puts on long-term U.S. Treasury notes and bonds are traded on the CBOE and the CBOT. The CBOE also trades options on long-term municipal bond index futures, options on 10-year, 5-year, and 2-year U.S. Treasury note futures, and options on 30-day interest rate futures based on federal funds held for 30 days.

Conclusion

Options on stocks are of interest to individual investors as a means of improving the yields from stocks in their portfolios. Selling calls on underlying stocks is a conservative strategy if you own several hundred shares in an optionable stock. Also, if you are a large investor in a number of individual stocks, you might benefit from buying puts or calls as a hedge against major stock market movements. Options on commodities and interest rate futures are of interest mainly to institutional money managers.

PART TWO

INVESTING

CHAPTER EIGHT

Buying and Selling Securities

KEY TERMS FOR THIS CHAPTER

broker	at the market	declaration date
round-turn	limit order	ex-dividend date
brokerage	GTC	record date
wire houses	stop order	payment date
security analyst	round lots	short selling
execution	odd lots	wash sale
cold calling	reverse stock split	churning
prospecting	DRIPs	arbitration
portfolio		

Investing in stocks and bonds calls for:

- selecting and dealing with a broker
- understanding the mechanics of trading stocks and bonds
- protecting yourself and your investments against abuse and understanding the avenues for correcting grievances
- recognizing the government agencies' roles in regulating securities markets and participants
- determining relative costs of market transactions.

We will examine each of these factors in turn.

Selecting and Dealing with a Broker

Picking a **broker** can be as important as picking your doctor or attorney. Unfortunately, brokers are handicapped from the outset by a conflict of interest, one you should be clearly aware of. The conflict of interest is simple—what is good for the broker may not be good for you. The broker earns a commission when he or she buys a stock for you and then earns another commission when the stock sells. The **round-turn** commission, buying in and selling out the same stock, can be a major cost to you in investing in individual issues of stocks and bonds.

Conditions in the stocks and bonds markets may be in the doldrums or in a downtrend. Under such adverse market conditions you may choose to be out of the market for two or three years, but your broker can't live with a lack of activity for such a long period—he or she needs a regular stream of commissions. So your broker may be influenced either by the need for income or by a supervisor's prodding to sell something, whether it is to the advantage of the investor or not. This conflict of interest is often the reason investors hold unsuitable securities.

How do you pick a broker who can rise above this conflict of interest? There are several steps you can take to increase the odds that your broker is responsible and will look out for your needs. Your first step is to choose between a full-service broker and a discount broker.

Full-service Brokers

Full-service brokers usually work for one of the major **brokerage** firms. Excellent brokers may also work for one of the smaller regional brokerages. Small firms may develop around a successful broker who breaks away from a major firm to set up his or her own firm. Major brokerages are also known as **wire houses,** because their many branch offices are tied to their headquarters (usually in New York City) by telephone trunks and, through these connections, to the major exchange floors and their own market makers for trading unlisted stocks in the over-the-counter (OTC) markets.

Full-service brokers receive extensive training if they are new to the industry.

They engage in selling securities underwritten by their firm and are backed by a staff of **security analysts** who provide a steady stream of data and information on companies along with recommendations on which companies to buy, sell, or hold.

Security analysts study individual companies to compute estimated earnings, monitor management changes, review new products on the horizon, and search out decisions on the acquisition of new companies or on research. They then develop sample portfolios for brokers to use in dealing with clients. Full-service brokers can offer investors a huge array of market and company reports from their research departments, as well as reviews of the investor's holdings with recommendations for changes and answers to specific questions.

If you are new to investing in stocks and bonds, you can benefit from access to the wide range of services offered by major brokerages. All of these services come with a price—higher levels of commissions on trades compared to discount brokers.

Discount Brokers

Discount brokers offer few of the services touted by major brokerage firms. Most discount brokers are salaried; thus, they need not depend on commissions for their income. As a result, they respond to your calls, but they seldom initiate calls to drum up orders. They provide little or no research data that an investor might use to make decisions about buying and selling securities. The discount broker's main function is the **execution** of trades. Execution is the action a broker takes to write a ticket (order) that is relayed to a floor broker on an exchange who finds a buyer or seller to complete a trade and confirms the trade back to the originating broker.

Some national discount brokers offer Individual Retirement Accounts (IRAs), Keogh plans, and asset management accounts. Often these plans cost less than similar managed accounts offered by banks or full-service brokerages. Advisory services offered by discount brokers are strictly limited. If you are able to do your own research and make up your own mind about which stocks or bonds to buy or sell, you can cut costs by using only the execution services of the discount broker, who can execute trades at far lower commission

rates than full-service brokers. Table 8A compares a sampling of trading costs between full-service and discount brokers.

Full-service and discount brokers are members of major exchanges and maintain tie-ins with major market makers for OTC stocks. Their sophisticated computer systems permit almost instant execution and confirmation of trades. Often, you can hold the line to wait for a confirmation of trades on major exchanges.

Tips on Choosing a Broker

If you decide to use the services of a full-service broker, select one only after en-

TABLE 8A	COMMISSIONS FOR FULL-SERVICE AND DISCOUNT BROKERS (SUMMER, 1991)				
FULL-SERVICE BROKERS					
Broker	200 @ $25[1]	300 @ $20	500 @ $15	500 @ $18	1,000 @ $14
Merrill Lynch	129.50	157.00	195.75	214.50	293.60
Shearson	128.00	154.25	199.00	222.25	347.75
Pru-Bache	140.92	167.08	211.60	232.60	348.95
Dean Witter	122.13	145.52	185.52	205.86	322.82
Waterhouse Securities	35.00	40.82	52.05	57.62	90.33

DISCOUNT BROKERS					
Broker	200 @ $25[1]	300 @ $20	500 @ $15	500 @ $18	1,000 @ $14
Charles Schwab	81.00	87.00	91.50	96.00	111.00
Fidelity Brokerage	80.75	86.75	91.25	95.75	110.75
Quick & Reilly	60.50	65.00	77.75	81.50	94.00
Olde Discount	60.00	60.00	80.00	80.00	105.00
Waterhouse Securities	35.00	40.82	52.05	57.62	90.33

[1] Number of shares and price per share

gaging in a bit of research and fact finding. Here are some tips:

● Avoid the broker of the day. If you call into the office of a major full-service brokerage firm where you have not been identified with a specific broker, the person at the switchboard will connect you with the broker assigned the duty for that day of taking calls from unknown callers. In a large office this duty is rotated among the new brokers or those actively looking for new clients. If this person is a new hire, he or she may be inexperienced. Inexperience is ample reason to avoid any broker.

All brokers dealing with individuals and institutions are licensed by the National Association of Securities Dealers (NASD) and by your state's securities licensing department. Before licensing, a broker applicant must pass a long and difficult examination. Preparing for the exam calls for extensive training. The prospective broker may attend classes taught either by a brokerage firm or by one of the tutors that specialize in teaching a cram course in brokerage and market activities, so all brokers who work for full-service or discount brokerages have a basic understanding of the business. There is no substitute for experience, however. Pick a broker who has been in the business for at least 10 years. New brokers may not have experienced a bear (down) market. Unless a broker has survived a full market cycle, he or she may not offer balanced advice.

● Look for a busy broker, one who deals with a customer base ranging from 400 to 500 customers; such a broker has built a confident working relationship with his or her clients. You find one of these busy brokers only by asking your friends and associates for referrals.

● Avoid the broker who calls unannounced, usually in the evening and often in the middle of your dinner. **Cold-calling** brokers, those who work from a list and possibly even the telephone directory, hope to add to their client base. Cold calling is one form of **prospecting,** of finding new customers. Cold calling is strictly a numbers game. If a broker makes 100 calls, he or she may attract interest in an offering from one or two respondents. Once you respond with any show of interest, you are a serious prospect.

Cold calls are scripted and rehearsed to gain maximum advantage from the few seconds a person may be listening. The usual cold call begins with a greeting and a question about your well being ("How are you this evening?"), followed by an attention-grabbing question, such as, "If I can show you an investment that will return $9\frac{1}{2}$ percent tax-free, would you be interested?" Cold-calling brokers are not usually busy or they would not be engaged in that difficult form of prospecting.

● Interview your prospective broker. Once you have a list of three to six names, set up appointments to talk with each of them personally. Time your appointments for the afternoon after the market closes, as the hours from 10 A.M. through 4 P.M. Eastern time are the productive hours for brokers who make their money writing tickets to be executed when the markets are open.

Appraise the chemistry between the two of you. You want someone who is friendly, who does not attempt to intimidate you, who will answer questions easily and fully, and who is accessible. Far too many brokers are curt, arrogant, impatient, and difficult to reach once you become a client.

Search out these characteristics during your interview. Finally, since you will deal with your broker mainly on the telephone, make sure you can get through quickly, as accessibility can be important.

• Recognize that your broker is, first of all, a salesperson. He or she does not personally analyze stocks, does not develop the detailed performance data you may request, and is not a data bank of facts. Ask how your prospective broker works. Does he or she use research data from the firm's analysts to help build your **portfolio**? Will the broker review your holdings, or portfolio, regularly? How often? Will your broker track your holdings and warn you if one or more of your holdings appears headed for trouble? Brokers are typically stronger on the buy side—that is, offering securities for you to buy—than on the sell side. Both are important if your program is to prosper.

Once you have selected a broker, you are ready to trade in the market.

Mechanics of Trading Stocks and Bonds

Once you have decided on a broker, you are ready to discuss your options in the stock market. Suppose you have decided to buy an issue listed on one of the exchanges. Consider the following elements of the transaction with your broker.

Trading Price

As a buyer you tell your broker how you want your order executed. You could au-

thorize him or her to buy shares **at the market.** This is a market order and means that your order will be filled, or completed, at the best price available. Your order may be filled at the same price as the last trade or close to it if stock is not available at the last traded price. When you authorize your broker to buy at the market, you don't know how much you will be paying for the stock.

An alternative is the **limit order.** Here you specify the price you expect to pay. You might offer to buy shares at a price below the most recent trade. Your order might fill at the lower price if a willing seller offers the stock; if no such seller can be found, your order will not be filled. A limit order may be a day order—one limited to the day you place it—and will expire at the market's close; or the limit order can be left open until it is cancelled, in which case the order is **GTC**—good 'til canceled. If you place a GTC order, remember it, as it could be filled weeks later.

Two other types of orders can help to protect your investments: the stop order and the limit order to sell.

The **stop order** is a special form of limit order that tells the broker's representative on the exchange floor to sell your shares if the price drops to a level you specify. Thus, you can avoid a major loss on shares you own by entering a GTC stop order.

Suppose you own shares bought at $35, but they are now trading at $45. You decide to protect at least some of your profit against a possible future drop in price and enter a stop order to sell your shares at $40. A reasonable profit margin is 10 percent to 15 percent of the price you originally paid. A stop order set too close to a current price could be tripped off by a temporary blip down, after which the price rises again. This brief movement down followed quickly by a move up is known as a whipsaw. If the market turns against you, and the price drops to $40, your stop order automatically becomes an active order and is executed. Although you have lost $5 per share from a recent price, you protected $5 per share of your profit above its cost basis.

Stop orders can be changed at will, so the trailing stop order may protect more of your profit if you monitor prices regularly. A trailing stop order is one that moves up as the price rises. Suppose, continuing the example, that the price of your stock moves up to $50 from $45. With the stop order set at $40, you could lose 20 percent of your profit in a serious downturn. To protect more of your profit, you could move the stop limit up from $40 to $43. If the stock continues to move up, call your broker and change the limit again. If you wish to continue holding the stock, track prices and move the limit price down if the stock declines closer to the stop limit.

Stop orders are available only for listed stocks and a limited number of OTC stocks. The specialist at the exchange records the stop order in his book. The specialist on the New York Stock Exchange (NYSE) operates at a post on the floor and trades all shares in a limited number of companies. The specialist is the key person who is charged with maintaining an orderly market in the shares of a company. All buy and sell orders clear through the specialist for that stock. If an order is entered to buy shares of IBM, for example, the floor broker takes the order to the post maintained by the specialist in IBM. There, the buy order is matched with sell orders on the spe-

cialist's books. A stop order is entered on the specialist's book as available at a set price. If the price declines to that level, the stop order automatically becomes a live order and is matched with a buy order. At times the price may be declining so fast that a stop order cannot be filled at the specified price. Stop orders are filled in the order received. If the specialist holds stop orders for 1,000 shares at $40, and buyers are willing to take only 600 shares at that price, 400 shares remain unsold. If the next price at which buyers appear is $39 and your order is among the 400 shares remaining unfilled at $40, then your stop order will be filled at $39 rather than the $40 you expect. You have no control over that mechanism once you authorize a stop order. A similar system, but without a specialist, handles stop orders on the National Association of Securities Dealers and Automated Quotation (NASDAQ) system for stocks traded on the OTC market.

Limit order to sell functions like a stop order to protect you in a sale. If you are holding stock currently trading at $45 and wish to lock in a profit on a rise, you may place a limit order to sell if your stock reaches $50 or some other price you specify. If the stock's price rises to 50, the limit order to sell becomes a live order and will be filled if buy orders for the stock are available at that price. It will not be executed at a price under $50 (or whatever price you specify).

Round Lot versus Odd Lot

Shares typically trade in **round lots,** or blocks of 100 shares. A larger order will usually be a multiple of 100 shares. Block trades, usually between institutions, are 10,000 shares or more.

Odd lots comprise some number of shares other than a multiple of 100. Odd numbers of shares may accumulate from stock dividends or participation in a dividend reinvestment plan, or an investor may not have enough money to buy 100 shares. He or she may buy 50, 74, or some other number, and thus be buying an odd lot. Unfortunately, odd lots trade at a penalty, usually $\frac{1}{8}$–$\frac{1}{4}$ point more if you are buying and $\frac{1}{8}$–$\frac{1}{4}$ point less if you are selling. This odd-lot differential depends on the price, with shares above $40 marked up or down by $\frac{1}{4}$ point. The $\frac{1}{8}$-point differential applies to shares priced under $40. The break point, where the differential increases or decreases, may change from time to time.

Investors should either plan to buy in round lots or, if too little cash is available, buy shares in a mutual fund. The odd-lot differential is not only costly, but it slows the process of trading, particularly in the OTC market. For example, a quantity of shares above 100 but less than 200 will be traded as two transactions, one for the 100 shares as a round lot and one for the odd lot at a different price. Let's say you own 213 shares of XYZ Corporation and wish to sell all. Your execution will be broken into two parts, one for 200 shares at one price and another for 13 shares at $\frac{1}{8}$–$\frac{1}{4}$ point less than the price for the round lot.

Share Prices

Price changes and levels are still quoted in fractions, usually with $\frac{1}{8}$ as the minimum tick. Tick is the minimum price vari-

ation either up or down, usually $\frac{1}{8}$ point, or $0.125 cents. (A point is $1.) A few stocks in the low price categories of $1 to $5 per share may trade in $\frac{1}{16}$-point, or even $\frac{1}{32}$-point, ticks because a $\frac{1}{8}$-point tick would represent a substantial percentage of the price.

Penny stocks, those typically priced at less than $1 per share, may trade in pennies, as even $\frac{1}{32}$-point ticks are too big. Some brokerages treat any stock priced under $3 ($5 in some brokerages) per share as a penny stock. Penny stocks, despite their title, are not cheap to trade. In order to meet their minimum requirements on fees for transactions, some brokers may levy a minimum per-share commission that could exceed the firm's minimum requirement dollar amounts from the commissions alone. If a penny stock trades at $.50, a $.04-per-share commission represents 12½ percent of the share's value— far higher than commissions as a percentage of value for higher priced stocks. As a result of the poor reputation of penny stocks, many brokerages refuse to handle them and will sell them out of portfolios brought to them for management.

If a company's fortunes decline and the price of its stock falls below $1 per share, the company may institute a **reverse stock split.** Under this maneuver the company's board of directors initiates a plan whereby some number of shares is exchanged for a single new share. A 10-for-1 reverse split, for example, would exchange 10 existing shares for 1 new share. Presumably a stock that had been selling for $.50 per share would sell for $5 per share after a 10-for-1 reverse split. To effect the reverse stock split, the company, through its transfer agent, calls in existing certificates and replaces them with new certificates with a proportional number of new shares. Odd numbers of shares that are not multiples of the old shares are cashed out, as fractional shares are not issued. At the new $5 price, shares in the company would again be acceptable for trading by most brokerages.

Stock Splits and Stock Dividends

Stock splits and stock dividends complicate trading, performance monitoring, and tax reporting.

Stock splits and capital gains. A normal stock split occurs when a company elects to reduce share price by issuing more shares to existing stockholders. Companies split shares mainly to reduce trading prices to a reasonable range. If a company's stock rises to $80–$100 per share, an investor must put up $8,000–$10,000 to buy a round lot. So the company splits the stock two-for-one, issuing two new shares for every existing share. If you owned 100 shares before the split, you would now own 200 shares. Other splits are also common—three-for-two, three-for-one, and even five-for-one. Instead of calling in existing certificates, the transfer agent simply sends additional certificates to register ownership of additional shares. The market responds by reducing the trading price of the shares in proportion to the new number of shares outstanding.

When a stock splits, the capital value of the shares remains the same, but the value of each split share drops by the ratio of the split. If you owned 100 shares of XYZ Corporation trading at $50 per share, their capital value would be $5,000. After the shares split two-for-one, you would own 200 shares and they would trade at $25 per share. At $25 per share, your 200 shares are still worth $5,000. If your cost basis on unsplit shares was $20 per share, the cost basis on the split shares would drop to $10 per share. (Cost basis for shares is their original cost plus commissions and/or trading costs.)

The cost basis for shares is the base for figuring capital gains or losses. If you sell your split shares of XYZ Corporation trading at $25 per share, your gain is $25 less the cost basis of $10, or $15 per share. Your investment of 200 split shares shows a current capital gain of $3,000 (200 shares times $15) less selling costs.

Stock dividends and capital gains. Stock dividends may be distributed by a corporation as a tidbit to stockholders, or they may be distributed by a company that has grown in total value but is strapped for cash. If you owned 100 shares in XYZ Corporation and it sends out a 10 percent stock dividend, you receive another certificate for shares boosting your stake in the company to 110 shares. The market will adjust XYZ's trading price accordingly. If the original cost basis of the shares was $10 per share, the 110 shares now have a cost basis of $1,000 divided by 110, or $9.09 per share. You pay no taxes on stock dividends unless you sell them.

Capital gains or losses are figured as in the stock split above. In fact, most investors consider a stock dividend a mini stock split, as capital value remains constant while the cost basis is distributed over more shares. Also, as in a stock split, you receive cash for any shares not a multiple of the distribution to avoid fractional shares. Expect to pay taxes on such cash payments.

Reinvesting cash dividends. Reinvesting cash dividends can be an inexpensive way to acquire additional shares in a company. Over 1,000 companies in the United States offer dividend reinvestment plans, or **DRIPs.** The company may charge a minimum fee in the range of $2.50–$5.00 for the exchange, or the company may encourage stockholders to reinvest dividends by charging nothing, subsidizing the transaction by absorbing brokerage costs. Some companies, particularly utility companies, reinvest declared dividends in additional shares at a 5 percent discount and charge no fees for the exchange. Be aware, however, that the Internal Revenue Service (IRS) considers the 5 percent discount to be taxable income.

Additional shares acquired by reinvesting dividends are kept as data entries in a computer with confirmations sent to shareholders quarterly following payment of dividends. Dividends are converted into fractional shares maintained to three decimal places to avoid cash distributions. If you wish to sell the shares acquired in a DRIP, you must request certificates for full shares and cash for any leftover fractional shares. Some companies will cash out shares acquired by a DRIP in response to a written request without going through a broker and at no cost. An information folder from the company spells out its policy when offering a dividend reinvestment plan.

Calculating the cost basis for your original shares plus shares acquired by a DRIP can be a hassle. Even though dividends are reinvested in additional shares, you are liable for income taxes on the dollar value of the dividends distributed each year. Most investors pay taxes on dividends reinvested in additional shares from other cash. All reinvested dividends then increase the original cost basis.

Suppose your original investment of $1,000 in XYZ Corporation bought 100 shares. Over the years you invested another $500 in dividends and acquired 40 additional shares. Your cost basis for the 140 shares would be $1,500, or $10.71 per share. If you sold all shares, you would figure any gain or loss on the cost basis of $1,500. If you sold only the 40 shares acquired by DRIP, your cost basis at the first sale would be $10.71 per share. If you continue to reinvest dividends from the original 100 shares, calculating the cost basis becomes complicated. Ask your tax advisor for help. You can avoid the problem of readjusting the cost basis for shares acquired by a DRIP by selling your complete stake in XYZ Corporation at one time.

Important dividend dates. Four dividend dates are important. The first, the **declaration date,** is the date when a company announces a dividend on its stock. The announcement specifies three additional dates. (See box below for an example of dividend distribution dates.) Dividends

---

DIVIDEND DISTRIBUTION DATES

Declaration date—Board of Directors announces dividends will be distributed to shareholders of record Friday, March 29

Ex-dividend date—Monday, March 25

Record date—Friday, March 29

Payment date—April 22

Stockholders on record March 25 (Monday) receive the declared dividend.

payable on high-dividend stocks can become an important income source, so pay attention to these dates to protect that income.

The **ex-dividend date** will be four days ahead of the record date. If you buy a share of stock in the regular way on the ex-dividend date or later, you will not receive the declared dividend because five days later is one day after the record date. (Regular way transactions are required to close in five business days.) If you make a cash trade rather than a regular-way trade, it clears on the same day and you can even buy shares on the record day and still receive the dividend. See your broker about the additional costs and restrictions on cash trades. The market price of shares normally drops on the ex-dividend date because regular-way buyers on that date are not entitled to the dividend.

Record date is the cutoff date for shareholders to receive the dividend. Stockholders of record (that is, registered as owning stocks at the end of the business day on the record date) will receive the dividend. The transfer agent, usually a bank, maintains the list of shareholders.

Payment date is when the bank mails checks to shareholders entitled to receive dividends. The payment date is often two or more weeks after the record date.

Spreads, Bids, and Asked Prices

Spread, bid, and asked are terms you should be familiar with in trading stocks and bonds. When you buy shares, you pay the asked price because that is the price the seller is asking for his shares. When you sell, you receive the bid price because this is the price a buyer is willing to bid for your shares. The spread is the difference between the bid and asked prices. Spreads may be practically nonexistent for shares traded on the NYSE due to the ready availability of buyers and sellers plus the volume of trading. In fact, prices you see quoted in *The Wall Street Journal* and other newspapers or magazines are one figure rather than bid and asked prices. In the specialists' book, however, a small spread may exist and is used in trading.

Spreads are more apparent in OTC stocks and bonds. Quotations for OTC stocks note both bid and asked prices with the spread typically in the $\frac{1}{8}$- to $\frac{1}{2}$-point range. Issues trading at low price levels usually have smaller spreads than higher priced issues. Volatility tends to increase spreads, as some issues jump around in price more than others, and a wider spread compensates the market maker for volatility risk. Activity level also affects spreads, as active OTC stocks carry a smaller spread than stocks that trade infrequently, say, only once in several days.

Bonds trade mainly on the OTC market, and the spread can be substantial, possibly in the range of 1–3 points ($10–$30 for a $1,000 bond). A broker will also charge a commission on each trade. Thus, a round-turn involves three costs: a commission on the buy, a commission on the spread, and a commission on the sale. For small quantities of corporate bonds, round-turn costs could run 4 percent to 6 percent of the dollar amount of the trade. Spreads and commissions are less on government bonds.

Buying on Margin

A margin account allows you to buy up to twice as many shares with your investable dollars as you would if you paid full price from a cash account by allowing you to use credit advanced by your broker. The Federal Reserve Board (the Fed) limits margin trading in stocks to 50 percent of the value of the trade. As little as a 5 percent margin is the norm for commodities and futures trading. For example, if the price of XYZ Corporation stock is $50, you could buy a round lot of 100 shares for $5,000 in cash, plus commission. Using a margin account, you deposit $5,000 with your broker, arrange to borrow another $5,000 from the broker, and buy 200 shares at $50 per share, plus commission.

With margin you double your profit potential because you bought 200 rather than 100 shares. If the market declines, however, you double your loss. This expansion of profit or loss potential is called leverage. If the market decline drops the price too far, your broker will call for additional margin.

How far is too far? The maintenance margin limit may be 35 percent or some similar limit defined by the brokerage. If the price declines to the point where your original margin deposit amounts to 35 percent or less of the value of the stocks, the infamous margin call goes out for more cash. For example, if the price for XYZ Corporation stock declined to $40, your position would be worth $8,000; you owe $5,000, leaving $3,000 for your equity interest. Your $3,000 amounts to 37.5 percent of the total. Another slight drop and

you would reach the 35 percent maintenance margin limit.

You can calculate this margin limit in dollars by dividing the margin by 1 minus the margin limit. In the example above, divide $5,000 by .65 (1–.35) for stock value of $7,692.31. At this point in the example, your broker would call for more cash to be added to the account.

All of these figures are made more complicated in an actual account by introducing commissions and interest accruals. In addition to the deposit, you must pay interest on the money borrowed from the broker at his broker loan rate, usually in the range of ½ percent above the bank's prime rate. The box on page 128 follows the dollar flows of a typical margin trade for stock and compares it with an investment without margin.

Margin investing is not for everyone. To profit from buying stocks on margin, you must sense changes in the direction of market prices. Complicating the profit picture from margin investing is the drag of interest rates; that is, your stocks must gain some increment over time just to pay for the interest on the money borrowed to buy stocks. Your potential for profit from a margin account depends heavily on the broker loan rate. A high interest rate makes profits harder to achieve. Discount brokers tend to charge slightly lower interest rates and to set maintenance margin limits as much as 5 percent below those for full-service brokers.

Short Selling

Short selling involves trading for profit in a declining market. Most investors are op-

MARGIN TRADING OF STOCKS

Investment without margin		Investment with margin	
Price per share = $50		Price per share = $50	
		100 shares @ $50	$ 5,000
		100 shares on margin	5,000
100 shares @ $50	($5,000*)	200 shares @ $50	(10,000)
Share price rises to $60	6,000	Share price rises to $60	12,000
Profit	$1,000	Profit	$2,000
100 shares @ $50	(5,000)	200 shares @ $50	(10,000)
Share price drops to $40	4,000	Share price drops to $40	8,000
Loss	($1,000)	Loss	($2,000)

The maintenance margin limit for the investment with margin is calculated as follows:

$$\text{Margin} = \frac{\$8{,}000 - \$5{,}000}{\$8{,}000} = \frac{\$3{,}000}{\$8{,}000} = 37.5\%$$

Thus, the investment with margin does not reach maintenance margin limit of 35%. If maintenance margin is 35%,

$$\frac{\text{Value of stock} - \$5{,}000}{\text{Value of stock}} = 35\%$$

then price value can be calculated as follows:

$$\frac{\text{Margin}}{1 - .35} = \frac{\$5{,}000}{.65} = \$7{,}692.31,$$

or $38.46 per share.

If price drops to $38.50, broker will call for more margin.

*All transactions incur commissions that are omitted in this example.

timists; they buy shares and hold them with the expectation that prices will climb and they can sell shares at a price to gain a profit later. You end up in a long position when you own shares; this is known as going long. Short selling is the reverse and involves selling shares you don't own with the intent of buying back shares later at a lower price for a profit. Short sellers are pessimists and expect to profit as the market heads south, an expression derived from the movement of the stock market average toward the bottom of a page, which is south on a map.

How can you sell shares you don't own? You borrow them from your broker. For example, suppose you sell 100 borrowed shares at $10 per share. A few weeks later the price has declined to $8 per share. If you buy back the shares and replace those you borrowed from your broker, you have gained a gross margin of $2 per share, or

$200 for the 100-share transaction. Out of this gross margin you must pay two commissions.

As a popular Wall Street rhyme goes, "He who sells what isn't his'n, must pay it back or go to prison." If you go short (sell a quantity of shares you don't own), you must buy them back within some reasonable period negotiated between you and your broker. You can sell short only from a margin account, as the broker wants money on deposit to cover a possible loss. A short sale leaves you liable for a potentially unlimited loss, since there is no limit on how high the price of the shares could go. If you should be unlucky enough to be trapped in a situation where the price of the shares you bought at $10 per share rises to $30 per share, you could lose $20 per share, or twice as much as you received from the original sale. A long purchase, buying shares at $10, for example, limits your loss to $10 per share, as the price can never drop below zero.

Interest on the shares borrowed from your broker tends to set a practical limit on how long you can hold those shares. The longer you hold shares sold short, the more the price must decline for you to break even. Further, the owner of shares borrowed by the broker continues to receive any dividends declared while you have borrowed the stock. The owner of the shares has parked them in street name with the broker and may not be aware that the shares are loaned out for a short sale. Stocks kept in street name are held by a broker with the owner identified as the beneficial owner, and no certificates are issued.

Covering short positions is often advanced as a reason for a particularly steep rise in the market. When the overall market enters an upward trend, investors in short positions get nervous. If price rises continue, they can lose heavily. If prices rise rapidly, they panic and buy shares to replace those borrowed at whatever price they can. Buying shares pushes up prices and pressures the shorts even more. The result can be a sharp rise over a few trading hours. *The Wall Street Journal* reports monthly on the number of shares in short positions on both the NYSE and the American Stock Exchange (Amex). This allows you to see how many other investors believe a certain stock is headed down before you invest.

Generally, short selling is a losers game for two reasons. First, the long-term bias for the stock market is up—about 4 percent to 6 percent yearly on average. Major and small movements up and down relate to the underlying trend. Second, costs associated with short selling (commissions and interest) require shorts to do better than average just to break even. Costs impose what is known as negative leverage. These disincentives plus the potential for huge losses make short selling a relatively minor activity engaged in mainly by professional traders.

Selling Short Against the Box

Selling short against the box is a tactic used by some investors to lock in a profit but transfer it to a following year for tax purposes. Suppose you have owned shares in XYZ Corporation for more than a year (ownership for over a year qualifies for a long-term capital gain). Near the end of the year you consider selling for a capital gain because you believe the price is due to decline, but you would prefer to move the gain into the following year. You sell short against the box by selling XYZ shares borrowed from your broker and putting your shares into your margin account to meet the broker's need for security or collateral. After the new year, you replace the shares borrowed with the shares in the box you own to close out your short position if the market remains relatively unchanged. If, as you perceived, the market declines, you can profit from the borrowed shares sold short and maintain your long position.

Wash Sales

Wash sale rules can trip up the unwary investor. A wash sale is one where you sell and rebuy the same security within 30 days. The rule, imposed by the IRS, voids the practice of taking capital losses to offset gains followed by immediately rebuying the stock or mutual fund because you are confident of future gains. If you sell XYZ Corporation shares to take a loss for tax purposes, you cannot rebuy shares in XYZ corporation for 31 days. If you do, the IRS defers the loss, if any, until a later sale.

A key element of the wash rule is the phrase "same or essentially the same security." Obviously, if you sell and then rebuy shares in the same XYZ Corporation, those securities are identical. If you sell shares of XYZ Corporation, you can immediately buy shares in UVW Corporation without violating the wash sale rule. But

if you wish to continue holding XYZ Corporation, you must wait for 31 days, during which time the price of shares could rise.

Selling and rebuying shares in mutual funds is easier. You could sell shares in Fund A, for example, and immediately buy shares in Fund B, where the two funds have essentially the same objectives and performance. Switching funds does not violate the wash sale rule. The wash sale rule applies only to losses. You may sell a security at a higher price than you bought it to take a gain and immediately rebuy the identical security without a problem.

Abuses in the Market

A broker's license is sometimes referred to as a "license to steal" by those initiated into the broker fraternity. Indeed, the opportunity for abuse in dealings between securities firms and investors is always present to tempt the greedy. Newspaper accounts of the abuse of fiduciary responsibility in selling and buying junk bonds; fraudulent multi-million dollar real estate deals by savings and loan association (S&L) officers; and insider trading scandals involving high company officials, major players at brokerages, and institutions responsible for the savings of small investors appear regularly. While such large-scale, unsavory activities make headlines, abuses in the relationships between retail brokers and individuals are common and little publicized. Your best defense is to be aware of the tricks and tactics and avoid them. Not all brokers are given to shady practices by any means, but there are enough to require watchfulness on your part.

Much of the abuse between broker and client results from the conflict of interest noted earlier: The broker needs a steady stream of commissions. Common activities that tend to enhance the income of brokers to the possible disadvantage of investors are outlined below.

Churning

Churning refers to excessive trading in an account. The broker, with the tacit approval of the client, engages in frequent trading for the express purpose of generating more commissions. Selling one block of stock in order to generate cash to buy a different block of stock yields two commissions. Churning often peaks near the end of each month when a broker may feel pressed to meet a goal or a quota. Often the broker will sell a stock that has advanced in price and shows a profit, citing the gain to the client. The pitch may be that the price for that stock has moved up and is now likely to stall—better to get out and move into another stock that the broker believes is about to move up.

In a bull market, one that is moving up, such tactics may appear reasonable to the unsophisticated investor who relies on the broker for advice. The reverse may occur in a bear market, one that is moving down, when the broker advises getting out of a stock that is declining to avoid a greater loss. The pitch may then be to move the cash generated from the sale into a defensive stock, one likely to retain its value in a downtrending market. A defensive stock may be one of the major food companies or a utility. Both industries tend to hold their value during a recession, as people must eat and they still turn on the lights. What may not be apparent to the casual investor is the price level of defensive stocks. Many will have been bid up in price by others taking positions in those same stocks months earlier when early signals of a declining economy appeared.

Ordinarily, according to the usual agreement signed between client and broker, the broker must obtain the client's approval for each transaction. However, some brokers fail to follow procedure and make trades on their own, often to the disadvantage of the client.

Your defense against churning is to pay close attention to the paperwork you receive from the broker. It is designed to simplify the work of the firm's computer rather than to inform the client, so learn how to read the monthly reviews of account activity. Check that every transaction had your approval. If you find transactions that you did not approve prior to execution, complain promptly. If you sense an unproductive volume of trading, advise your broker to stop it.

A discretionary agreement allows your broker to use his own discretion in trading for your account without your prior approval. A broker operating with a discretionary agreement can more easily churn your account and may invest in companies riskier than you might approve. If you now have a discretionary agreement with your broker, revoke it. Requiring a broker to check with you before trading is one way of keeping the broker's feet to the fire. If he has to check with you, he will most likely engage only in trades in whose outcome he has confidence.

Unsuitable Investments

When you hook up with a broker, you will be asked to spell out your goals and operating parameters. You may be asked about your interest in capital gains versus income, about whether your attitude is conservative or aggressive, and about acceptable risk levels. This form goes into your record as a statement of your intentions and goals.

A broker may recommend investments far outside the limits on your disclosure. You may have indicated that you are conservative and desire to invest for income with liquidity. A broker who sells you a limited partnership to finance some real estate, oil development, or apple orchard is not following your expressed goals, as these investments tend to be extremely risky, long-term, and illiquid. Further, limited partnerships require investors to meet suitability limits, such as a minimum net worth outside one's residence and a high salary level. Such suitability requirements are established by the Securities and Exchange Commission (SEC) and state security departments to limit partnership offerings to sophisticated investors with enough financial resources to withstand a loss if the project goes sour. However, the broker may push such partnerships because they generate higher commissions than stocks and bonds.

Your defense against unsuitable investments is to question your broker about the details of any investment he or she recommends. Learn enough about various alternatives to rate the risks on your own. Before you venture into an unknown field of investing, do your homework. Before committing to a large investment, ask your accountant or a knowledgeable friend to review it. Don't depend entirely on recommendations from your broker.

Initial Public Offerings

Shares in an initial public offering can be a risky investment with little promise of a big payback to compensate for the added risks. An initial public offering, or IPO, may be one of two kinds: a public offering by a company seeking funds for expansion or an initial offering on a closed-end mutual fund.

Underwriting IPOs enables small companies to grow. A company making a public offering of shares to raise funds for expansion usually has an excellent track record—years of steadily rising sales, rising profits, proved managers in place, and promising business plans for expansion once new funding is available. Many IPOs go on to unqualified successes, such as Nordstrom and Microsoft. However, despite the rosy projections featured in the prospectus issued by the IPO underwriters, not all companies prosper after raising new cash. (An underwriter is a brokerage firm or group of firms that offers the new stock to the public and distributes it to their clients.)

One way to judge the general opinion of the professionals about an IPO is to ask your broker about shares. If many shares are available and your broker offers you as many shares as you want, the issue is probably a dog and should be avoided. Other investors, possibly more knowledgeable than you, have passed on purchasing the shares, and this accounts for their ready availability. On the other hand, if a forthcoming IPO generates considerable media attention, the shares may become a hot issue. Unless you are a frequent investor who buys and sells in large dollar terms, your broker will not offer shares to you. When a hot issue hits the market, many investors enter buy orders even before the share price is announced. Brokers swamp the market with orders. Too few shares are available to satisfy the demand and may be rationed to brokers.

The quick summary on IPOs is: If you can buy IPO shares readily and in any quantity, don't. If IPO shares are likely to be profitable, you won't be able to buy them unless you have a close relationship with your broker.

The second type of IPO is the closed-end mutual fund. These IPOs are probably one of the biggest rip-offs in the investment business. You should avoid buying shares in closed-end funds at the initial offering for one simple reason—they are overpriced. Let's say your broker offers you shares in a new closed-end fund without a commission. You buy at the asking price. But your broker earns a concession (commission) from the fund manager equal to 6 percent to 8 percent of the money invested. If you take 7 percent as an average, what you bought for each $100 invested is $93 of assets.

For a few weeks, until all of the shares have been sold, the underwriters will probably support the price, mainly by buying any shares being offered at a price lower than the IPO price. After the initial period, shares are left to find their own price level. Many decline to a discount relative to their net asset value (NAV). Discounts of 15 percent to 25 percent are common. If you are interested in a closed-end fund, wait

for several months and buy shares at a discount.

Boiler-room Sales

Fraudulent sales activities are engaged in by high-pressure salespeople who operate at some remote location. These salespeople are particularly adept at promoting oil and precious metals, either as stock or as commodities. They may contact you because your name appears on a list of subscribers to some financial publication, because you asked for information in response to a sales piece you received in the mail, or simply because you live in an area known to be affluent. Telephone swindlers can sound authentic and may offer unbelievable deals. The standard response to such offerings is, "If it appears too good to be true, it probably is."

Refuse to deal with anyone unknown to you who approaches you by telephone. Don't be tempted by promises of huge profits. If special deals were available in platinum or obscure oil stocks, you would be able to access them through your local broker at a lower cost. If a boiler-room solicitor contacts you, simply hang up; it's your best protection.

Other Problem Areas

Some unfortunate happenings are the result of risks inherent in the trading process and are not the results of abuses by brokers. The main question that arises between brokers and clients is "Who is responsible for losses?"

If your broker recommends a stock and you approve the transaction with a full understanding of the facts, and the price of the stock declines, can you take your broker to arbitration? Probably not. You can't expect to earn a profit on every transaction. Brokers may work with some undisclosed ratio of profitable to losing trades, but a 70 percent ratio of profitable trades represents a high success ratio. This means that out of every 10 transactions, three may go sour. If you suffer one of these losses following full disclosure by your broker, you have no actionable recourse.

Overall market declines are not the responsibility of the broker either. During the wild selloff on October 16, 1987, some clients were unable to reach their brokers to enter a sell order. Brokers were sometimes unable to reach a market maker in an OTC stock to enter a sell order. Problems of this magnitude occur only when the market is in a free fall, and everything and everybody is in an uproar. You may believe you have cause for complaint in these unusual situations, but the status of the environment can be cited as a defense if you take a case to arbitration.

Settling Disputes

If you believe you have a legitimate grievance, consider taking a stepped approach as you seek resolution. Every brokerage has a written policy for resolving disputes and grievances. Any defense under this policy requires you to retain all paperwork, confirmations, certificates, and monthly statements. Armed with solid documentation, you can attempt to resolve your problems in two ways.

Resolving Problems In-house

If you discover a problem in your monthly statement from the broker, call it to your broker's attention. You may discover a trade you did not authorize, a trade you authorized but which was not made (through the negligence of your broker), a violation of your margin agreement, or some misrepresentation. If you discover a trade you did not authorize and you have not signed a discretionary agreement, notify the broker within a day or two if possible. Undoing a trade must be handled quickly. Other problems can be brought to your broker's attention within a couple of weeks. If your complaint is legitimate, the broker's firm should resolve it promptly.

If your broker can't or refuses to resolve your complaint, your best recourse is to try to have your complaint resolved through the broker's grievance resolution process. Set up an appointment with the broker's supervisor or the office manager. (Sometimes a single person serves both functions.) At this meeting, explain your problem and back up your complaint with documentation.

If the office manager cannot resolve your grievance, contact the firm's Compliance Department, which may be located at a headquarters office if the firm maintains a number of branch offices. If this proves unsuccessful, your next stop is the regional manager or the firm's president. Exhaust every avenue within the brokerage firm before taking your complaint to outsiders.

If you fail to get satisfaction within the firm, you can file complaints with the SEC, the NASD, your state's securities department, and, if the security is traded there, with the NYSE. Be prepared for delays if you take your grievance to a state securities regulatory body, as investigations are often backed up. Once a grievance with these bodies is in the investigatory hopper, a filing for arbitration or a suit in court which you may subsequently initiate will be held pending resolution of the investigation.

Arbitration

Your final step is to take an unresolved complaint to **arbitration** or court. The agreements presented by many brokers to new clients contain an arbitration clause that effectively precludes the client from taking a case to court. In separate decisions in 1987 and 1989, the U.S. Supreme Court affirmed these broker agreements. Attempts to delete these arbitration clauses from broker agreements are seldom accepted. Arbitration rules may be those of the American Arbitration Association, the Board of Arbitration of the NYSE, or the NASD. Arbitration decisions are final and may not be appealed.

Going to arbitration is not all bad. In fact, arbitration offers a number of advantages:

1. Disputes are almost always resolved far more quickly in arbitration than in state or federal courts.
2. Costs for arbiters, attorneys, and arbitration hearings are lower than similar costs in court.
3. According to the SEC, investors receive a higher percentage of their claim for damages against brokers in arbitration than they do in court cases.

You should be aware of your rights to choose the forum, either the NASD, NYSE, or American Arbitration Association. Consult an attorney who is knowledgeable about securities arbitration. NASD arbitration hearings are held in large cities around the country; most NYSE arbitrations occur in New York City. You or your attorney should obtain the rules or procedures and all the necessary documents for filing a claim from the forum you select. You will be charged filing fees.

An arbitration case begins by filing a Statement of Claim in the form of a detailed letter with supporting documentation. The party bringing the claim is called the claimant.

A small claims procedure (for amounts of less than $10,000) limits costs and time. Small claims are typically decided by a single arbitrator from submitted written data. At the arbitrator's discretion, he or she may hold a hearing and/or request additional documentation. Claims of $10,000 or more are conducted by a panel of three arbitrators—two public arbitrators and one industry arbitrator. An industry arbitrator is one who currently works within the brokerage industry or has recently worked in the industry. Public arbitrators have no current or past ties to the brokerage industry and may be attorneys or others with a knowledge of legal procedure and securities trading.

The arbitrator or arbitration team renders its decision either immediately or within a few days. There is no appeal from an arbitration decision. If your claim is considered valid and damages are specified, the brokerage pays and that is it. In some blatant cases of broker mischief, attorney fees incurred by the claimant are charged to the broker. Otherwise, you are liable for your own expenses. Thus, you must assess the costs of bringing a case to arbitration with the prospect of recovery versus accepting a loss and dropping your complaint.

Conclusion

Learning the mechanics of investing in stocks, bonds, and mutual funds is a mat- ter of experience. The best way to learn is by engaging in a number of small trades of different types and asking your broker to explain each step. If your broker is impatient, switch to one who is willing to explain what is going on and to expand your know-how. Investing can be a fascinating hobby or business, one that is challenging and potentially profitable, but only if you understand what is going on. Sources of information abound; it is up to you to exploit them.

CHAPTER NINE

What's Happening: Using Indexes and Averages as Market Indicators

---

KEY TERMS FOR THIS CHAPTER

averages
indexes
market indicator
benchmark
simple mean
relative value
unweighted

capitalization
base value
weighted
index fund
arithmetic average
geometric average

How's the market today? What's happening in the market? If you were to scan the many small print entries in newspapers reporting daily results of stock, bond, commodities, futures, and options trading, you would gain little insight into the overall movements in the market. You would need some sort of summary, and that is the reason for **averages** and **indexes.** Averages and indexes have been around since 1884 to summarize what happened either in one day or over a period of years.

Statisticians call averages an "indicator of central tendency." Indexes are averages related to a base. These **market indicators** provide useful information to investors and market watchers. They indicate price and volume trends and cycles over a period. Technical analysts pore over historical data in search of clues to movements that may be forthcoming, but averages and indexes are essentially a history, not a guide to the future. Historical perspective and comparability are important in the analysis of indexes and averages. The over-100-year history of the Dow Jones Industrial Average, for example, is a major key to its use and popularity.

Indexes also provide a **benchmark** for stock and portfolio comparison. If you own a portfolio of stocks or mutual funds, you can compare how your holdings are doing to an index. Frequently, money managers and mutual fund managers compare their performance to the Dow Jones Industrial Average or the Standard & Poor's 500 Index.

Another more modern use of indexes has been as a base for futures and options contracts. A number of the popular indexes were created specifically for the purpose of trading futures and options.

Many specialized and obscure averages and indexes are available, but the most important of the major averages and indexes are noted below.

Dow Jones Averages

Dow Jones & Company* is a financial publisher of *The Wall Street Journal* and other publications.

The Dow Jones Industrial Average. The Dow Jones Industrial Average (DJIA) is recognized as the granddaddy of "indicators of central tendency." The DJIA is the most quoted single indicator of market activity, as in the report that "the market was up with the Dow climbing 6.34 points." The report assumes the listener will recognize that "Dow" means the industrial average. The DJIA represents what happened over the course of the day to 30 major stocks listed on the New York Stock Exchange (NYSE). (See page 139 for listing of companies)

* The Dow Jones Industrial Average, Dow Jones Transportation Average, Dow Jones Utility Average, and Dow Jones Composite Average are trademarks of Dow Jones & Company.

What is now called the Dow Jones Industrial Average was started on July 3, 1884, when Charles Henry Dow issued his Dow Jones Average (DJA) of 11 stocks—9 railroad stocks, a steamship company, and Western Union. The closing prices of the 11 stocks were totaled and divided by 11 for a **simple mean,** or average, of the 11 closing prices. The DJA was distributed as part of the *Customer's Afternoon Letter*, the forerunner of *The Wall Street Journal*. The DJA first appeared in the initial edition of *The Wall Street Journal* on July 8, 1889.

The composition of the DJA (that is, the companies included in the average) changed several times until 1896 when Dow issued an index of 12 industrial stocks. The average was still computed as a simple mean of the closing prices each day. Companies continued to be deleted and added over time, and in 1916 the list was expanded· to 20. Due to stock splits, the average of stock prices was no longer comparable to what it had been in the past, and, beginning in 1916, the compilers changed the value of prices to reflect stock splits or stock dividends. If a company's stock split two-for-one, for example, the price was doubled and the divisor remained at 20. By that time General Electric and Sears, Roebuck had split for a total of four-for-one.

On October 1, 1928, 30 stocks were listed in the DJIA, which appeared for the first time in *The Wall Street Journal*. The average aimed to indicate market action among major big capitalization corporations.

Components of the DJIA are chosen according to undisclosed criteria. Over the years, the stocks included in the magic 30 have changed occasionally to reflect mergers and to improve representation. How-

COMPOSITION OF THE DOW JONES INDUSTRIAL AVERAGE (DJIA)*

Alcoa	Goodyear
Allied-Signal	International Business Machines
American Express	International Paper
American Telephone & Telegraph	McDonald's
Bethlehem Steel	Merck
Boeing	Minnesota Mining & Manufacturing
Caterpillar	Morgan, J.P.
Chevron	Philip Morris
Coca-Cola	Procter & Gamble
Disney	Sears, Roebuck
DuPont	Texaco
Eastman Kodak	Union Carbide
Exxon	United Technologies
General Electric	Westinghouse
General Motors	Woolworth's

* In 1991.

ever, the problem of maintaining a continuity with previous averages became more complicated as companies continued to split shares and to declare stock dividends that affected share prices. The compilers of the DJIA at *The Wall Street Journal* corrected for these splits by changing the divisor. About 1986 the divisor had drifted

COMPOSITION OF THE DOW JONES TRANSPORTATION AVERAGE (DJTA)*

AMR	Federal Express
Airborne Freight	Norfolk Southern
Alaska Air	Roadway Services
American President	Ryder System
Burlington Northern	Santa Fe Pacific
CSX	Southwest Air
Carolina Freight	UAL
Consolidated Freight	Union Pacific
Consolidated Rail	USAir
Delta Air	XTRA

* In 1991.

COMPOSITION OF THE DOW JONES UTILITY AVERAGE (DJUA)*

American Electric Power
Centerior Energy
Columbia Gas
Commonwealth Energy
Consolidated Edison
Consolidated Natural Gas
Detroit Edison
Houston Industries

Niagara Mohawk Power
Pacific Gas & Electric
Panhandle Electric
Peoples Energy
Philadelphia Electric
Public Service Enterprises
SCE

* In 1991.

---

down to slightly over 1. Because the divisor is close to one, relatively small changes in prices can produce large changes in the DJIA. Remember, the DJIA does not reflect either the true dollar value of the stocks in the average or the dollar value of an increase or decrease; it represents a continuation of an average that measures market action of major stocks. Thus, changes in the DJIA should be noted as points, not dollars. The continuity of **relative value** remains one of the major strengths of the DJIA, which continues to provide a consistent view of changes in the market into the second century of its existence.

Companies that make up the DJIA are listed below. The DJIA is **unweighted;** that is, each price carries equal weight regardless of the size or **capitalization** (a combination of equity and debt) of the company. Without a weighting for size, those companies whose stock prices are highest exert the greatest influence on the average, a weakness according to some market watchers.

The DJIA is also criticized as being unrepresentative, because it includes only 30 out of about 1,700 stocks traded on the NYSE. Many of the stocks included in the DJIA represent the older "smokestack" issues. Thus, the DJIA fails to record how high-tech or smaller fast-growth companies are doing in the market. However, since the 30 stocks include about 35 percent of the total capitalization of stocks on the NYSE, stocks in the DJIA carry a lot of weight in what happens to the overall market.

Dow Jones Transportation Average. The Dow Jones Transportation Average (DJTA) is an offshoot of the DJIA. Nine of the eleven companies making up the original DJA were railroads because they were the dominant corporations of the day. A Railroad Average was begun in 1896 when the DJIA was reconstituted to include only industrial concerns. In 1970 the Railroad Average became the DJTA, recognizing the growing importance of trucks and airlines in transportation. The 1970 DJTA included nine airlines, eight railroads, and three trucking companies. Early in 1991 a major change occurred when Pan American went into Chapter 11 bankruptcy and was replaced in the DJTA with Roadway Services, the first over-the-counter (OTC) stock to appear in any Dow Jones average. The DJTA is also unweighted and consists of the 20 stocks listed on page 139.

Dow Jones Utility Average. The Dow Jones Utility Average (DJUA) consists of 15 utilities, including electric power generating companies and natural gas companies. No telecommunications companies are included in the average. From 1970 through 1990, oil crises, high interest rates, and environmental concerns caused the DJUA to gyrate wildly without moving in a sustained trend. Companies that make up the DJUA are listed on page 140.

Dow Jones Composite Average. A combination of the three basic Dow Jones averages (the DJIA, the DJTA, and the DJUA) make up the Dow Jones Composite Average. The 65 stocks in the three basic averages provide a broader view of market activity than any one of the three alone.

Standard & Poor's Indexes

These indexes are the most representative of all market indicators, according to many market watchers who recognize the limits of the DJIA. Standard & Poor's Corp. (S&P)* is a major stock and bond analysis firm that publishes detailed information for use by investors. S&P indexes are listed below.

* S&P, Standard & Poor's, and S&P 500 are trademarks of the Standard & Poor's Corporation.

Standard & Poor's 500 Composite Index. Standard & Poor's 500 Index, commonly known as the S&P 500, differs from the Dow Jones averages in three important ways:

1. It is an index and not an average of stock prices. Daily changes in the index reflect the **base value** of 10 from the 1941–43 period. That is, the value of the market in the 1941–43 period was averaged and given a value of 10. When the market doubled from that period, the S&P 500 reached 20. It has been moving up dramatically since that period, as the stock market has advanced.

2. Index values are **weighted.** The price of each stock in the index is multiplied by the number of shares of each stock outstanding, and the total is divided by the total number of shares included in the index. This weighting means that major corporations have a greater influence on index values than smaller corporations. Thus, a stock that makes up 1 percent of the S&P 500's valuation exerts 10 times as much influence on the index as a corporation with .1 percent of the S&P 500's valuation.

3. Because it includes a greater number of stocks, the S&P 500 more accurately reflects overall market activity than any of the Dow Jones averages. Within the S&P 500 are four subindexes of 400 industrial companies, 40 public utilities, 40 financial companies, and 20 transportation companies. The S&P 500 reflects a broad sampling of the market, similar to the Dow Jones Composite Average but with a wider spread.

The S&P 500 includes a great variety of new companies in telecommunications, computing technology, and biotechnology. High-tech companies, once they are established on a profitable operating basis, tend to grow faster than more mature corporations in basic industries. Composition of the S&P 500 changes more frequently than that of the Dow Jones averages due to leveraged buy-outs, mergers, and declines in company fortunes. When a corporation merges with another corporation, is bought out by management or outsiders, or ceases to be a leader in its category, the corporation is dropped from the S&P 500 listing. With 500 corporations in the list, these changes occur more frequently in this index than in the DJIA. Criteria for selecting stocks to be included in the S&P 500 are confidential.

Ordinarily, when a company is dropped from the S&P 500, the replacement company's shares climb in price during the next market day as a result of buying by **index fund** managers because the new company must be represented in the index fund in the same proportion as in the index itself. If you want to "buy the market," that is, to buy a piece of the total stock market, the most logical tactic is to buy shares in an index mutual fund.

Listing all of the stocks included in the S&P 500 is neither practical nor desirable, as the mix changes. However, the 10 biggest companies included in the S&P 500 in 1991 were IBM, Exxon, General Electric, Royal Dutch Petroleum, American Telephone & Telegraph, General Motors, DuPont, Ford, Merck, and Amoco. Companies whose stocks are traded on the NYSE, the American Stock Exchange (Amex), and the OTC markets are included in the list of 500 companies.

Standard & Poor's 100 Index. Standard & Poor's 100 Index (S&P 100) is a special list of stocks on which options are traded on the Chicago Board Options Exchange (CBOE). Most of the stocks in the S&P 100 are traded on the NYSE; they are mainly industrials with a few transportation, utility, and financial stocks. Futures on the S&P 100 are traded on the Chicago Mercantile Exchange (Chicago Merc). Options on the futures are not traded.

Other Standard & Poor's Indexes. Standard & Poor's 400 Index (S&P 400) is a subindex of the S&P 500. The S&P 400 is limited to industrial companies traded on the NYSE, the Amex, and the OTC markets.

Additional subindexes of the S&P 500 include an index of 40 utilities companies including electric power, telecommunications, and gas transmission companies; an index of 40 financial companies including banks, savings and loan associations (S&Ls), and insurance companies; and an index of 20 transportation companies including railroads, trucking companies, and airlines. Although the subindexes of the S&P 500 are reported in the financial press, they are less important than the S&P 500.

Major Market Indexes

A number of indexes were created for underlying securities for futures and options trading. In addition to providing reports on those securities, the indexes also provide a useful guide to what is happening to the overall market or segments of the market.

NYSE Composite Index. The NYSE Composite Index includes all common stocks listed on the NYSE, a total of about 1,700. Daily closing prices of the NYSE Composite Index have been computed and reported since May 1964. The NYSE Composite Index is based loosely on an earlier Securities and Exchange Commission (SEC) index of NYSE stock activity. Adjusting the statistics from the earlier SEC index allows the NYSE Composite Index to claim a history going back about 45 years.

Since the NYSE Composite Index is the basis for futures and options trading, it is now computed every half-hour, with four subgroup indexes—industrial, transportation, utility, and finance—reported every hour. The base value of the NYSE Composite Index is 50, which was close to the average closing price of all common stocks traded on the NYSE on December 31, 1965.

The NYSE Composite Index is weighted similarly to the S&P 500 and is computed as follows: Each common stock's price is multiplied by the number of shares outstanding to determine the stock's current aggregate (total) value. These aggregate values are totaled and compared to the aggregate value of all stocks for the base period. If the current aggregate value of all common stocks listed is double the value of all stocks for the base period, then the Composite Index is 100—double the base level of 50. Rising market prices are indicated by an index number higher than 50. Daily percentage changes may be computed by subtracting yesterday's index from today's index and dividing by yesterday's index. For example, if the NYSE Composite Index is 51 today and was 50 yesterday, the computation would be 51 less 50 divided by 50, or 1 divided by 50, for a 2 percent increase. If today's index is lower than yesterday's, then the result will be negative, indicating that the market declined.

The NYSE Composite Index effectively measures changes in the total value of NYSE common stocks after adjusting for additional share issues, additional listings of companies, and delistings. Index values are generally available in media reports of market activity.

Value Line Index. The Value Line Index differs from both the S&P 500 and the NYSE Composite Index in that it is price weighted. Each stock's price exerts the same effect as that of every other stock. Company A may be 100 times bigger than Company B and have 100 times more shares of stock outstanding, but a $1 change in Company B's stock has the same effect on the Value Line Index as a $1 change in Company A's stock. For example, if Company A's stock changes in price from $100 to $101 and Company B's stock changes in price from $10 to $11, the effect on the average is the same.

The Value Line Index is exceptionally broad-based, including about 1,650 stocks. About 35 different industry groups are represented ranging from machinery to computer and insurance to mining, with a broad base of commercial activities. The divisions, which are not computed as subgroups, include about 89 percent industrials, 10 percent utilities, and 1 percent railroads. Nearly three quarters of the stocks included in the Value Line Index are listed on the NYSE, 21 percent in the OTC market, 6 percent on the Amex, and a small number on the Toronto Stock Exchange (TSE).

Daily changes in the Value Line Index are computed by first adding together all of the price changes of each stock in the index. Each daily price change is calculated as that day's closing price divided by the previous day's closing price to provide an index. Increases in some stocks are balanced by decreases in others. The sum of all the price changes is divided by the number of issues in the index, which changes from time to time as issues are added or deleted. This **arithmetic average** of the individual stock indexes has been used since March 9, 1988. Before that date the Value Line Index was computed as a **geometric average** from a base level of 100 that was equated to the prices as of June 30, 1961. A geometric average is the nth root of a product of n numbers (where n equals the number of issues). The difference between an arithmetic change and a geometric change is detailed in the box on page 145. Given the same data, the arithmetic average will always vary more widely than a geometric average using the same data.

CRB Futures Price Index. The Commodities Research Bureau (CRB) calculates an index, the CRB Futures Price Index, based on the futures prices of 21 commodities—including live cattle, gold, heating oil, and wheat—traded on commodities exchanges in the United States.

The CRB Futures Index, or CRB Index, reflects the changing percentage values of the unweighted geometric average of 21 arithmetically averaged sets of future prices. Begin first with the arithmetic average of each set of prices for the 21 commodities. As an example, consider the live cattle average. Futures contracts expire at various times, and prices quoted for all periods through the end of the ninth calendar month from a current date are included in a set of prices. All of the prices quoted for each expiration period are added together to reach a total for the set; that total is then divided by the number of prices for a simple arithmetic average or mean. These 21 means are then multiplied together and the 21st root of the total is extracted to yield the geometric mean. The geometric mean is then divided by 53.0615, which was the value of the 1967 base year. A further adjustment is to multiply the base-adjusted figure by .94911, a factor that accounts for the changeover on July 24, 1989 from 26 commodities averaged over 12 months to 21 commodities averaged over 9 months. This adjusted number is multiplied by 100 to obtain the CRB Index. Computers perform these complex operations in a flash.

The CRB Index is used by analysts as a guide to inflation trends. Increases in the cost of living roughly follow what happens to the future prices for the 21 raw materials that are used to produce the goods we buy in quantity. The CRB Index is also the base for futures and options contracts traded on the New York Futures Exchange (NYFE).

The Major Market Index (MMI). This index is a product of the Amex. The MMI began in September 1973 with a base level of 100, replacing a previous index called the Price Change Index that had begun in April 1966. On July 5, 1983, the MMI was changed to reflect a base level of 200, in effect doubling index values. The MMI includes 20 stocks, 15 of which are also included in the DJIA. Index options are based

---

COMPUTING ARITHMETIC AND GEOMETRIC AVERAGES
FOR THE VALUE LINE INDEX

$$\text{Individual stock price change (PC)} = \frac{\text{Today's price}}{\text{Yesterday's price}}$$

$$\text{Arithmetic average} = \begin{array}{c}\text{Yesterday's}\\ \text{Closing}\\ \text{Index}\end{array} \times \left(\frac{PC_1 + PC_2 + \cdots PC_n}{n}\right)$$

$$\text{Geometric average} = \begin{array}{c}\text{Yesterday's}\\ \text{Closing}\\ \text{Index}\end{array} \times \sqrt[n]{PC_1 \times PC_2 \times \cdots PC_n}$$

Up Market

	Stock A	Stock B	Stock C
Today's price (T)	45	100	120
Yesterday's price (Y)	30	75	100
Price change (T ÷ Y)	1.500	1.333	1.200

$$\text{Arithmetic average} = \frac{1.500 + 1.333 + 1.200}{3} = 1.344$$

$$\text{Geometric average} = \sqrt[3]{1.500 \times 1.333 \times 1.200} = 1.339$$

New Value Line Index
  Arithmetic average = 200.00* × 1.344 = 268.80 (+34.4% change)
  Geometric average = 200.00 × 1.339 = 267.80 (+33.9% change)

Down Market

	Stock A	Stock B	Stock C
Today's price (T)	40	65	120
Yesterday's price (Y)	50	75	125
Price change (T ÷ Y)	.800	.867	.960

$$\text{Arithmetic average} = \frac{.800 + .867 + .960}{3} = .8757$$

$$\text{Geometric average} = \sqrt[3]{.800 \times .867 \times .960} = .8732$$

New Value Line Index
  Arithmetic average = 200.00 × .8757 = 175.14 (−12.4% change)
  Geometric average = 200.00 × .8732 = 174.64 (−12.7% change)

* 200.00 is the starting index value in both examples

---

on the MMI trade on the Amex and are second in volume only to the S&P 100, which trades on the CBOE.

The MMI is another weighted index that measures changes in the aggregate value of common stocks. One factor differentiates it from other weighting methods, however: Each day's price is multiplied by the original issue of shares. Stock splits, stock dividends, trading halts, new listings, additional listings, delistings, suspensions, or cash dividends do not figure in the computation of the MMI. Since dividends do not change the MMI, the index reflects the return of the underlying issues and not just its price performance.

International Market Index. The International Market Index (IMI), a product of the Coffee, Sugar, and Cocoa Exchange (CSCE) and the Amex, offers continuous real-time pricing throughout the trading day in the United States for a representative sample of stocks of major international companies. The index is calculated and disseminated every 15 seconds. The IMI measures the performance of 50 foreign stocks traded in the United States through a direct listing or as an American Depositary Receipt (ADR) on the NYSE, the Amex, or the National Association of Securities Dealers and Automated Quotation (NASDAQ) OTC market. Because the foreign stocks are traded on U.S. exchanges, prices are always denominated in U.S. dollars. Further, because the underlying securities are regulated by the SEC and may be traded individually by U.S. investors, a portfolio of index securities can be assembled for trading against the index futures contract. Options and futures based on the IMI are traded on the CSCE and the Amex.

The IMI includes stocks from 10 countries that are distributed into 20 industry groups. To be listed with the IMI, stocks must actively trade in the United States and represent a minimum worldwide market value of $100 million when converted to U.S. dollars. Minimum trading volumes must also be maintained.

The IMI is weighted according to capi-

tal value, similar to the S&P 500. The base of 200 for the index represents the starting value of the IMI on January 2, 1987. The IMI provides a benchmark for evaluating international market movements and futures based on the index to provide a means for hedging foreign transactions.

NASDAQ Indexes. NASDAQ indexes report actions in the OTC market. The NASDAQ system is actually divided into two major groups. First is the top tier of major OTC companies that have millions of shareholders and trade in volumes that match many of the listed companies. This is the National Market System Composite Index (NMS) of NASDAQ. The second is the NASDAQ Composite Index, which covers about 2,900 issues plus the NMS top-tier issues. The six specialized NASDAQ indexes are: the Bank Index, Insurance Index, Other Finance Index, Transportation Index, Utilities Index, and Industrial Index.

All eight of the NASDAQ indexes began on February 5, 1971 with a base of 100. They are weighted by capitalization, similar to the S&P 500. Since there is no single closing figure with OTC stocks quoted as bid and asked prices, the NASDAQ indexes use a median bid price. The indexes are adjusted for stock splits and stock dividends but not for cash dividends. None of the NASDAQ indexes are used as a base for index futures or options.

Wilshire 5000 Equity Index. The Wilshire 5000 Equity Index encompasses more issues than even the NASDAQ Composite Index. More than 6,000 common stocks traded on the NYSE, the Amex, and the OTC markets make up the index. The

Wilshire began in 1974 and is maintained by Wilshire Associates of Santa Monica, California. The Wilshire 5000 is unique in one respect: A 1-point change in the index represents roughly $1 billion of assets, so that a 10-point drop in the index would represent a $10 billion decline in the aggregate value of the stocks within the Wilshire 5000.

The Financial News Composite Index (FNCI). This is a price-weighted index of 30 blue-chip stocks and tracks the DJIA closely. The FNCI was developed by the Financial News Network (FNN) to include many stocks with active listed options and is now maintained by CNBC/FNN. Index option contracts based on the FNCI are traded on the Pacific Stock Exchange (PSE).

Shearson Lehman Hutton Treasury Bond Index. This is the most publicized of several bond indexes. It is limited, as the name indicates, to U.S. Treasury notes and bonds. The Shearson Lehman Index measures the performance of all U.S. Treasury notes and bonds outstanding, except for flower bonds. The index is capitalization weighted by multiplying the gross principal value of a bond issue by its closing market price. Index values relate to the base level of 1,000 at the end of 1980.

Solomon Brothers Broad Investment-Grade Bond Index (SBI). SBI includes U.S. Treasury and foreign government issues, U.S. government agency bonds, corporate and mortgage bonds, plus such pass-through certificates as those of the Government National Mortgage Association (GNMA) and other agencies of the U.S. government. Unlike most other indexes, the SBI is calculated monthly rather than daily. Index values relate to the base level of 100 on December 31, 1979.

Standard & Poor's Bond Yield Averages. S&P maintains four corporate composite bond yield indexes, one for each of the top four rating groups: AAA, AA, A, and BBB. These averages began in January 1937 and produce an effective measure of the yields according to rated risk levels. Bonds used as bases for the four corporate composite indexes are about evenly divided between industrial and utility issues. Indexes are calculated weekly as arithmetic averages. S&P began calculating and reporting two indexes of junk bonds in 1988, one for a group of bonds rated BB and another for a group of bonds rated B.

Finally, S&P computes and reports on municipal bonds (muni-bonds) in two indexes. One is based on prices of 15 bond issues rated AAA to A with typical maturities of 20 years. Prices are obtained in a telephone survey of muni-bond dealers. The second index is one based on yields of 15 issues rated AAA to A as surveyed by telephone.

Using Market Indicators

Stock and bond averages and indexes can be useful guides to trends and cycles of general and specialized markets. Obviously, which index you select depends on how you plan to use it. The S&P 500, for example, is an accurate measure of what is happening across the broad market. If you are a market watcher, you can follow the ups and downs by glancing at a chart of the S&P 500 over a specific period. If you are involved in stock index futures or options investing, you may use the S&P 500 as an underlying security. If you would like to invest in a cross section of the market, index mutual funds offer a proxy for the market by tracking the performance of the S&P 500 closely. These are only a few examples of how investors use averages and indexes to monitor the market for their own purposes.

Conclusion

Market indicators, in the form of a wide variety of averages and indexes, serve a number of purposes. They offer a quick summary of market activity; they form the underlying securities for futures and options contracts; and, finally, they provide technicians with basic data for price and trend analysis that can be useful in forecasting what might happen to the markets in the future.

CHAPTER TEN

Keeping Tabs

KEY TERMS FOR THIS CHAPTER

ticker tape

stock symbol

composite transactions

EPS

relative strength

closing price

warrants

voting issue

preemptive right

unit

when issued

composite tick

More than half of the adult population in the United States is involved in investing in one form or another. As a result, the demand for information on how stocks, bonds, certificates of deposit (CDs), and mutual funds are doing is intense and growing. To satisfy this demand, a never-ending stream of financial information flows out of exchanges, banks, government, and media covering financial centers. Major metropolitan newspapers devote entire sections to trade and financial news and offer daily reports on stocks, bonds, and mutual funds.

Here are the sources of information you can use to keep tabs on your investments.

The Tape

Before the computer age and the availability of electronic displays, individual trades on the New York Stock Exchange (NYSE) were reported on a mechanical **ticker tape**, hence the origin of the term, the tape. Thin ribbons of paper snaked out of the ticker seconds after a trade on the trading floor was recorded. Because of the huge amount of data that must be transmitted in a short time, transactions appeared on the tape in a form of shorthand. Even so, during high activity periods, the tape sometimes fell behind actual floor trading.

Today, the tape no longer spews out of a noisy mechanical ticker. Instead, a similar flow of information in much the same format moves steadily across an electronic reader board at several locations around the NYSE and other exchange floors. This electronic data is transmitted to local brokers' offices, where one or more exchange transactions appear on a moving display similar to those on an exchange floor. Financial News Network and Consumer News and Business Channel, now combined into a single cable television network FNN/CNBC, displays trades and summaries every hour the exchange is open, but data is delayed 15 minutes by agreement with the exchanges.

This is how the electronic tape, or ticker, works. Two rows of data appear on the ticker (see the box below). Symbols consisting of one to five letters denote the company on the upper row. A few companies, 22 in all, are identified with a single letter, such as *C* for Chrysler Corporation, *S* for Sears, Roebuck & Co., and *T* for American Telephone & Telegraph Co. Most companies' **stock symbol** consists of two to four letters, such as *BA* for The Boeing Co. (originally Boeing Airplane Co.), *Wy* for Weyerhaeuser, *BP* for British Petroleum, *AMX* for Amax, Inc., and *CHMX* for Chemex Pharmaceuticals.

Ticker symbols tend to be collections of letters with some mnemonic significance, such as *EK* for Eastman Kodak Co. Ticker symbols also appear after the alphabetical listing in stock tables in *The Wall Street Journal*. Additional symbols on both the upper and lower rows on the ticker display other information in abbreviated format, such as whether a stock is a preferred issue.

Trades march across the reader board displays at a fairly rapid pace, and unless you recognize the symbols in the blink of an eye, you can miss much of the information. Few traders can recognize all symbols, but investors interested in a few stocks can easily pick out those symbols

---

REPRESENTATIVE TICKER TAPE

DCY   BA[1]   ASPr[3]   GTE   ACK   TIS
$2\frac{1}{4}$ 25s$7\frac{7}{8}$[2] $16\frac{1}{8}$ 10.000s28$\frac{1}{8}$[4] $9\frac{1}{4}$ $7\frac{7}{8}$

Explanatory notes

[1] BA, tape symbol for The Boeing Co.

[2] 25s before price indicates 2500 shares traded—25 round lots of 100 shares. $7\frac{7}{8}$ price omits 4, as total price is $47\frac{7}{8}$. Investors must know trading range for stock and supply additional number.

[3] Pr following AS (symbol for Armco Steel) indicates stock is preferred issue A. If B followed Pr, as in PrB, stock would be preferred issue B.

[4] 10.000s indicates a block trade of 10,000 shares. Numbers of 10,000 and greater are not multiplied by 100 to register number of shares in trade.

from the mix of trades and extract the information needed.

Computer Displays

Detailed information on all stocks traded on exchanges and National Association of Securities Dealers and Automated Quotation (NASDAQ) system are generally available on computer screens in brokerage offices. Individual brokers will have their own screens, and many public rooms at brokers' offices include a running ticker display plus one or more computer work stations where customers can punch up specific companies and study the information presented. NASDAQ mainly lists those over-the-counter (OTC) stocks that meet National Association of Securities Dealers (NASD) minimum requirements. A company must have a minimum of 1,000 shareholders plus minimum net worth and asset totals, for example, to qualify for NASDAQ listing.

Newspaper Stock Tables

The many lines of densely packed small type that comprise a newspaper report of stock prices and trade data may appear formidable, but they can be interpreted if you know what each number and symbol means. In addition to the financial publications, major metropolitan newspapers report the complete NYSE listing, most of the important companies listed on the American Stock Exchange (Amex), and abbreviated listings of OTC issues, usually those of major OTC stocks along with those

of local interest. Some foreign or regional issues may also be reported, but coverage is uneven among general interest daily newspapers.

NYSE Tables

The box on pages 152–153 displays a small section of a typical day's report of NYSE **composite transactions** from *Investor's Daily*. *Investor's Daily* appears Tuesday through Saturday, with each day's reports covering the market through the close of the previous day. Here are explanations of different bits of information noted by number in the table.

1. On the far left is a listing of the stock's **EPS** rank, which is a measure of a company's earnings per share (EPS) growth over the past five years and the stability of that growth. The EPS rating is computed as follows: The percent change in earnings in the last two quarters is compared to the percent change in earnings in the same two quarters of the previous year and combined and averaged with the five-year record. Those absolute results are compared with all other companies' EPS ratings and ranked on a scale of 1 through 99, with a rating of 99 the highest. A 90 rank means the company produced earnings results in the top 10 percent of all listed companies. Companies with EPS rankings of 80 and above are considered to have superior earnings records.

2. Next to the EPS rank is a figure for **relative strength**, which is a measure of a company's relative price changes

INTERPRETING DAILY STOCK TABLES FOR THE NEW YORK STOCK EXCHANGE

EPS Rnk	Rel. Str.	52-Week High	Low	Stock Name	Closing Price	Chg.	Vol. % Change	Vol. 100s	PE	Day's High	Price Low
				Common stocks for Monday, Aug. 27, 1990							
				— A —							
61	14	$37\frac{1}{2}$	$15\frac{1}{4}$	AAR Corp	$16\frac{1}{8}$	$+\frac{3}{8}$	−50	285	10	$16\frac{1}{4}$	$15\frac{3}{4}$k o
	52	$9\frac{3}{4}$	$7\frac{3}{4}$	ACM Gvt Opp	$7\frac{7}{8}$	....	+21	217	..	8	$7\frac{3}{4}$
	65	$11\frac{5}{8}$	$9\frac{3}{8}$	ACM Gvt Incm	$9\frac{3}{4}$	$-\frac{1}{8}$	−27	386	..	10	$9\frac{3}{4}$
	54	$9\frac{3}{4}$	7	ACM Mgd Inc	$7\frac{7}{8}$	....	−52	154	..	$7\frac{1}{4}$	$7\frac{7}{8}$
	80	$12\frac{1}{8}$	10	ACM Mgd Mlt	$11\frac{1}{4}$	....	−38	103	..	$11\frac{1}{4}$	11
	62	$11\frac{1}{2}$	$9\frac{3}{8}$	ACM Gvt Sec	$9\frac{1}{2}$	$+\frac{1}{8}$	−15	×798	..	$9\frac{5}{8}$	$9\frac{1}{2}$
	60	$9\frac{3}{8}$	$7\frac{3}{4}$	ACM Gvt Spct	$8\frac{1}{8}$	$+\frac{1}{4}$	+2	578	..	$8\frac{1}{8}$	$7\frac{7}{8}$
88	81	$24\frac{5}{8}$	$14\frac{5}{8}$	AL Labs Inc	$19\frac{1}{2}$	$+\frac{3}{4}$	−61	90	17	$19\frac{1}{2}$	19
21	9	$5\frac{3}{4}$	$1\frac{5}{8}$	AM Int Inc	$1\frac{3}{4}$	....	−65	211	..	$1\frac{7}{8}$	$1\frac{5}{8}$k
39	**26**	**$107\frac{1}{4}$**	**$43\frac{3}{8}$**	**AMR Corp**	**47**	**$+1\frac{1}{4}$**	**+90**	**1.0m**	**11**	**$47\frac{5}{8}$**	**$46\frac{3}{4}$o**
79	60	$4\frac{1}{4}$	$2\frac{3}{8}$	ARX Inc	$3\frac{1}{8}$	....	−39	49	10	$3\frac{3}{8}$	$3\frac{1}{8}$
	86	$72\frac{3}{4}$	$41\frac{3}{8}$	ASA Ltd	$48\frac{1}{8}$	$-4\frac{3}{8}$	+136	3060	..	$50\frac{5}{8}$	$48\frac{1}{8}$k o
91	**88**	**$45\frac{5}{8}$**	**$30\frac{3}{8}$**	**Abbott Labs**	**$39\frac{1}{4}$**	**+2**	**+13**	**8736**	**19**	**$39\frac{1}{2}$**	**$38\frac{1}{2}$o**
29	85	$15\frac{3}{8}$	$11\frac{1}{4}$	Abitibi Price	$13\frac{3}{4}$	....	+13	61	..	14	$13\frac{3}{4}$
12	24	$11\frac{5}{8}$	$6\frac{1}{2}$	Acme Clevlnd	$6\frac{5}{8}$	....	−58	65	8	$6\frac{7}{8}$	$6\frac{5}{8}$
60	38	$9\frac{5}{8}$	$6\frac{7}{8}$	Acme Electric	$6\frac{7}{8}$	....	−5	21	9	7	$6\frac{7}{8}$
96	**88**	**$49\frac{1}{8}$**	**$28\frac{3}{8}$**	**Acuson**	**$41\frac{3}{4}$**	**$+1\frac{7}{8}$**	**−35**	**480**	**23**	**$41\frac{7}{8}$**	**$40\frac{1}{2}$o**
	60	**$16\frac{7}{8}$**	**$14\frac{1}{8}$**	**Adams Exprs**	**$15\frac{1}{8}$**	**+1**	**+10**	**165**	**. .**	**$15\frac{1}{4}$**	**15**
59	71	$15\frac{3}{8}$	10	Adobe Rsrces	$11\frac{1}{2}$	....	−1	290	..	$11\frac{1}{2}$	$11\frac{1}{4}$
42	16	$11\frac{3}{8}$	$4\frac{7}{8}$	Adv Micro Dvc	$5\frac{3}{4}$	$+\frac{1}{4}$	+21	5817	23	$5\frac{7}{8}$	$5\frac{5}{8}$o
21	11	$9\frac{1}{4}$	$3\frac{1}{8}$	Advest Group	$3\frac{3}{8}$	$+\frac{1}{4}$	**+54**	×238	42	$3\frac{1}{2}$	$3\frac{1}{4}$
84	42	$62\frac{1}{2}$	$43\frac{3}{8}$	Aetna Life	$44\frac{1}{8}$	$+\frac{5}{8}$	+0	1663	7	$44\frac{1}{8}$	$43\frac{5}{8}$o
27	38	$13\frac{3}{4}$	$8\frac{1}{4}$	Affiliated Pub	$8\frac{7}{8}$	$+\frac{1}{4}$	−71	195	..	$8\frac{7}{8}$	$8\frac{3}{4}$
89	43	25	$15\frac{5}{8}$	Ahmanson HF	$16\frac{3}{4}$	$+\frac{1}{2}$	−47	1288	7	17	$16\frac{5}{8}$o
39	92	$3\frac{5}{8}$	$1\frac{7}{8}$	Aileen Inc	$2\frac{5}{8}$	....	**+97**	148	..	$2\frac{5}{8}$	$2\frac{1}{2}$k
71	**62**	**61**	**43**	**Air Products**	**$46\frac{1}{4}$**	**$+1\frac{5}{8}$**	**+21**	**1717**	**12**	**$46\frac{3}{4}$**	**$45\frac{1}{8}$o**
94	**64**	**27**	**$16\frac{3}{8}$**	**Airbrn Frght**	**$21\frac{1}{2}$**	**$+3\frac{3}{8}$**	**+26**	**993**	**12**	**$21\frac{1}{2}$**	**$20\frac{1}{4}$**
82	33	$24\frac{5}{8}$	$13\frac{7}{8}$	Airgas Inc	$14\frac{7}{8}$	$+\frac{3}{4}$	−10	114	27	$14\frac{7}{8}$	$14\frac{1}{8}$
69	65	$20\frac{3}{4}$	$16\frac{1}{2}$	Airlease Ltd	$17\frac{1}{2}$	$+\frac{1}{8}$	+3	35	9	$17\frac{5}{8}$	$17\frac{3}{8}$
50	27	$29\frac{7}{8}$	16	Alaska Air Gp	$17\frac{3}{8}$	$+\frac{3}{4}$	−15	375	9	$17\frac{1}{2}$	$16\frac{3}{4}$o
37	27	$22\frac{1}{2}$	$11\frac{7}{8}$	Albany Intl	13	....	−77	162	12	$13\frac{1}{8}$	13
94	**58**	**$27\frac{7}{8}$**	**20**	**Albrto Culvr B**	**$22\frac{3}{8}$**	**$+1\frac{1}{8}$**	**−36**	**87**	**18**	**$22\frac{3}{8}$**	**$21\frac{3}{4}$**
94	**54**	**$22\frac{1}{4}$**	**$15\frac{3}{4}$**	**Alberto Clv A**	**$17\frac{1}{8}$**	**$+1\frac{1}{8}$**	**+62**	**459**	**14**	**$17\frac{3}{8}$**	**$16\frac{1}{4}$**
94	**86**	**$37\frac{5}{8}$**	**$24\frac{3}{8}$**	**Albertsons**	**$33\frac{1}{8}$**	**$+2\frac{7}{8}$**	**−52**	**945**	**22**	**$33\frac{3}{8}$**	**$32\frac{3}{4}$o**
42	75	$25\frac{1}{8}$	$18\frac{7}{8}$	Alcan Alumin	$21\frac{5}{8}$	$+\frac{1}{2}$	−57	3338	8	$21\frac{7}{8}$	$21\frac{1}{2}$o
67	**54**	**$37\frac{7}{8}$**	**$27\frac{5}{8}$**	**Alco Standrd**	**$30\frac{1}{4}$**	**$+1\frac{1}{4}$**	**−57**	**211**	**11**	**$30\frac{3}{8}$**	**$29\frac{5}{8}$o**
32	33	34	20	Alex & Alex Sv	21	$+\frac{5}{8}$	−83	82	19	$21\frac{1}{8}$	$20\frac{5}{8}$o
27	15	$63\frac{1}{4}$	$30\frac{1}{2}$	Alexanders	$31\frac{1}{2}$	$+\frac{7}{8}$	+24	62	..	$31\frac{3}{4}$	$31\frac{1}{4}$
96	**52**	**$98\frac{1}{4}$**	**$76\frac{1}{2}$**	**Alleghany**	**78**	**+1**	**+77**	**55**	**7**	**78**	**77**
10	98	1	$\frac{7}{32}$	Allegheny Intl	$\frac{1}{2}$	$-\frac{1}{4}$	+51	437	..	$\frac{3}{4}$	$\frac{1}{2}$b
48	48	$34\frac{1}{4}$	$22\frac{3}{4}$	Allegheny Ldl	$23\frac{1}{8}$	$+\frac{3}{8}$	+137	×914	7	$23\frac{5}{8}$	23

Reprinted by permission of INVESTOR'S DAILY, *America's Business Newspaper*

EPS Rnk	Rel. Str.	52-Week High	52-Week Low	Stock Name	Closing Price	Chg.	Vol. % Change	Vol. 100s	PE	Day's High	Price Low
56	**56**	**42 1/2**	**34 1/4**	**Alleghny Pwr**	**35 1/2**	**+1**	**−55**	**293**	**10**	**35 1/2**	**34 3/4**
91	**84**	**20**	**9**	**Allen Group**	**14 5/8**	**+1 1/8**	**−55**	**146**	**13**	**14 5/8**	**14**
16	38	25 1/8	12 1/4	Allergan Inc	14	+1/8	−40	1007	20	14 1/8	13 7/8o
98	58	17 3/8	12 3/4	Alliance Cap	13 7/8	+5/8	+6	204	14	14	13 3/8
2	**13**	**17**	**8 5/8**	**Allinc Gibl**	**10 1/4**	**+1**	**−40**	**136**	**..**	**10 1/4**	**9 3/4**
2	47	12 1/8	8 7/8	Alli Nw Euro	9 1/2	+3/8	−45	460	..	9 7/8	9 3/8
34	24	14 1/4	4 5/8	Allied Product	5 1/2	−1/8	−57	46	7	5 7/8	5 1/2
65	**48**	**40 3/8**	**29**	**Allied Signal**	**31**	**+1 1/4**	**−13**	**2013**	**9**	**31 5/8**	**30 3/4o**
	73	10 3/4	9 3/4	Alst Muni Inc	10	....	**+55**	361	..	10 1/8	10
	73	10 1/8	9 1/4	Alst Muni II	9 3/8	−1/8	**+91**	532	..	9 5/8	9 3/8
	75	10	8 3/8	Alst Mun III	8 3/4	....	−7	103	..	8 7/8	8 3/4
	69	11 1/8	9 3/4	Alls Mun Inc	10 1/4	+1/4	−34	118	..	10 1/4	10 1/8
	69	10 1/4	8 7/8	Alls Mun OpII	9 1/4	+1/8	−14	133	..	9 1/4	9 1/8
2	71	**10 1/8**	9 5/8	Alst Muni III	9 5/8	....	+10	124	..	9 5/8	9 5/8
	71	**9 3/4**	8 5/8	Alst Mun Prm	9	+1/8	−64	113	..	9	8 7/8
73	31	41 7/8	24 3/4	Alltel Corp	25 1/2	....	**+92**	2168	11	26	25 1/4o
46	60	79 5/8	59 3/4	Alcoa	62 1/8	+7/8	−12	3772	8	63 1/8	61 5/8o
67	91	20 1/4	12 3/4	Amax Gold	16 3/4	−2 1/8	**+76**	427	47	18 5/8	16 3/4
41	80	29 3/8	20 3/4	AMAX Inc	25	+3/8	−42	1952	7	25 1/8	24 5/8o
16	1	16 1/4	1 1/2	Ambase Corp	2 3/8	....	+38	3789	..	2 5/8	2 1/4
48	27	12 7/8	7 1/2	Amcast Indstl	7 5/8	−1/8	−3	85	11	7 7/8	7 5/8
11	1	14 3/4	9/32	Amdura Corp	7/16	....	−95	7	1	7/16	7/16b
12	90	**54 1/2**	38 3/8	Amerada Hes	51 3/8	−1/2	−52	1689	46	52 3/8	51 o
2	73	**10 3/8**	9 1/8	Am Adj Rt	9 7/8	+1/8	**+74**	157	..	9 7/8	9 3/8
98	95	24 3/4	10 7/18	Am Barrick Rs	20 1/4	−1 7/8	**+250**	1.4m	49	21 3/8	20 o
91	64	79 5/8	61 3/4	Amer Brands	64 1/8	+7/8	−17	2030	9	65	64 o
79	52	41 5/8	31 5/8	Am Bldg Main	32 1/4	+1/4	−99	1	14	32 1/4	32 1/4k
69	52	25 3/8	19 1/2	AmBusn Prod	19 3/4	+1/2	−58	×20	10	19 3/4	19 1/2
	58	21 5/8	16	Am Cap Bond	16 1/8	−1/8	−15	67	..	16 1/4	16
	50	22 1/4	17 1/8	Am Cap Conv	17 3/8	+1/4	−63	10	..	17 1/2	17 3/8
	48	9 1/4	6	AmCap Inc Tr	6 1/4	+1/8	**+67**	421	..	6 1/4	6 1/8
48	93	**12**	8 1/4	AmCap Mgmt	11 1/8	....	−76	48	14	11 1/4	11 1/8
86	**60**	**61 1/2**	**46 1/4**	**Am Cyanamid**	**50 5/8**	**+1 3/8**	**−34**	**2890**	**17**	**51 1/8**	**50 1/4o**
60	58	33 3/8	26	Am Elec Powr	26 5/8	+3/8	+10	2805	9	27	26 1/2o
39	31	39 3/8	22	Am Express	24 3/8	+7/8	−33	8869	40	24 5/8	24 1/8o
87	**54**	**22 1/2**	**13 3/8**	**Amer Family**	**14 7/8**	**+1**	**−43**	**849**	**12**	**14 7/8**	**14 3/8o**
94	**84**	**50 5/8**	**28 1/8**	**Am General**	**40 7/8**	**+1 5/8**	**+17**	**5290**	**10**	**41**	**40 o**
	58	8 1/8	6 1/2	Am Gvt Inc Fd	7	+1/8	16	276	..	7	6 3/4k
	64	10	8 1/2	Am Gvt Inc Prt	8 5/8	....	−21	160	..	8 3/4	8 5/8
	71	10 5/8	9 1/4	Amer Gvt Trm	9 5/8	−1/8	−84	13	..	9 5/8	9 5/8
73	64	24 1/4	19 3/4	Am Hlth Pptys	21 1/4	+7/8	+16	319	12	21 1/4	20 3/8
84	65	24 1/2	20	Am Heritage L	21 3/8	+3/4	**+410**	51	8	21 3/8	21 1/8
86	**52**	**55 1/8**	**43**	**Am Home Prd**	**45**	**+1**	**+21**	**6408**	**12**	**45 3/8**	**44 3/4o**

over the past 12 months compared to all other stocks in the tables. Results are ranked from 1 through 99. Stocks ranked below 70 are usually considered weak or lagging in relative strength performance.

3. Highs and lows for the past 52 weeks offer a range of prices for comparison with that day's high, low, and closing prices to provide some idea of the volatility of the stock—that is, how much its price varies from a high to a low.

   Important information may be obtained from the high and low figures but won't be specifically noted in the tables. The ratio of the high and low figures is a further indication of volatility. Also important is the percentage difference between a low price and a high price for the past 52 weeks and how much the daily change amounts to percentagewise. For example, a $2 drop in a $10 stock represents a loss of 20 percent; a $2 drop in a $50 stock represents only a 2 percent decline.

   An *NH* next to a company indicates the stock hit a new high for the 52-week period. An *NL* next to the stock indicates a new low. Tables in *The Wall Street Journal* indicate a new high with an up-pointing arrow and a new low with a down-pointing arrow.

4. The stock name is abbreviated but is more recognizable than a ticker symbol.

5. **Closing price** is the last price at which the stock traded for the day.

6. Important to stock watchers is the change in the closing price compared to the closing price for the previous day. Both the amount and direc-

tion of the change are important to technicians.

7. Volume (shares traded) change in percent relates that day's volume to an average volume for the last 50 trading days. This figure shows if a major price change came on a big change in volume. A +50, for example, indicates the stock's volume of trading for that day was 50 percent higher than the 50-day average.

8. Volume of trading is abbreviated to the number of round lots—100 shares. Thus, a figure of 285 for AARCorp indicates 28,500 shares traded. Some technical analysts consider volume one of their most important tools when assessing prospects of future stock action. A daily number of shares traded is less significant than a series of daily or weekly volumes that could point to a trend.

9. Price/earnings (P/E) ratio provides a valuable tool for analysts in evaluating stocks. The P/E ratio is price divided by earnings (not shown in the tables). The P/E ratio is important because it assesses the value of a stock in terms of company earnings without the influence of the share price. For example, a stock with $1 in earnings and a price of $15 per share will have the same P/E ratio as a stock with $6 in earnings and a price of $90 per share. Thus, P/E ratios can be compared directly without factoring in a price per share. Growth stocks tend to have low P/E ratios because they plow a larger percentage of income back into research and investment for growth. Investors will often bid up the

prices for growth stocks—that is, buy shares of stocks at a P/E ratio of 25 rather than 15—because they are buying future value; they expect higher prices or higher dividends later. They are, in effect, "investing for the future" or "betting on the come." No entry (. .) in the P/E column indicates negative earnings or that the security is a fixed-income instrument.

10. High and low prices for the day indicate the range of volatility and how the closing price figures in the range. A stock that closes on its high for the day appears to be heading higher and could open at a higher price the next day.

Each Friday *Investor's Daily* includes a column in its report of stock prices that lists dividends as a percentage yield (dividends as a percent of closing price). Symbols at the far right of the listings provide additional information.

• A *k* means an earnings report is due within the next four weeks.

• A hyphen (-) indicates an earnings report in that day's edition of *Investor's Daily*.

• An *o* means the stock is an underlying security for options trading.

• A *b* indicates the company is bankrupt, in receivership, or in reorganization.

• Other letters include *n* for new issue, *un* for units, *wi* for when issued, *wt* for **warrants**, and *x* for ex-dividend, or ex-rights. Entries in bold indicate a new high price or an increase for the day of $1 per share or more. Ex-rights indicates prices are for securities that no longer include a

particular benefit, such as the right to buy more shares.

Barron's reports weekly data similar to that reported daily in *The Wall Street Journal*. It appears on Mondays to report results from the previous week through the Friday close. *Barron's* tables are particularly useful as a data bank for analysts who chart weekly data.

Amex and Other Exchange Tables

The Amex reports appear in *The Wall Street Journal* in the same format as the NYSE reports. Reports for other United States exchanges (such as the Pacific and Midwest exchanges) and the Canadian exchanges appear in abbreviated tables. The most complete reports appear in *The Wall Street Journal*, *Investor's Daily*, and *Barron's*.

OTC Tables

Reports for OTC stocks are similar to those for exchange issues except that different issues of stocks may be identified. Prices are on the bid side and no asked prices are noted for national issues. Ticker symbols for use by brokers on their NASDAQ screens are limited to four letters with a fifth letter available for noting special information. Here is an explanation of the symbols following the company ticker symbol.

• The letter *A* indicates the stock is a Class A issue.
• The letter *B* indicates a Class B issue.
• The letter *C* indicates the stock is exempt from NASDAQ listing specifications for

a limited period. If you need more information, check with a broker who can determine the period from information available on the computer screen.

- The letter *D* indicates the issue is new.
- The letter *E* indicates the company is delinquent in filing required data and documents with the Securities and Exchange Commission (SEC).
- The letter *F* indicates the issue is a foreign issue.
- The letter *G* indicates the issue is a first convertible bond issue.
- The letters *H* and *I* indicate the issue is a second or third convertible bond, respectively.
- The letter *J* indicates the issue is a **voting issue**; that is, holders of these shares are entitled to vote on company policy issues.
- The letter *K* indicates the issue is a nonvoting issue.
- The letter *L* may indicate any of several situations, such as an issue that is second class (not carrying all rights), a third class of warrants, or other information that might affect trading or stock value. Check with a broker to find the full particulars about a stock with an *L* after its ticker symbol.
- The letters *M, N, O,* and *P* distinguish various issues of the same company's preferred stock, with *P* representing the first preferred issue and *M* the fourth.
- The letter *Q* indicates the company is in bankruptcy.
- The letter *R* indicates the issue is for rights. Rights are sometimes issued by a company to finance an additional block of stock for expansion or recapitalization. Existing stockholders may be entitled to **preemptive rights,** a privilege that permits them to buy more shares on a priority basis and usually at a reduced price to retain their original percentage ownership in the company. For example, if a company has issued one million shares and Shareholder A owns 10,000 shares, he owns a 1 percent equity share of the company. If the company decides to issue 500,000 additional shares for whatever reason, Shareholder A may be issued rights to buy 5,000 shares to retain his 1 percent equity position. Not all company bylaws require the issuance of preemptive rights. If the rights permit the holder to buy shares at a reduced price, then they have some value. A holder issued preemptive rights may decide not to exercise them and offer them for sale; the rights may then trade separately in the OTC market. When an issue is identified with the letter *R* following the ticker symbol, then the security is a right to buy shares at the current shareholder's discounted price. The rights price will be determined by supply and demand according to the perceived value of the right.

- The letter *T* indicates the issue includes warrants or rights along with shares in the company. A broker can supply the backup details for these issues.
- The letter *U* indicates the issue is a **unit**, or combination package of securities. Sometimes a company will offer a share of stock, a fractional interest in a bond, a warrant, or rights in some combination. The defined package of security pieces is called a unit and is traded as a single entity.
- The letter *V* indicates an issue to be re-

leased later. The price quote is for the stock when issued. Other media may label such stock as *WI* for **when issued**.

- The letter *Y* indicates the issue is an American Depositary Receipt (ADR).

The Wall Street Journal reports transactions for NASDAQ-listed OTC stocks plus a number of secondary issues that do not meet the full NASD requirements in a different format. The main difference between these listings and those of the general NASDAQ listing is the inclusion of bid and asked prices for a company. Note the difference, as a large spread (difference between bid and asked prices) indicates the issue may be volatile and/or risky.

Issues normally listed on the NASDAQ but not traded that day may be omitted from the listing. Not every issue trades every day, and you can see that some of the reported trades in secondary issues involve only a few round lots. Also not reported are those OTC shares that trade only through the pink sheets. These are the stocks of companies too small to meet even the minimum requirements for secondary companies on NASDAQ. For information on pink sheet issues you must call a broker or the company.

Newspaper Mutual Fund Reports

Mutual funds operate from offices all over the United States. Shortly after the markets close, each fund notifies the NASD of its numbers for the day. The NASD compiles the data and transmits the day's results to the print and electronic media. For a mutual fund to be included in the NASD list, it must have a minimum of 1,000 shareholders. If you own shares in a mutual fund that does not make the NASD list, you must call the fund for closing prices for the previous day or wait for quarterly reports from the fund.

Newspaper listings are grouped alphabetically by fund group (see Table 4B). Unless you know the fund group, you may experience difficulty in finding a fund the first time. Partners Fund, for example, is one of the Neuberger & Berman group and appears under the group's alphabetical listing rather than under *P*.

Mutual funds that operate as no-loads report only one price, the net asset value (NAV). A second number may appear under Offer Price if the fund is a load fund. The higher price is the NAV plus the commission. A third column indicates what happened to the NAV since the close of the previous session. A number of additional letter codes provide information about extra expenses, redemption charges, and data on dividend distributions.

Electronic Media

Radio and television reports can keep you up to date on what is happening in the market anecdotally, but these are less successful in providing detailed data for analysis. Here are a few of the helpful electronic media sources.

The "Nightly Business Report" (NBR) airs nationally on Public Broadcasting System (PBS) stations. Check local listings for time and station. The NBR originates in Miami and usually airs for a half hour between 5 and 8 P.M. Monday through Friday.

Typically, the NBR reports on happenings that could affect the stock markets, such as current negotiations for mergers between companies, possible bankruptcies, court decisions, tax law changes, and economic forecasts. NBR also reports closing stock prices for the 10 most active stocks on the NYSE and NASDAQ markets, with highlights from the Amex, commodities, and futures markets. Reports on changes in bonds, the federal funds rate, currencies, and changes in the market averages in Japan, England, Canada, and France provide a broad review of world economic and financial activity. On-site reports from around the United States and the world by NBR correspondents in collaboration with Reuters, an international news-gathering agency, provide international scope.

"Moneyline" appears on Cable News Network (CNN) for a half hour at 4 P.M. Eastern time, with a repeat at 7 P.M. Times do not change with time zones; the airing at 7 P.M. Eastern time appears at 4 P.M. Pacific time. "Moneyline" originates in New York with occasional remote reports. Typically, this program reports much of the same data as the "NBR."

Financial News Network (FNN) and Consumer News and Business Channel (CNBC) combined operations in a merger to air financial information full time. Many cable operators include FNN/CNBC in their line-up. The ticker indicating trades on the NYSE flows across the bottom of the screen during the hours the exchange is open, with a 15-minute delay. Summaries of the Dow Jones Industrial Average (DJIA), NYSE Composite Index, Amex, **composite tick**, and interest rate data appear every 90 seconds to provide an update of overall market action. Interviews with market gurus, economists, government officials, and reports from overseas correspondents fill the time between market updates for commodities, futures, and options markets that are not part of the moving display. Most investors find the complete day of financial information to be more than they need or want. But tuning in from time to time can keep you abreast of fast-moving developments.

Financial news reported on network and local radio stations tends to be limited to a current reading for the DJIA and possibly some indication of the direction of short-term interest rates. A few radio stations in major markets that feature all-talk programming may devote several hours to financial news during a 24-hour period. A favorite program is the call-in program featuring a knowledgeable professional who answers a wide range of investment and financial questions on the air. While these programs can be interesting, they seldom provide hard data on which you might base investment decisions.

Newsletters

At one time an estimated 1,900 newsletters on various aspects of financial news and investments were being published regularly in the United States. A number of these proved unprofitable and are no longer around. Newsletters provide a mix of reports, commentary on market activity, and forecasts of future market activity.

See Chapter 13 for ideas on how to use newsletters in planning your investments. Some of the better newsletters are listed in Resources.

While not exactly a newsletter, *Standard & Poor's Stock Guide* is a veritable treasure trove of information updated monthly. A recent edition comprised 256 pages of densely packed performance price data on common and preferred stocks and mutual funds. Many of the brokerages use the *Stock Guide* as a promotion piece. If you are a regular customer you can ask your broker for a free copy. A few of the discount brokerages also offer it as a service to clients. Even if you don't happen to have the most recent copy of the *Stock Guide*, it serves as an index to corporations, with information about where their stocks are traded, a two- or three-word description of their businesses, 10-year price ranges, dividends paid, and earnings over the past five years.

Magazines

A number of magazines report on happenings on Wall Street and other financial centers around the globe. A few of the more prominent and well read magazines are discussed below.

Forbes appears biweekly except for two weeks in October. One of *Forbes'* most popular issues is the "Annual Fund Ratings" issue that usually appears in early September. Those funds that make the *Forbes* Honor Roll are reported on newspapers' financial pages each year. Both load and no-load funds are rated for their perform-

ance in bull and bear markets. The reports provide an annual base for comparison.

Money appears monthly and is published by Time Inc. Issues include the "Money Scorecard," with a roundup of financial information on CD interest rates, mortgage rates in different areas, and current information that could affect investment strategies. The "Fund Watch" highlights mutual funds' performances over the course of recent months and as far back as five years. *Money*'s monthly mutual fund data is one of the most useful departments of the magazine.

Kiplinger's Personal Finance Magazine is another monthly magazine published by the Kiplinger Washington Editors, Inc. *Kiplinger's Personal Finance Magazine*'s "Mutual Fund Monitor" provides market averages for various categories of stock and bond funds for the past month, a year ago, and the highs and lows over funds' histories. Reports on the top-performing stock, bond, and closed-end funds keep you up to date on what's happening in mutual funds.

Conclusion

Information on stocks, bonds, and mutual funds is everywhere. Information on the general market is broadcast hourly on radios, several times daily on television, and is reported in newspapers. Indexes and averages of various kinds summarize market activity, but for information on specific stocks or mutual funds you need to consult a newspaper, magazine, or newsletter.

CHAPTER ELEVEN

How Are Your Investments Doing?

KEY TERMS FOR THIS CHAPTER

return on investment
confirmation
cost basis
acquisition cost
annualized
cumulative

fractional share
Form 1099-DIV
Form 1099-B
first in-first out
principal

Wall Street runs on paper. Any glimpse of the trading floor at one of the exchanges reveals a veritable thicket of paper scraps discarded in the heat of action. Eventually you may receive some of the paper stream that floods out of the back offices of Wall Street firms. Some is essential—keep it handy for tax reporting or figuring your returns. Some is useful but not essential. Some you can toss into the round file. A few clues as to which pieces of paper are important and how to use the information can be helpful.

Return on Investment

Accurate records will reveal prices and other data about your stocks, bonds, mutual fund shares, or other investments, but you must usually calculate the **return on investment** (ROI), or how much of a return in dollars or percentage terms is profit on an investment. A $5 return on an investment of $100 would be a 5 percent ROI. Mutual funds, for instance, provide a mass of information on returns, but they will not report on how your individual account is doing. If you are serious about knowing how your investments are faring in the market, relying on general interest rates or what happened to stock averages is not good enough. Before you abandon one investment strategy, you should know exactly how it has been performing for you. Otherwise, you won't know whether the change has been of any benefit to you.

Calculating ROI on Stocks

Stocks may be evaluated on the basis of price, dividends, and total return. Total return is a term you will hear often. It combines the dividends paid with changes in the price of shares. Total return is more applicable to mutual fund shares than to most stocks. If a stock pays no dividends, then the change in the price of shares during some period and total return are the same.

To calculate ROI, first you must know what your cost basis was. The **confirmation** of your order for stocks from the broker is your starting point, as it tells you what you paid for the stock. Keep every confirmation until six years after you sell the shares. These records could be vital to you in an income tax audit. When determining your **cost basis,** you must adjust your investment to include **acquisition costs;** that is, the costs for commissions and fees for buying the stock.

Suppose you buy 100 shares of XYZ Corporation stock at $10 per share on April 1; the broker's commission is $35. Your total investment is $1,035, and that is your cost basis. (See the box on page 162 for details about the following calculations.) On De-

cember 31, XYZ closes at $12 per share. Since XYZ Corporation is a small growth company, it pays no dividends. The value gain on a per-share basis for 39 weeks is $2 per share ($200), or 20 percent for the period, without considering acquisition cost. The ROI is less on a total investment basis, however, due to the commission. The value gain (which includes acquisition cost) would be the value at year end ($1,200) versus cost basis ($1,035), divided by cost basis, for a 15.9 percent return.

Comparisons of performance for odd periods, such as 9 months, 250 days, 2 quarters, or some other period, are meaningless without a common time component to compare returns on different investments. For this reason, performance figures are **annualized**—they are figured on what they would have been for a full year (365 days).

The easiest method of annualizing a return is to first divide the ROI by the number of days in the period to get the daily rate of return; then multiply the daily return by 365. In our example, the 20 percent gain on the shares for 9 months (39 weeks of 7 days, or 273 days) is equivalent to 26.75 percent over a full year. You can figure the ROI with acquisition cost similarly by dividing the 15.9 percent by 273 and multiplying by 365 for an annualized ROI of 21.3 percent.

Suppose the next year XYZ Corporation's directors declare a quarterly dividend of $.04 per share, payable on the last day of the middle month of the quarter. You hold the shares until July 20 and sell on that date. You collected $.04 per share, ($4 for your 100 shares) twice, once on February 28 and once on May 31. When you sold your shares, the price had gone up

RETURN ON INVESTMENT AND TAX CALCULATIONS
FOR STOCK IN XYZ CORPORATION

April 1 (first year)

Buy 100 common shares @ $10 per share — $1,000.00

Broker's commission (acquisition cost) — 35.00

Total investment (cost basis) — $1,035.00

December 31 (first year)

XYZ closes at $12 per share — $1,200.00

Value gain (without acquisition cost) — $200.00

$$ROI = \frac{(1,200 - 1,000)}{1,000} = \frac{200}{1,000} = 20\%$$

Value gain (with acquisition cost) — $165.00

$$ROI = \frac{(1,200 - 1,035)}{1,035} = \frac{165}{1,035} = 15.9\%$$

Annualized ROI (without acquisition cost)

Daily ROI

$$\frac{20\%}{(39 \text{ weeks} \times 7 \text{ days})} = \frac{20}{273} = .0733\%$$

Annual equivalent ROI (without acquisition cost)

.0733 × 365 = 26.75%

Annualized ROI (with acquisition cost)

Daily ROI

$$\frac{15.9\%}{(39 \text{ weeks} \times 7 \text{ days})} = \frac{15.9}{273} = .0582\%$$

Annual equivalent ROI

.0582 × 365 = 21.3%

February 28 (second year)

Dividend $0.04 per share — $4.00

May 31 (second year)

Dividend $0.04 per share — 4.00

Total dividends received on 100 shares — $8.00

July 20 (second year)

Sell 100 shares @ $13.20 per share — $1,320.00

Selling costs — (35.00)

Net proceeds — $1,285.00

Total (second year) — $1,293.00

ROI (second year only)

Total ROI

$$\frac{1,293 - 1,200}{1,200} = 7.75\%$$

Annualized ROI

$$\frac{7.75}{201} \times 365 = 14.07\%$$

(Continued)

ROI (first and second years)
Total ROI

$$\frac{1,293 - 1,035}{1,035} = 24.93\%$$

Annualized ROI (average)

$$\frac{24.93}{414} \times 365 = 21.98\%$$

Income Tax Calculations

First year	No taxable income
Second year	
Capital gain (1,285 − 1,035)	$250.00
Dividends	8.00
Total taxable gain & income	$258.00

again to $13.20 per share and the selling costs were $35. Receipts were $1,320 less $35 for the selling commission, or $1,285. What was the return on your investment? There are two component questions here: What was the annualized ROI for the current year and what was the return for the period you owned the stock—total and annualized?

First, figure the annualized ROI for the current year. At the end of the first year, your investment was worth $1,200 (100 shares at $12 per share). During the second year you received $8 in dividends. When you sold your shares, your net receipts were $1,285, so your total return for the second year was $1,285 minus $1,200 (or $85 plus $8) for a total of $93. During the second year you owned the stock for 201 days. ROI was equal to the total return divided by the value at the beginning of the year ($93 divided by $1,200), or 7.75 percent. To annualize, divide 7.75 percent by 201 days to find the average daily total return and multiply the daily return by 365 days to get the annualized return of 14.07 percent. Even though XYZ Corporation

started paying dividends, the total return dropped off from the previous year and could be one reason for selling the stock.

Total return for the period you owned the stock, with acquisition costs, was $1,293 (net receipts from the sale after paying commissions plus dividends) minus the cost basis of $1,035 for a total return of $258, which is equal to a 24.93 percent total return ($258 divided by $1,035). To annualize, divide 24.93 by 414 (213 days in the first year plus 201 days in the second year) and then multiply by 365. Your average annual ROI was 21.98 percent.

Calculations for Taxes

Calculating what you owe for income taxes calls for different figures. Using the example of XYZ Corporation once again (see box above), note that at the end of the first year, you still owned the stock, but you had no reportable income. Your total return of $165, or the difference between $1,200 and the cost basis of $1,035, was not an actual profit because you did not sell the shares. You had a paper profit but not a taxable profit. When you sold the shares on July 20 of the second year, you had a capital gain of $250 ($1,285 minus $1,035). You also received $8 of taxable dividends. While you report the capital gain separately from the $8 of taxable dividend, the rates are the same, so your taxable income was $258.

To collect the information you need to track your investments accurately, you need record sheets similar to the ones below.

Impact of Stock Splits and Stock Dividends on ROI

Calculating your ROI is relatively simple until you run into stock splits and stock dividends. If a stock splits two-for-one, you end up owning twice as many shares with the same capital value. If your company declares a stock dividend, again you end up with more shares but with no change

of capital value. Furthermore, no income taxes are due unless you sell some or all of the split shares or the dividend shares.

Suppose you own 100 shares of MNO Corporation; your cost basis is $10 per share, or $1,000 for the 100 shares (see the box on page 166). For this example ignore acquisition costs, just to keep the numbers simple. The directors of MNO Corporation decide the price of shares in the $10 neighborhood is too high, so they split the stock two-for-one. The company's transfer agent sends you another certificate indicating your ownership of an additional 100 shares. You now own 200 shares at a price of $5 per share. Your total investment is still valued at $1,000—200 shares at $5 each.

The price rises to $7 per share, and you decide to sell half of your holdings, or 100 shares. Your gain is $2 per share over the adjusted cost basis of $5 per share, or $200. To calculate your ROI on the shares that you sold, divide $200 (your profit) by $500 (your investment). Your ROI is 40 percent if you sold half of the split shares exactly one year after you bought the original 100

Stock Record													
	PURCHASE					SALE				GAINS OR LOSSES			
										NET GAIN		NET LOSS	
Company	No. of Shares	Price/ Share	Cost	Acqui- sition Cost	Total Cost Basis	No. of Shares	Price/ Share	Cost	Total Receipts	Short Term	Long Term	Short Term	Long Term

Dividend Record					
Company	No. of Shares	Dividend Share	Total Dividend	Date Paid	Yearly Receipts

shares. If you sold at some different time, you could adjust the gain to an annualized figure.

Six months later, on June 30, you sell the second lot of 100 shares of MNO Corporation at $8 per share. You may now compute the ROI for the gain on those shares, which was $300 over the cost basis of $500, or 60 percent, and adjust the gross number to an annualized return.

Each sale will show a different ROI. You may find the return for the original investment by averaging the two annualized ROIs. However, the average will be of only general interest because the $700 received from the sale of the first lot of 100 shares would probably have been reinvested or earning interest in a savings account or money market fund (MMF) and would show some gain or loss for the period until

the second lot of 100 split shares was sold. You can only legitimately compare each lot's ROI with other investments, not both lots sold at different times.

Computing the taxable gains on the two sales is relatively easy as long as you consider each lot of 100 shares separately.

Making tax calculations for stock dividends can be a little trickier but is not difficult as long as you maintain precise records. Suppose you own 100 shares of DEF Corporation with a cost basis of $10 per share. (Again, we'll ignore acquisition costs to keep the numbers simple for this example.) The directors of DEF Corporation declare a 10 percent stock dividend. Now you own 110 shares, but your cost basis remains at $1,000 total, or $9.09 per share ($1,000 divided by 110 shares). If you sell all 110 shares, your gain or loss will be the difference between the net price you

---

ROI AND TAXES ON SPLIT SHARES

January 2 (first year)	
Buy 100 shares MNO Corp. @ $10 per share	
(ignore acquisition costs)	$1,000
Stock splits 2-for-1	
100 additional shares from transfer agent	
Owned after split	
200 shares with cost basis @ $5 per share	$1,000
December 31 (first year)	
Sell 100 shares @ $7 per share	$700
Cost basis @ $5 per share	500
Net gain	$200
ROI	

$$\frac{200}{\$500} = 40\%$$

June 30 (second year)	
Sell 100 shares @ $8 per share	$800
Cost basis @ $5 per share	500
Net gain	$300
ROI (second year)	

$$\frac{\$300}{\$500} = 60\%$$

Annualized ROI

$$\frac{60}{(365 + 182)} \times 365 = .1097 \times 365 = 40.04\%$$

Taxes	
First year	
Capital gain	$200
Second year	
Capital gain	$300

receive and $1,000. Suppose you sell all 110 shares at $12 per share for a total of $1,320—your gain is $320.

The 10 dividend shares are not taxable until you sell them. If you sell only the 10 shares, your gain is the difference between the net proceeds and the adjusted share price of $9.09. If the shares sell for $11 per share, your gain is $19.10 ($11.00 times 10 shares minus $9.09 times 10 shares). The $19.10 is taxable income and must be reported. If you sell the remaining 100 shares, use the same $9.09 per share cost basis for computing any gain or loss.

Stock dividends can be a nuisance. A few companies declare small stock dividends each year as their way of rewarding shareholders without disbursing any cash. Of course, the number of shares outstanding as shown on the balance sheet of the corporation will be adjusted to reflect the additional shares. If you hold shares in a company that declares one or a series of stock dividends or splits, you must retain good records that will enable you to compute the cost basis for figuring any gain or loss on the shares when you sell.

Calculating ROI on Mutual Funds

Mutual fund records and the records you keep for them differ substantially from those for individual stocks. Mutual funds seldom issue certificates of ownership of shares. Instead, you receive a confirmation that is a copy of the data entered into the mutual fund's computer. (See Table 11A

for an example of a mutual fund confirmation.) Note that entries are **cumulative**. Each new dividend, withdrawal, or addition to capital rates a new line, and the number of shares is adjusted to reflect the change. You must keep at least the last confirmation. Records for your individual stocks will not be all in one place, as are mutual fund transaction records.

Generally, mutual funds will report only those transactions that can be printed on one page, dropping earlier transactions to make room for the new ones. Thus, you need to retain one or more confirmations with the details of your holdings and trans-

---

TABLE 11A   MUTUAL FUND CONFIRMATION

Investment Statement/1999 Calendar Year
THE GENERIC GROUP   GENERIC
                                                   INCOME FUND

CURRENT ACCOUNT SUMMARY
JULY 27, 1999
SHARES OWNED   405.836
SHARE PRICE $ 16.21
ACCOUNT VALUE $ 6,578.60

Tele-Account No. 27   Account No.   When writing to Generic, please include your fund
For Account Service   Social Security No.   name and account number and mail to:
Call Toll-Free 1-800-000-0000   Tax ID No.   THE GENERIC FINANCIAL CENTER
                                                   P.O. BOX 0000
                                                   ANYTOWN, USA 0000

Trade Date	Transaction Description	Dollar Amount	Share Price	Share Amount	Shares Owned
	BEGINNING BALANCE				390.277
03/28	INCOME REINVEST .28	109.28	16.21	6.742	397.019
03/28	CAP GAIN REINVEST .08	31.22	16.21	1.926	398.945
06/27	INCOME REINVEST .28	111.70	16.21	6.891	405.836
07/27	INCOME REINVEST .28	113.63	16.34	6.954	412.790

PAID THIS CALENDAR YEAR	Income Dividends	or	Tax-Exempt Income	+	Short-Term Gains	+	Long-Term Gains	=	TOTAL DISTRIBUTIONS
	220.98						31.22		252.20

actions earlier in the year that may have been dropped to provide room for transactions later in the year. To be on the safe side, retain all confirmations until the end of the year before discarding those with repetitious entries. Keeping your mutual fund records as data entries permits reinvesting dividends and internal capital gains automatically; withdrawing funds by writing a check and depositing it in your local bank; and requesting a wire transfer of funds to your bank by telephone. These transactions would be much more complicated if you had to submit certificates for each transaction.

Mutual funds also maintain records of **fractional share** holdings, usually to three decimal places. The use of fractional shares simplifies record keeping and provides greater flexibility for managing mutual fund investments.

About 84 percent of mutual fund shareholders sign up for the automatic reinvestment of dividends. Some mutual funds declare dividends monthly; most of the others declare dividends quarterly. Realized capital gains from internal transactions are usually distributed annually, near or at year end. Recent tax law changes require mutual funds to pay out 98 percent of their income and realized capital gains to shareholders each year to avoid paying taxes on income and gains at the corporate level. Capital gains may be computed at year end and paid before January 31 of the following year. Even though they are paid after December 31, dividends and gains are taxable for the year in which they were earned.

Any internal losses from market transactions are not passed along to shareholders. Losses offset capital gains first. If gains exceed losses, the net gains are distributed to shareholders. If losses exceed gains, the net losses are retained by the fund to offset gains in the next or following years until used up.

An up-to-date and accurate cost basis for shares is critical in the computation of your ROI or taxes due on your mutual fund holdings. Suppose you invest $10,000 in no-load Fund W on January 2 (see Table 11B). The share price at day's end on January 2 for Fund W was $9.50 per share, and your $10,000 bought 1,052.632 shares. At the end of each quarter the fund passes through your share of the accrued fund income as dividends. Let's say Fund W pays $125 in dividends after the first quarter, $150 after the second, $175 after the third, and $200 at year end and credits your account on the last day of each quarter. (Some of the increase in dividends as the year progresses results from the compounding of dividends paid on prior dividends posted to your account.)

Some time in January following a full year of investment, Fund W distributes $200, representing your share of the capital gains realized from internal transactions. Thus, over the year your account has grown by $650 in dividends and $200 from capital gains realized from internal trading, for a total of $850. In addition, during the year share prices rose from $9.50 to $12.19. Dividends were credited to your account according to the share price at the close of business on the last day of each quarter. These dividends increased the number of shares owned to 1,128.405. For example, on March 31, dividends of $125 were reinvested at a share price of $9.79 to buy 12.768 shares (125 divided by 9.79 equals 12.768) that brings the total shares

TABLE 11B   SAMPLE MUTUAL FUND TRANSACTIONS

Trade Date	Transaction	Dollar Amount	Share Price	Shares Owned
	Beginning Balance			0
01/2	Shares purchased by check	10,000.00	9.50	1,052.632
03/31	Income reinvest	125.00	9.79	1,065.400
06/30	Income reinvest	150.00	10.43	1,079.782
09/30	Income reinvest	175.00	11.07	1,095.591
12/31	Income reinvest	200.00	12.19	1,111.998
12/31	Cap gain reinvest	200.00	12.19	1,128.405
12/31	Account value $13,755.26			

Taxable Income

Income reinvested	$650
Capital gains reinvested	$200
Total taxable	$850

Cost Basis

Original investment	$10,000.00
Income reinvested	$650.00
Capital gains reinvested	$200.00
Cost basis =	$10,850.00

Taxable Income (if shares sold at year end)

Year end account value	$13,755.26
Cost basis	$10,850.00
Total taxable	$2,905.26

ROI

Year end account value	$13,755.26
Original investment	$10,000.00
Total return	$3,755.26

$$ROI = \frac{3,755.26}{10,000.00} = 37.55\%$$

owned to 1,065.400 shares. Similar reinvestments at the end of each quarter increase the number of shares owned to 1,111.998 before the reinvestment of the $200 in realized capital gains. Total value of the fund at year end, after crediting capital gains, is $13,755.26 (1,128.450 shares multiplied by $12.19). Dividends of $650 and capital gains of $200 reinvested increase the cost basis to $10,850. Reinvesting the dividends and gains was the same as if you had added those sums to your original investment from other income. Your total year's return was $650 from dividends, $200 from realized capital gains, and $2,905.26 from an increase in the net asset value (NAV), or $3,755.26. Your ROI

for the year was 37.55 percent ($3,755.26 divided by original investment of $10,000). Only the $850 earned in dividends and capital gains is taxable, as you did not sell the shares to record a gain at the increased value.

Calculating Mutual Fund Income and Gain for Taxes

Taxation of mutual fund income and capital gains can be divided into two parts. As long as you hold onto your shares, only income and capital gain distributions are subject to tax, even though they were reinvested. Your mutual fund makes that even easier by providing you with a **Form 1099-DIV** for each account; a copy of the form is also sent to the IRS. Form 1099-DIV lists the taxable dividend and capital gains separately. Capital gains are taxed at a maximum rate of 28 percent; dividend income is taxed progressively at 15, 18, and 31 percent, based on your tax bracket.

The following general information about calculating taxes on the ownership and sale of mutual fund shares is not intended as a substitute for professional tax advice. You may find more information in IRS Publication 564, "Mutual Fund Distributions," available free from IRS offices or by mail from the IRS forms supply source that serves your area.

That said, you should be aware of the general rules for compiling the cost basis of mutual fund shares. If you sold or exchanged shares in a stock or bond mutual fund, you must submit a Schedule D along with your Form 1040. Exchanging shares in a stock or bond fund for shares in a MMF by telephone or letter constitutes a sale for tax purposes.

Figuring any capital gain or loss on the sale can be confusing. Your mutual fund will likely send you a **Form 1099-B** indicating the number of shares sold and their gross value at the time of the sale. MMFs and tax-exempt fund shareholders will not receive Form 1099-B, as the former maintains a constant $1 per share capital value and income from tax-exempt funds is, as the name says, exempt from federal income taxes.

You will have to determine the cost basis of the shares sold if you expect to pay taxes only on the capital gain or use any capital loss to offset other gains. Four different methods for establishing the cost basis for mutual fund shares are acceptable to the IRS:

- Specific shares may be identified by the date and price paid. You must identify those shares to be sold when you notify your mutual fund manager. You may direct the manager to sell or exchange "100 shares of Fund Y purchased on (date)." The purchase date and the price paid establish the cost basis of the shares sold. Be sure to document this sale in writing if you authorize the sale by telephone. If you should be audited by the IRS, you will need the documentation to establish the exact number of shares sold, the date sold, and the price of the shares when you purchased them (that is, your cost basis). But not all of your shares can be specifically identified and the documentation to back up such sales can be difficult to establish, so some other method may be more useful.

- **First In-First Out** (FIFO) is an accounting term meaning that the oldest shares are sold first—those shares you acquired first are the first to be sold. If the first sale of shares is a partial sale, a later sale starts from the basis of the oldest shares remaining after the first sale. At some point you may be advised to sell all shares and start fresh. If you do, remember the wash sale rule that prevents you from reporting a loss on a sale if you subsequently rebuy essentially the same securities again within 31 days. Buying shares in the same fund within 31 days would violate the wash sale rule; buying shares in a similar but different fund would be okay.

One problem with FIFO is that you are selling the oldest shares first. In a bull market those early shares may have cost considerably less than the prices you are selling at now. Your capital gain is higher and your taxes will be too. You may groan, but remember, "The IRS never takes it all." The more profit you make, the higher taxes you pay—and the more after-tax, spendable dollars you gain from the investment. Using another method, the average cost method, could reduce immediate taxes.

● The average cost method—single category—first computes the average cost basis of shares by dividing the total amount invested plus any dividends and distributed capital gains reinvested by the number of shares owned. Taxes are computed by deducting the average cost basis from the value of shares to find the taxable gain or loss. The term single category refers to a single capital gain figure regardless of how long you may have owned the shares. See the computation in Table 11C, which begins with the 1,128.405 shares owned at the end of the year in Table 11B. Note the initial investment of $10,000 in Table 11B with subsequent quarterly reinvestments of dividends (income) and realized capital gains reinvested at year end. An additional cash investment of $5,000 on January 2 increases shares owned to 1,538.577, and income continues to be reinvested in additional shares. The transfer of $12,000 to a MMF has the same effect tax-wise as a sale of 966.184 shares ($12,000 divided by the price per share of $12.42). Money in a MMF does not appreciate, as the share price remains a constant $1 per share. MMFs earn interest income, but that is not a factor in the capital gains calculation.

To compute the average cost basis of shares, begin by determining the total investment, which is the cumulative value of the original $10,000, additional share purchase of $5,000, plus the reinvested div-

idends and capital gain, from both years, for a total of $16,470. Average cost basis for shares equals the total investment ($16,470) divided by the shares sold (966.184—as a transfer to the MMF—plus the 621.659 shares remaining to close out the account). The capital gain is computed by subtracting the cost basis ($16,470) from the total value of shares sold ($19,596.67), for a gain of $3,126.67.

● The average cost method—double category—divides any gains into long- and short-term categories (see Table 11D and boxes on page 172). Currently the tax on gains for stocks, bonds, and mutual fund shares held for different periods is the same. Even so, you must report short- and long-term gains separately on Form 1040 Schedule D. Long-term refers to securities held for a minimum of six months before selling if you acquired them between 1/22/84 and 12/31/87. For shares acquired after 12/31/87, the long-term holding period is one year. Long-term and short-term capital gains are still taxed at the same rate, but the IRS requires that capital gains be divided between short- and long-term periods.

In the example in Table 11E, follow the flow to separate short-term from long-term gains. Original investment plus income reinvestments on 03/31/01 and 6/30/01 acquire a total of 1,079.782 shares that were sold (transferred to MMF) over a year later, and thus, qualify for long-term gain treatment. (The 01 designates first-year transactions and 02 second-year transactions.) Note that the long-term gain includes the sale of the 1,079.782 shares—partially on 08/20/02 and the remaining shares on 09/15/02. Since the $12,000.00 transferred to the MMF on 08/20/02 did not

Trade Date	Transaction	Dollar Amount	Share Price	Shares* Owned
	TABLE 11C AVERAGE COST METHOD: SINGLE CATEGORY			
01/1	Opening balance	10,850.00		1,128.405
01/2	Share purchase	5,000.00	12.19	1,538.577
03/31	Income reinvested	250.00	12.90	1,557.957
06/30	Income reinvested	260.00	12.45	1,578.841
08/20	Transfer to MMF	12,000.00	12.42	612.657
09/15	Income reinvested	110.00	12.22	621.659
09/15	Transfer to MMF	7,596.67	12.22	0
	Account value – 0			

$$\text{Average cost basis} = \frac{\text{Cost basis}}{\text{No. of shares}} = \frac{\$16,470.00}{(966.184 + 621.659)} = \$10.37 \text{ per share}$$

CAPITAL GAIN: SINGLE CATEGORY

Capital gain = (Number of shares sold × price/share) – cost basis

= (966.184 × \$12.42) + (621.659 × \$12.22)–\$16,470.00

= (\$12,000 + \$7,596.67)–\$16,470.00

= \$3,126.67

CAPITAL GAIN: DOUBLE CATEGORY

Shares purchased 01/2 (first year) through 6/30 (first year) and sold on 8/20 (second year) qualify for long-term capital gain treatment (shares held one year or longer).

Shares purchased 09/30 (first year) through 9/15 (second year) are short-term gains (shares held less than one year).

---

involve all 1,079.782 shares, a portion (113.599 shares) were sold on 09/15/02 to complete the sale of all shares qualified for long-term gain treatment.

The long-term gain is calculated by totaling the value of the 1,079.782 shares at their sale and subtracting the cost basis for a total gain of \$3,113.17.

Continuing the example through 9/15/02 enables you to compute the short-term gain on shares remaining after those qualified for long-term gains were sold. Short-term gains are those remaining after long-term gains are deducted from total gains (3,326.67 – 3,113.17 = 213.50). Partial sales during different tax years can com-

TABLE 11D	CAPITAL GAIN: DOUBLE CATEGORY			
Trade Date	Transaction	Dollar Amount	Share Price	Shares
	Beginning Balance			0
01/2/01	Shares purchased	10,000.00	9.50	1,052.632
03/31/01	Income reinvest	125.00	9.79	1,065.400
06/30/01	Income reinvest	150.00	10.43	1,079.782
08/20/02	Transfer to MMF	12,000.00	12.42	(966.184)
09/15/02	Transfer to MMF	1,388.17	12.22	(113.599)

$$\text{Long-term gain} = (12{,}000.00 + 1{,}388.17) - (10{,}000.00 + 125.00 + 150.00)$$
$$= 13{,}388.17 - 10{,}275.00$$
$$= 3{,}113.17$$

$$\text{Shares @ 06/30/01} = 1{,}079.782$$

$$\text{Shares transferred 08/20/02} = \frac{12{,}000.00}{12.42} = 966.184$$

Remaining shares for long-term $= 1{,}079.782 - 966.184$
Long-term $= 113.599$
Shares transferred 9/15/02 $= 113.599 \times 12.22 = 1{,}388.17$

plicate capital gain or loss reporting. If your transactions are more complicated than this simple example, contact your accountant.

Whichever method you choose for tax purposes, remember these three points:

• Be sure to include any shares purchased with reinvested dividends or capital gains. If you forget, your cost basis will be lower and you will end up paying taxes on those amounts a second time, something you certainly want to avoid.

• Once you have selected one or the other of the average cost methods, you must stick to it. You cannot use it one time and then sell identified shares another time. This limitation applies to the shares you might own in one fund at a time. You may, for example, use the average cost method—single category when determining the cost basis for shares in Fund Q and FIFO for shares in Fund R even if Fund Q and Fund R are in the same fund family.

• When using either the single or double category of the average cost method, you must advise the IRS which method you are using. (See box on page 172.) Later, if you wish to change the average cost method, you must request permission for the change from the IRS.

ROI for Load and No-load Mutual Funds

Remember that mutual funds may be sold as load or no-load. Included in the load category are those low-load funds that distribute shares directly to investors rather than through brokers. The load can be a significant part of your acquisition cost for those shares acquired through a broker.

TABLE 11E	CAPITAL GAIN: DOUBLE CATEGORY SHORT-TERM PORTION			
Trade Date	Transaction	Dollar Amount	Share Price	Shares
09/30/01	Income reinvest	175.00	11.07	1,095.591
12/31/01	Income reinvest	200.00	12.19	1,111.998
12/31/01	Capital gain reinvest	200.00	12.19	1,128.405
01/2/02	Share purchase	5,000.00	12.19	1,538.577
03/31/02	Income reinvest	250.00	12.90	1,557.957
06/30/02	Income reinvest	260.00	12.45	1,578.841
08/20/02	Transfer to MMF	12,000.00	12.42	612.658
09/15/02	Income reinvest	110.00	12.22	621.660
09/15/02	Transfer to MMF	7,596.67	12.22	0

Cost basis = Original investment + additional investment + income and capital gain reinvestment
= 10,000.00 + 5,000.00 + 1,270.00
= 16,270.00

Total gain = Shares sales − cost basis
= (12,000.00 + 7,596.67) − 16,270.00
= 19,596.67 − 16,270.00
= 3,326.67

Short-term gain = Total gain − long-term gain
= 3,326.67 − 3,113.17
= 213.50

When figuring your ROI on a sale of shares, the load increases the cost basis and reduces the total return. The general formula applies—net proceeds minus cost basis divided by cost basis. See Table 11F for an example of how ROI is figured for load mutual funds.

Note that $10,000 is paid in to the broker for investment in Fund L (for load fund), but only $9,150 (after $850 commission, or load) is invested at $10 per share for 915.000 shares. Although $2,000 of income was paid on December 31, only $1,830 is invested in new shares because the broker took the 8½ percent commission. (Not all brokers deduct commissions on reinvested dividends; ask before investing.) At $12 per share, because the price of shares advanced, the $1,830 of reinvested dividends increases the number of shares owned to 1,067.500. On the first business day of the new year, the 1,067.500 shares were sold at $12 per share for a total of $12,810. ROI is calculated from the investment value ($12,810.00) less amount invested ($12,000) divided by the amount invested for an ROI of 6.75 percent.

Similar performance and calculations for an investment in a no-load Fund NL are shown on the lower half of Table 11G. Since the broker deducts no commission, the full amount of the investment is used

TABLE 11F   ROI FOR LOAD MUTUAL FUND SHARES

FUND L

Trade Date	Transaction	Dollar Amount	Share Price	Shares Owned
First year				
01/02	Shares purchased	10,000.00 (9,150.00)*	10.00	915.000
12/31	Income reinvested	2,000.00 (1,830.00)*	12.00	1,067.500
Second year				
01/02	Sell all shares	12,810.00	12.00	0

$$ROI = \frac{12,810.00 - 12,000.00}{12,000.00} = \frac{810.00}{12,000.00} = 6.75\%$$

FUND NL

Trade Date	Transaction	Dollar Amount	Share Price	Shares Owned
First year				
01/02	Shares purchased	10,000.00	10.00	1,000.000
12/31	Income reinvested	2,000.00	12.00	1,166.667
Second year				
01/02	Sell all shares	14,000.00	12.00	0

$$ROI = \frac{14,000.00 - 12,000.00}{12,000.00} = \frac{2,000.00}{12,000.00} = 16.67\%$$

*Amount invested after commission (load).

to buy shares and the ROI is 16.7 percent following calculations similar to those for the Fund L. Typically, the ROI for no-load mutual funds exceeds the ROI for load funds because there is no load added to the cost basis and there is more cash to purchase shares on which gains and income can be expected.

Comparing the ROI for load and no-load mutual funds without a sale requires an additional adjustment. Suppose you bought shares in both Fund L and Fund NO on January 2. At the close of the market on December 31, you want to compare the ROI on both funds. If you compare the true acquisition costs with total returns at year end, Fund L suffers a distinct disadvantage if you include the full load. Comparing a load fund that includes an $8\frac{1}{2}$ percent load with a no-load fund is like giving the no-load fund an $8\frac{1}{2}$-yard head start in a 100-yard race. The load fund must run faster than the no-load fund just to break even.

A more reasonable comparison would allocate the load to more than one year's total return. If you were to allocate or distribute the $8\frac{1}{2}$ percent load equally over $8\frac{1}{2}$ years, the penalty would amount to only 1 percent per year. Compared to the penalty of 8½ percent for the single year, the distributed load improves ROI. If you were to sell Fund L after two years, the load could be allocated to each year of ownership at 4¼ percent per year—half of the load for each of the two years. Tables 11F and 11G show the results of a typical comparison between load and no-load mutual funds assuming the same performance for two years.

Failure to allocate the cost of acquiring load funds sometimes traps unwary investors who depend on the NAVs reported in various financial magazines and newspapers. Since the reporting agencies have no idea how long you may own shares in load funds, there is no rational way of diminishing returns by some portion of the load.

Thus, returns reported for load and no-load funds for specific periods are not comparable. Only you can compare results based on your own holding period for load funds. You may legitimately compare reported results of no-load funds directly, as loads do not affect their returns; what you see is what you get.

TABLE 11G	ROI FOR NO-LOAD FUND SHARES				
		FUND L			
Trade Date	Transaction	Dollar Amount	Share Price	Shares Owned	
Alternative second year					
01/02	Opening balance	12,000.00 (10,980.00)	12.00	1,067.500	
12/31	Income reinvested	2,000.00 (1,830.00)	14.00	1,198.214	
Third year					
01/02	Sell all shares	16,775.00	14.00	0	

$$ROI = \frac{16,775.00 - 14,000.00}{14,000.00} = \frac{2,775}{14,000} = 19.82\%$$

		FUND NL			
Trade Date	Transaction	Dollar Amount	Share Price	Shares Owned	
Alternative second year					
01/02	Opening balance	12,000.00	12.00	1,166.667	
12/31	Income reinvested	2,000.00	14.00	1,309.524	
Third year					
01/02	Sell all shares	13,333.34	14.00	0	

$$ROI = \frac{18,333.34 - 14,000.00}{14,000.00} = \frac{4,333.34}{14,000.00} = 30.95\%$$

Bonds and Debt Instruments

Record keeping and tax reporting for bonds are much the same as for stocks. You receive a confirmation from your broker to define acquisition costs. When you sell, you receive another confirmation. The confirmation may or may not include a separately stated commission. If the broker sells from inventory as a **principal** rather than as an agent, his commission will be part of the markup, and your acquisition cost will be stated as a single number. (The brokerage firm may have bought bonds with its own money; these bonds then become part of the firm's inventory, just as a lumber dealer buys 2×4s for resale. When the broker acts as a principal, he sells bonds owned by the brokerage firm. The broker may also act as an agent; in this case he buys bonds from another investor and marks up the bond before selling to a client.) The broker who is acting in the role of agent also charges a commission on the sale.

One important distinction applies to bonds. Consider the long-term bond of ABC Corporation you buy on the secondary market from your broker. The price will differ from the par or face value of the bond in accordance with general interest rates. The price will also include the amount of interest earned since the last interest payment date. When you buy the bond, you pay the previous owner for the interest earned; later you get the interest back from the bond issuer. You must identify that interest as part of the cost or you could pay taxes on more interest than you earned. For example, suppose you buy a bond on May 1 that pays interest quarterly on the last day of each quarter. From April 1 through May 1 the bond will have accrued 30 days' interest. If the $1,000 bond pays 8 percent (or $80) per year, daily interest is $0.221 and the interest accrued over 30 days amounts to $6.63.

Conclusion

Knowing your position and monitoring the progress of your investments are key functions in managing your money. Keeping records, checking on investments at regular intervals, and switching investments as needed to keep your money working at a rate that exceeds taxes and inflation are key tasks you must learn to do for yourself. Make sure you keep the information you need to track your investments and to document your gains and/or losses in a tax audit.

Paper records are essential. Without the facts and figures you find on confirmations, dividend reports, and Form 1099s, you can hardly expect to have more than a fragmented view of your investments. Calculating and tracking your return on invested capital is the true bottom line for your financial program.

CHAPTER TWELVE

Tools For Investing

KEY TERMS FOR THIS CHAPTER

fundamental analysis   *support*
technical analysis   *resistance*
indicators   *break-out*
bottom line   *reversal*
balance sheet   *trends*
technicians   *penetrations*
advance-decline line   *market timing*
moving average   *trend following*
weighted average   *dollar-cost averaging*
exponential average   *value-cost averaging*

How do you go about making investments? The process is much like building a house: You need tools and materials plus a plan. Three major groups of tools have been used by savvy investors since the late 1800s and perhaps before that.

• **Fundamental analysis** calls for a thorough understanding of a company before investing. This is what many in investing call the bottom-up approach. The emphasis is on the fundamentals of a specific company—its product, operating efficiency, management, and financial performance.

• **Technical analysis** is the study of **indicators** and patterns of price and volume behavior, practically without regard for a company's fundamentals. The emphasis is on movements of a company's stock relative to activity in the overall market, rather than on what a company makes or how well it functions.

• Mechanical or rote systems have been around for years. At certain times the systems work better than at other times; they often work better than the hit-or-miss investing practiced by many individuals. Two excellent systems, dollar cost averaging and value cost averaging, are described later.

Fundamental Analysis

Examining a company's performance from the bottom up to determine its value as a potential investment can be time-consuming. Fortunately, much of the data collection and presentation is done by financial reporting organizations, such as Value Line and Standard & Poor's (S & P). Getting to know a company, however, calls for more than a detailed look at its balance sheet and statement of earnings.

Obtaining General Information

Before you tackle the job of analyzing a company's financials (reports of sales, earnings, liabilities, balance sheet, and profits), you need to examine what a company does and how well it does it. Is it a manufacturing company or a service-oriented company? Manufacturing companies make a product to be sold. Car companies are manufacturers; so are steel companies, computer makers, and nut and bolt factories. They turn raw materials or small parts and subassemblies into finished goods for sale. Service-oriented companies make nothing; they serve the public with something it wants or needs. McDonald's serves hamburgers; J.C. Penney sells goods; doctors and dentists offer health services. All are part of the service economy. While governments provide services, they issue no stocks. Govern-

ments do, however, issue billions of dollars worth of bonds and debt instruments. The interest paid on various kinds of bonds reflects how efficiently various governments provide services, and you should understand the government or agency that issues bonds before you loan them your money.

Learning about a company isn't difficult. Various sources of data and general information about a company are readily available.

• Newspapers and magazines write about individual companies constantly. Profiles of major companies appear in *Fortune*, *Forbes*, the *New York Times*, and many other publications. If you are researching a particular company, check the index to magazine articles in your library for articles that may have appeared.

• Annual reports issued by the company usually include lengthy descriptions of a company's activities along with colorful photographs of facilities and products. Annual reports are also sources of recent financial data. Current stockholders receive an annual report automatically. If you are interested, send a postcard to the company or telephone to request a copy. Companies are pleased to send nonshareholders copies of their annual reports. *Business Week*, *The Wall Street Journal*, and other business journals include advertisements by companies soliciting requests for annual reports from readers as part of their public relations program.

• Annual meetings are a good source of information, and they are not limited to shareholders. Some companies stage extensive dog and pony shows to advise attendees about operations and display their activities and results with slides or movies.

• Analysts' reports dig beneath the glossy surface of company reports to present data that has been collected and analyzed. These reports from brokerage company analysts can be obtained on request if you are an active client of that broker. These special reports are less available to the public unless a broker attempts to use them to build a client base.

• Subscription sources of company data, such as Value Line and S & P, report regularly on stocks traded on the New York Stock Exchange (NYSE), American Stock Exchange (Amex), and the larger over-the-counter (OTC) stocks. Continuing subscriptions to the detailed reports and up-

dates can be expensive, but most large libraries maintain these sources and update them regularly.

Obtaining Financial Information

A company's income statement and balance sheet represent the keys to evaluating its financial performance (see box below). These two accounts are important documents you need to understand. Even if you use data prepared by others, you should be aware of the fundamental figures that represent the results of a company's ac-

---

ABC Distributing Co.
Income Statement
Year ending December 31

Revenues		
Sales	$9,780*	
Rights	42	
Interest	30	
Other income	28	
		$9,880
Costs and Expenses		
Cost of goods sold	$4,840	
Operating profit		$5,040
Sales expenses	1,525	
General admin. expenses	430	
Interest on debt	1,920	
Depreciation	104	
Miscellaneous expenses	40	
	$4,019	
Gross Profit (before taxes)		$1,021
Federal taxes	$549	
State & local taxes	39	
	$588	
Net Profit (earnings)		$433

* 000 omitted in all amounts.

tivities, whether it is a manufacturing company or a service company.

• The income statement summarizes yearly results starting with gross revenues from all sources and ending with net income after expenses. The **bottom line** in a company's financials is the net profit, or earnings. The box on page 180 is a sample income statement for ABC Distributing Co. Revenues do not necessarily represent sales alone, although distributing a variety of products is ABC's primary activity. Interest from cash invested is another source of revenue along with rents, royalties on subsidiary rights sales, and unspecified income that could include tie-ins to books, toys, and other products, such as T-shirts based on toy characters. All of these are part of total revenue.

Costs usually break down into the following components:

1. Cost of goods sold. For ABC Distributing Co. the production costs of products purchased from manufacturers make up the main cost of goods sold. Subtracting the cost of goods sold from total revenues yields an important number called Operating Profit, or the profit on sales before selling and general administration costs are deducted.
2. Sales expenses include salaries and travel expenses for salespersons, warehousing of the products, rent for wholly owned store outlets, and similar expenses.
3. General administration expenses include staff salaries plus accounting and other overhead costs that cannot be attributed to specific product lines.
4. Interest on debt is the cost for money borrowed by selling bonds.

5. Depreciation is the amount deducted to recover the annual cost of previous capital expenditures.
6. Miscellaneous expenses is a catch-all for many identified costs too small to warrant a line of their own.

Before-tax profits (or losses) fall out after deducting all costs from total revenues. Federal, state, and local taxes are deducted from the before-tax total to leave the net profit, or net earnings—widely referred to as the bottom line, for the obvious reason that it appears at the bottom of the income statement.

• The **balance sheet** (see box on page 182) also greatly simplified, includes a list of assets owned by ABC Distributing Co. and an offsetting list of liabilities and stockholders' equity. The two lists must balance—that is, they must add up to equal dollar amounts. In analyzing a company's balance sheet, it is important to relate current assets and liabilities to long-term assets and liabilities. Current assets are those assets expected to be sold or converted into cash within the next 12 months. Current liabilities are expected to be paid within the next year. Long term refers to assets and liabilities with an expected life in excess of 12 months.

On the asset side, cash is just that: cash in a checking account at a bank. One element of the sample income statement shows interest on investments, and these investments by ABC Distributing Co. are U.S. Treasury bills (T-bills), noted among the current assets. Rather than keep large amounts of cash in a checking account drawing no interest, the company's financial officer invested excess cash in T-bills to earn income from the asset. T-bills

ABC Distributing Co.
Balance Sheet
Year ending December 31

Assets			Liabilities		
Current assets			Current liabilities		
Cash in bank	$306*		Accounts payable	$1,670	
Securities (T-bills)	375		Loans & notes payable	3,100	
Accounts receivable	1,680		Royalties payable	680	
Inventories	9,337		Other	375	
Prepaid royalties	50		Total current liabilities	$5,835	$5,835
Other current assets	33		Long-term bonds	1,752	
Total current assets	$11,781	$11,781	Total liabilities	$7,587	7,587
Long-term assets			Stockholders' equity		
Plant & equipment	430		Common stock	4,600	
Investment property	100		Retained earnings	124	
Total long-term assets	$530	530	Total stockholders' equity	$4,724	
Total assets		$12,311	Total liabilities and stockholders' equity		$12,311

* 000 omitted in all amounts.

are quickly convertible into cash when needed. Accounts receivable represent sales that have not yet been paid for by customers. Inventory is a big asset for a product distributor and represents the stock of unsold goods stored in a warehouse. It also includes products in various stages of production, known as work in progress. The inventory is valued at the products' production or purchase cost. Prepaid royalties are early payments to owners of protected property for rights to produce and sell a product. Other current assets are a catch-all for small asset items, such as office supplies and equipment.

An analyst examining the income statement and balance sheet in a company's annual report will look for telltale signs of the company's financial condition. A number of the important points are:

1. Earnings. If a company produces a profit, that's good. How good? Two signs are watched closely: earnings per share and earnings as a percentage of revenues. Let's say ABC Distributing Co. has 500,000 shares of stock outstanding. Earnings per share are earnings ($433,000) divided by shares (500,000), or $0.87 per share. If an analyst figures that a stock in the distributing industry is conservatively priced at 10–15 times earnings, the stock of ABC Distributing might be fully priced at $8.66–$12.00 per share. ("Fully priced" is a euphemism for a stock price that will probably not rise until earnings rise.) Second, in the case of ABC Distributing, net earnings of $433,000 represent 4.4 percent of gross revenues ($9,880,000)—proba-

bly a bit better than the industry average.

Another sign is return on equity calling for figures from both the income statement and the balance sheet. Again take the net earnings ($433,000) and divide by stockholders' equity ($4,724,000) to get 9.17 percent—an average return on the equity invested by shareholders. A 10 percent to 15 percent return on equity can be considered a likely target.

2. Growth. A major characteristic of growth companies is a plowing back of earnings to expand business. How did ABC Distributing do for the year in question? One measure is the retention rate, the amount of net earnings ABC Distributing retained for growth. ABC Distributing, like many growth companies, does not pay dividends to stockholders. Retention rate is calculated by deducting dividends from net earnings and dividing that number by net earnings. Since ABC did not pay dividends, its retention rate is 100 percent.

   If ABC had paid dividends, say $100,000, to shareholders, the hypothetical retention rate would have been $433,000 less $100,000 divided by $433,000 ($333,000 divided by $433,000), or 77 percent. Of course, not all net profits are likely to be reinvested for growth; a major portion of after-tax profits may go for paying off portions of the debt principal.

3. Dividend payout percentage. Since many investors expect some immediate return, they may look at how much a company pays out in dividends. The percentage of net earnings paid out in dividends is called the dividend payout. In the case of ABC Distributing, no dividends were paid, so the dividend payout was 0 percent. Assuming a $100,000 hypothetical dividend payment, the dividend payout would be calculated by dividing $100,000 by $433,000 for a payout percentage of 23 percent—low by many standards, but not unusual for a company dedicated to fast growth. A mature company with stable earnings might pay as much as 40 percent to 50 percent of its earnings to shareholders as dividends.

4. Reinvestment rate. Another measure of how much a company is plowing back for growth is the reinvestment rate, calculated by multiplying the return on equity by the retention rate. For ABC Distributing, a 9.17 percent return on equity (net earnings divided by stockholders' equity) multiplied by 1.00, representing a 100 percent retention rate, equals 9.17 percent, an average figure.

5. Current ratio. The relationship of current assets to current liabilities is a widely watched figure. It is obtained by dividing current assets by current liabilities. For ABC Distributing, it is $11,781,000 divided by $5,835,000, or 2.019. A current ratio of 2.0 or greater is considered good. Inventories, which are part of current assets, tend to lower the current ratio for distributors because inventory amounts to a large value.

6. Long-term debt ratio. Strong balance sheets are those with high percentages of equity (shareholder ownership) and small percentages of long-term debt.

A common sign of balance sheet strength is the long-term debt ratio, or long-term debt divided by total liabilities. For ABC Distributing, the figure is $1,752,000 divided by $7,587,000, or 23.09 percent. A 50–50 ratio (50% debt and 50% equity) is a common goal, because a heavy debt load leaves a company vulnerable to low sales, as in a recession.

7. Long-term debt/stockholders' equity ratio. Another measure of long-term debt is its relationship to stockholders' equity. Conservative financing calls for equity to equal or exceed long-term debt. For ABC Distributing, calculate this percentage by dividing long-term bonds ($1,752,000) by stockholders' equity ($4,724,000) for a ratio of 37.09 percent.

8. Cash flow. Almost as important as net earnings is how much cash flows into the company. Even if a company is profitable, it cannot continue without a positive cash flow. Depreciation figures heavily into cash flow calculations, as it is a nontaxable source of cash. The formula for cash flow is net earnings plus depreciation. For ABC Distributing, add $433,000 and $104,000 for a cash flow of $537,000—not a particularly good figure. Higher cash flows result from previous investment in depreciable assets.

9. Cash flow per share. Another meaningful number for analysts is how much cash is flowing into the company for each share of stock outstanding. For ABC Distributing, the cash flow of $537,000 is divided by 500,000 shares to yield $1.07 per share. This figure is only important as it relates to previous years' results. Cash flow or profits per share are dependent on the number of shares, so comparisons with other companies' results are meaningless.

10. Book value per share. Another simple calculation divides the stockholders' equity (assets minus liabilities) by the number of shares outstanding. For ABC Distributing, the figure is $4,724,000 divided by 500,000, or $9.45 per share. This figure relates to a value of shares based on earnings. At $8.66 per share (from No. 1 above), the shares might be considered undervalued, as shares typically sell at 1½–2 times the book value per share.

Using these and other fundamentals an analyst can draw a broad range of figures and impressions from the raw numbers presented in a company's financial statements. Numbers are not absolute, however. Judgment and experience are critical to the analyst's conclusions—there is no substitute for either when appraising the potential value of stocks.

Technical Analysis

Technicians are market analysts who examine the technical elements of the market in search of clues to future action. They are the gurus of indicators, over- or undersold markets, and market timing signals. Just as fundamental analysts study the performance of individual companies, technicians study the performance of stock price and volume behavior of individual companies in relation to the market itself.

From these studies the technicians attempt to find past patterns of behavior that may be repeated under similar conditions. For example, when the general level of short-term interest rates has declined, prices for stocks have risen. Given this relationship, it is worth exploring when the decline starts and how much of a stock rise can be expected. This information can then be charted and used to predict future stock price trends.

According to the general consensus of market participants, about 70 percent of the change in direction of individual stock prices is due to the total market. The remaining 30 percent is due to supply and demand for the stocks. Thus, even when the overall market rises, many stocks decline for a day or longer. Technical analysts attempt to forecast what will happen the next day, over the next few weeks, or even during the next year on the basis of what has happened before.

Technicians operate on the assumption that the market takes into account all information, and they presume that the fundamentals of a company are known to all participants. No analyst has an advantage over others through knowing something the others don't. Nevertheless, technicians agree that a truly efficient market does not and cannot exist. They sense the strength or weakness of the market by reading its vital signs—price and volume action.

Technicians use a variety of indicators or characteristics of the market that reflect specific aspects of market activity. Two of the most often used indicators are the daily summaries of a major average, such as the Dow Jones Industrial Average (DJIA), and concurrent daily volume. Charts are important to technicians, as overall trends and patterns are more discernible in a graphic display.

Technicians are continually looking for the perfect indicator, one that would signal a rise in a stock's price a few days before the price actually rises. The technician could then buy the stock, wait for it to rise, and sell it at a profit at the new, higher price. No such reliable indicator exists, but that doesn't stop technicians from continuing their search. Since a single indicator can seldom be counted on for its predictive value, technicians look for combinations of indicators to help them predict changes in direction more reliably and consistently. One prominent technician is said to use 51 different indicators for predicting which stocks to buy and sell.

Technicians tend to keep their methods and indicators under wraps. Newsletters publish predictions of stock and market activity based on technical analysis but keep their systems and methods confidential or proprietary.

Charting Market Activity

Since much of technical analysis involves graphics, knowing how charts are constructed will aid your understanding of technical analysis and help you to interpret results.

Constructing charts. One of the simplest charts is a calendar line chart, in which days, weeks, or months form the base, also known as the X-axis. A sample of closing prices for the DJIA appears along the top of Chart 12A as a series of short vertical lines. Closing prices are plotted daily according to the calendar at the bottom (X-axis) and value is plotted according

Chart 12A   Calendar Line Chart

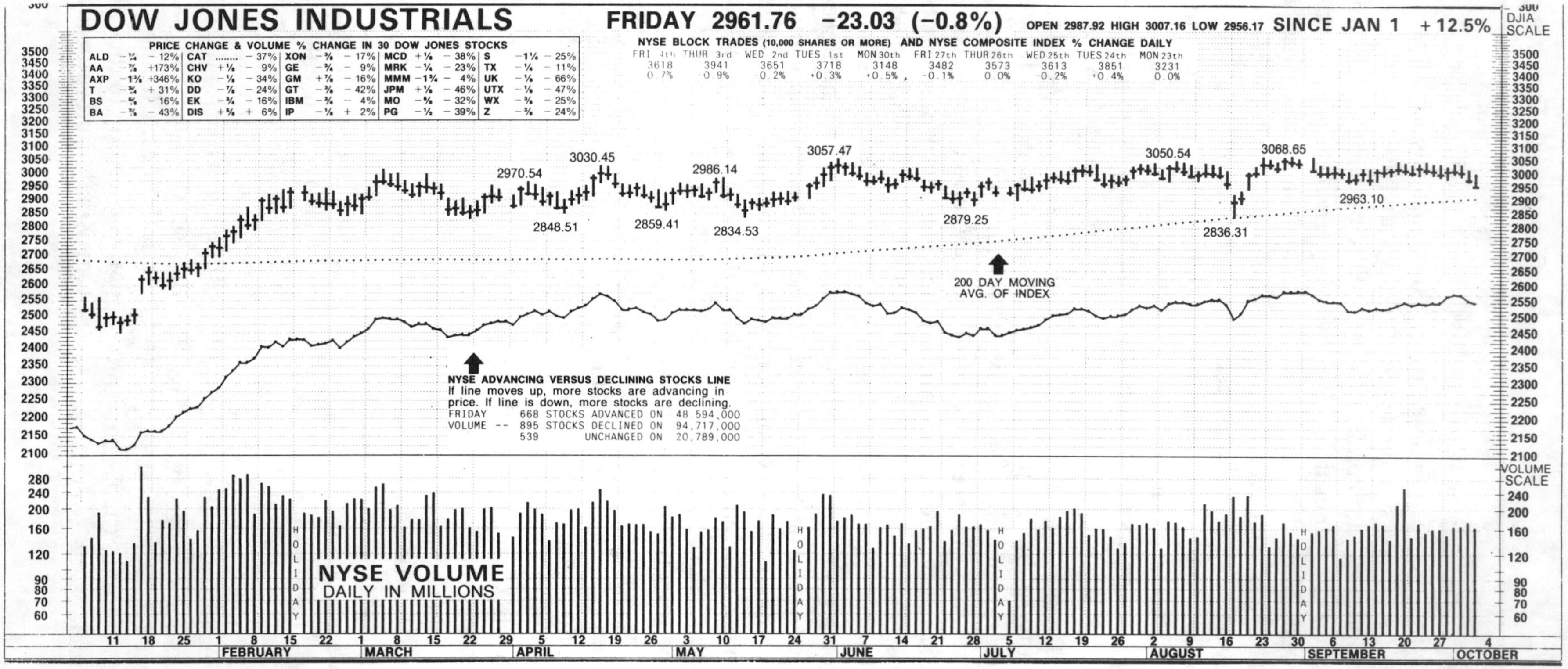

DOW JONES INDUSTRIALS

FRIDAY 2961.76 −23.03 (−0.8%)

OPEN 2987.92 HIGH 3007.16 LOW 2956.17 **SINCE JAN 1 + 12.5%**

NYSE BLOCK TRADES (10,000 SHARES OR MORE) AND NYSE COMPOSITE INDEX % CHANGE DAILY

	FRI 4th	THUR 3rd	WED 2nd	TUES 1st	MON 30th	FRI 27th	THUR 26th	WED 25th	TUES 24th	MON 23rd
	3618	3941	3651	3718	3148	3482	3573	3573	3851	3231
	0.7%	0.9%	0.2%	+0.3%	-0.5%	-0.1%	0.0%	0.2%	-0.4%	0.0%

PRICE CHANGE & VOLUME % CHANGE IN 30 DOW JONES STOCKS

ALD	−¼ − 12%	CAT − ½ − 17%	MCD + ⅛ − 38%	S − ⅜ − 25%
AA	+⅛ +173%	CHV +⅜ − 9%	MRK − ¼ − 23%	TX − ¼ − 11%
AXP	−1¼ +346%	GE − ¼ − 16%	MMM − 1½ − 4%	UK − ¼ − 66%
T	−⅜ + 31%	GM + ⅜ − 42%	JPM + ½ − 46%	UTX − ½ − 47%
BS	−⅜ − 16%	GT − ½ − 24%	IBM − ¼ − 32%	WX − ⅜ − 25%
BA	−⅜ − 43%	DIS +⅜ + 6%	IP − ½ − 39%	Z − ⅜ − 24%

3068.65

2963.10

3057.47

3050.54

2986.14

2836.31

3030.45

2970.54

2879.25

2859.41   2834.53

2848.51

200 DAY MOVING
AVG. OF INDEX

NYSE ADVANCING VERSUS DECLINING STOCKS LINE
If line moves up, more stocks are advancing in
price. If line is down, more stocks are declining.
FRIDAY   668 STOCKS ADVANCED ON 48,594,000
VOLUME -- 895 STOCKS DECLINED ON 94,717,000
         539 STOCKS UNCHANGED ON 20,789,000

NYSE VOLUME
DAILY IN MILLIONS

DJIA SCALE: 3500 3450 3400 3350 3300 3250 3200 3150 3100 3050 3000 2950 2900 2850 2800 2750 2700 2650 2600 2550 2500 2450 2400 2350 2300 2250 2200 2150 2100

VOLUME SCALE: 280 240 200 160 120 90 80 70 60

Months: FEBRUARY MARCH APRIL MAY JUNE JULY AUGUST SEPTEMBER OCTOBER

Reprinted by permission of *Investor's Daily.*

to the vertical scale at the left side (Y-axis). This series of short vertical bars is a variation of the simple line chart, as each bar represents one day's DJIA activity. The top of the daily bar represents the DJIA's high for the day, the bottom represents the DJIA's low, and the point somewhere between the high and the low (marked with a short cross bar) represents the closing price.

Also shown on the chart is a 200-day moving average plotted as a series of dots running through the bars representing the DJIA. The 200-day moving average smooths the up-and-down spikes of the daily prices.

Near the bottom of the upper chart, and separate from the DJIA, is the **advance-decline line**, a single line representing the ratio of advancing stocks to declining stocks.

To judge the breadth of the market, technicians rely on the advance-decline line, which is constructed by subtracting the number of stock issues traded on the NYSE that closed lower from the number of stock issues that closed higher. Unchanged issues are ignored. The difference is charted around a horizontal neutral line. If advancing stocks outnumber declining stocks, the line moves up and vice versa. Because of the many rapid changes up and down, a 10-day or 30-day moving average (an average that moves with time) may be used to smooth the data. The advance-decline line provides useful information to the technician on where the market is headed. For instance, it may caution that a rising DJIA is not confirmed by a broad market rise.

Vertical bars, one for each day, rise from the X-axis to indicate the number of shares of stocks traded that day on the NYSE. Prices are plotted above volume for the same day because technicians gain information from the relationship between daily price movement and volume.

Moving averages help technicians perceive trends or variations of market activity without the distractions of spiky daily highs and lows. Statisticians may use a variety of averages or "indications of central tendency." A simple mean is the one familiar to most people. To figure a simple mean, add up the numbers to be averaged and divide the total by the number of entries.

A **moving average** is one that moves with time. Each day a new data point is added and the earliest point is removed. Intervening points between earliest date and the most recent date are averaged and plotted at the most recent date. Technically, a moving average smooths the data, removing the daily rises and drops to allow the underlying movement to be seen; it eliminates the "noise" in an array of data. Moving averages may cover 5 days, 13 weeks, 200 days, or any other period. A common period is 39 weeks, with each of the 39 weekly closing prices forming the basic data points. A long period tends to remove more of the bumps and dips from the data, but many weeks may need to be studied to see any important change in direction. A shorter period smooths the data but may still move up and down in a pattern that could hide an underlying trend. Picking a reasonable period requires skill to match the moving average period with the purpose of the analysis.

Understanding how the simple mean moving average is constructed will help you interpret results. A **weighted average**

TABLE 12A	COMPUTING A SIMPLE MEAN MOVING AVERAGE		
Week No.	Stock Price	10-week Average	10-week Mean
1	42.11		
2	43.38		
3	44.00		
4	45.50		
5	45.13		
6	44.63		
7	44.50		
8	46.50		
9	47.75		
10	48.00	451.50	45.15
11	48.25	457.63	45.76
12	49.25	463.50	46.35
13	49.38	468.88	46.89
14	48.75	472.13	47.21
15	48.50	475.50	47.55
16	49.63	480.50	48.05
17	50.50	486.50	48.65
18	51.00	491.00	49.10
19	51.75	495.00	49.50
20	52.00	499.00	49.90
21	52.00	502.75	50.28
22	51.75	505.25	50.53
23	52.00	507.88	50.79
24	52.25	511.38	51.14
25	53.00	515.88	51.59
26	53.50	519.75	51.98
27	53.75	523.00	52.30
28	54.50	526.50	52.65
29	56.00	530.75	53.08
30	55.00	533.75	53.38
31	56.50	538.25	53.83
32	56.75	543.25	54.33
33	57.00	548.25	54.83
34	58.13	554.13	55.41
35	59.25	560.38	56.04
36	60.00	566.88	56.69
37	61.13	574.25	57.43
38	61.25	581.00	58.10
39	61.25	586.25	58.63
40	60.75	592.00	59.20
41	60.00	595.50	59.55
42	59.75	598.50	59.85
43	59.13	600.63	60.06
44	57.75	600.25	60.03
45	57.25	598.25	59.83
46	58.50	596.75	59.68
47	57.13	592.75	59.28
48	54.75	586.25	58.63
49	54.00	579.00	57.90
50	53.25	571.50	57.15
51	52.00	563.50	56.35
52	50.50	554.25	55.43
53	49.88	545.00	54.50
54	49.00	536.25	53.63
55	50.75	529.75	52.98
56	50.00	521.25	52.13
57	47.25	511.38	51.14
58	46.75	503.38	50.34
59	44.50	493.88	49.39
60	46.00	486.63	48.66
61	44.75	479.38	47.94
62	43.00	471.88	47.19

and an **exponential average** may also be used for special purposes. Each type has its uses and advantages for different kinds of technical analysis.

To construct a simple mean moving average, pick a period and average each of the groups of prices as the period moves. The example in Table 12A uses a 10-week mean and averages weekly closing prices of a generic stock. Adding the first 10 weekly numbers produces a total of 451.50. Dividing this number by the 10 data entries yields the first 10-week mean of 45.15. To construct a moving average, drop the top (earliest) number and add the next (latest) number in the array. The total of numbers from week 2 through week 11 is 457.63, for a 10-week mean of 45.76. The moving average proceeds one week at a time by repeating the process. Chart 12B shows how these 10-week averages move with a line connecting data points. Note that the moving average is plotted at the most recent week of the period and smooths the actual weekly price line represented by the Fund Price Line.

The problem with the common mean as a moving average is the need to add all of the numbers each day or week to compute the total from which the average is figured. A computer, of course, can simplify the process. Despite its cumbersome construction, the moving average is frequently used for 39-week and 52-week analyses.

Interpreting charts. Once you have constructed daily or weekly moving line or bar charts for a period, you can begin to see patterns. You may prefer to see charts already prepared in such publications as *Investor's Daily*. Chart 12C offers some simplified patterns. Here is how a technician might read these patterns as a prelude to action.

Patterns illustrating price **support** and **resistance** levels are shown in Charts 12C-1 and 12C-2. Price support and resistance levels begin from a trading range (a pattern of trading) between a low of, let's say, around 30 and a high of around 40. (Figures are for share prices in dollars.) For weeks or months the stock trades at prices that move up or down without much direction.

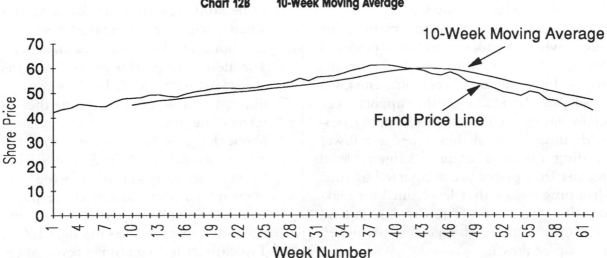

Chart 12B   10-Week Moving Average

The overall market may also be moving aimlessly in a similar trading range of its own. Prices within a trading range move from a price support level at the bottom end of the range to a price resistance level at the upper end of the range. When investors see the price reaching the resistance level, they may sell shares, knowing that the stock has retreated when it reached that level in the past. But when the stock price reaches the lower support level, investors may buy with the expectation that sometime it will reverse and climb to the resistance level again where they can earn a profit by selling. A stock that continues to trade within a fairly narrow range is not likely to generate any excitement until it breaks out. At the right end of Chart 12C-1, the price moves up sharply in what technicians call a **break-out.** This could be a time to buy, as once a stock breaks out of a trading range, it tends to continue until it establishes a new and higher trading range. Technicians have discovered that once a stock breaks out of a trading range in either direction, something is propelling it up or down. Forces that led to the break-out are likely to continue affecting the stock.

An opposite pattern appears in Chart 12C-2 with a break-out to lower prices. If an investor is holding stock, he or she would likely sell at a break-out. Thus, if a stock price breaks below the support level, chances are it will continue dropping, possibly until it establishes a new and lower trading range. The term support level means that prices are supported against dropping below that level until a break-out disturbs the pattern. Break-outs tend to occur on major changes in volume, either up or down.

Reversals can assume different patterns. A **reversal** occurs when a pattern of upward movement changes to a downward movement, as in the following examples:

1. If a stock's price moves steadily upward then suddenly drops and keeps on dropping, as in Chart 12C-3, the change is called a panic reversal. Such a pattern may have been apparent following the sharp market drop in October 1987.
2. A more likely reversal pattern is shown in Chart 12C-4. Prices may be rising, but the daily incremental rise begins to taper off until it stops rising and gradually begins to lose in price. This is known as the round-top reversal.
3. A double-top reversal, as shown in Chart 12C-5, can easily confuse technicians, as the direction of prices changes often.
4. Similar confusing signals can result from the head-and-shoulders reversal, as shown in Chart 12C-6. For a true head-and-shoulders, the middle hump (head) must rise higher than the shoulders on either side. The two bottoms between the head and shoulders tend to be similar, and a break-out occurs when prices drop below the level of the two bottoms. Then it's time to sell.
5. The descending triangle reversal, as shown in Chart 12C-7, displays two significant characteristics. First, the intermediate lows of each cycle reach about the same level. Second, the high points of each cycle are successively lower. When prices drop below the level of the intermediate low, it's time to sell.
6. Instead of a spiky top, a selling climax reversal may appear as in Chart 12C-8. Typically, a selling climax reversal oc-

Chart 12C   Price Patterns for Technical Analysis

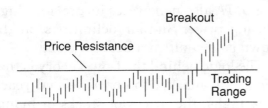

12C-1   Price Resistance

12C-2   Price Support

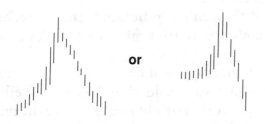

12C-3   Panic Reversal

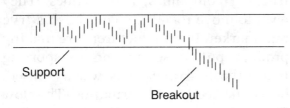

12C-4   Round-top Reversal

12C-5   Double-top Reversal

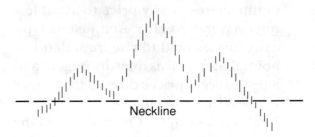

12C-6   Head-and-shoulders Reversal

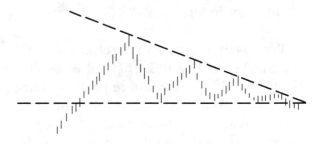

12C-7   Descending Triangle Reversal

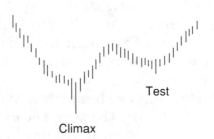

12C-8   Selling Climax Reversal

12C-9   Round-bottom Reversal

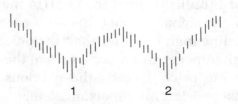

12C-10   Double-bottom Reversal

curs on high volume when shareholders dump shares at any price to avoid losing even more value. And just as typically, prices tend to rise from that low point. Later, prices may drop again and a test to see if prices drop to the former low level may occur.

7. The round bottom, Chart 12C-9, is the reverse of the round top. The double bottom, Chart 12C-10, is the reverse of the double top—and just as confusing to technicians.

Trends that appear in the charts are major market indicators. Instead of a horizontal trading range where prices bounce off the support level at the bottom and off the resistance level at the top, share prices may move about an inclining or declining trend line. Trends are extremely important because they may last for several years. Generally, stocks in the United States have been trending up at about 6 percent per year since 1900 or before.

Penetrations can be another important market indicator. The Dow Theory is one of the oldest technical systems in use. It aims only to indicate primary trend direction and is not used to forecast either the duration or height of an upward trend or the duration or depth of a downward trend. The theory uses variations in the DJIA and the Dow Jones Transportation Average (DJTA) as basic indicators. An upward (bullish) trend in the DJIA may appear to signal a rising market if each succeeding high is higher than the preceding high. A penetration occurs when the DJIA closing price exceeds the previous high closing price. An important element of the Dow Theory, however, is confirmation—a new upward trend is not confirmed until the DJTA also penetrates its previous high closing price. Similar definitions on the down side confirm a bearish trend.

The logic behind the Dow Theory is that for a bull market to continue and reach new highs, the prices of stocks of manufacturers must be bid up. Similar interest would bid up the prices of the stocks of transportation companies, railroads, trucking companies, and airlines. They need to move together to establish a true bull market. If manufacturers are making products but not selling and transporting them, the bull market is weakly based, hence the need for confirmation. The Dow Theory is one you may hear about from time to time, as it is widely followed. It continues to be used because it has been successful.

Other chart indicators. Only a technician's creativity limits the use of various chart indicators.

A short-interest chart follows the number of issues sold short, as short sellers (sellers of borrowed stock) believe the market is headed down. Short sellers must buy the stock back at some point, however, and some technicians see this as a bullish indicator.

A sentiment index surveys the opinions of a sample of newsletter writers. When a majority of the writers is forecasting a bull market, a contrarian may take a bearish position that the majority is always wrong. A contrarian is an investor who invests in stocks when others are selling and vice versa. The sentiment index has also proved to be a reasonably accurate indicator of market directions at times. A sentiment index is reported every day in *Investor's Daily*.

An odd-lot index relies on the collective action of small investors. Market watchers believe that small investors—those with too little money to buy in round lots—tend to be wrong most of the time. Thus, when many odd-lotters enter the market, indicated by the daily report of odd-lot trading, professionals and technicians believe the market will reverse and head down.

Market timing with moving averages compares daily prices with a long-term moving average. Numerous newsletters chart moving averages and announce timing changes according to their unique combination of charted data. The typical move occurs when a stock, mutual fund, or index penetrates a 33-, 39-, or 52-week moving average. Various systems may be used. For example, a 52-week moving average of the DJIA may be charted against a single mutual fund. Or a composite group of mutual funds may be charted as a 39- or 52-week moving average and a single fund or several individual funds compared to it.

A **trend-following** system calls for mov-ing into or out of a mutual fund according to specific rules. (Moving in means to invest cash in mutual fund shares; moving out means to redeem shares in mutual funds. One can move out of one fund and into another within the same family of funds. A family of funds is two groups of funds managed by the same fund distribution corporation, such as Vanguard, a family of 60-plus related funds.) Mutual funds are the typical vehicle for moving in or moving out, rather than individual stocks, because movements in or out cost less in broker's fees than timing individual stocks. If no-load mutual funds are the vehicles, moves may cost nothing. Start with the moving average above the daily or weekly closing prices for Mutual Fund A, noted in Chart 12D as the fund price line. Since the moving average lags the changes in share prices, gradual changes have minimal effects. As long as closing share prices remain below the moving average, investors remain out of the market. Typically, they will have parked their money in a

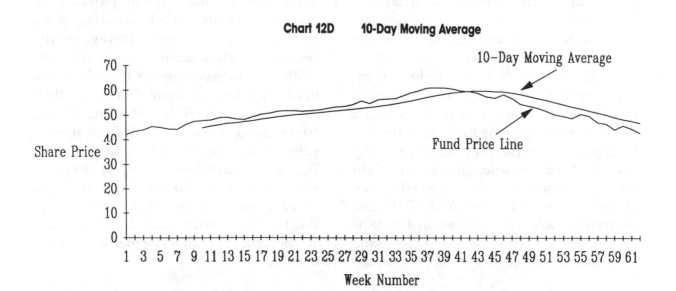

Chart 12D   10-Day Moving Average

money market fund (MMF) because MMFs maintain a constant share value. Thus, the investor incurs no risk of losing capital.

When the closing price moves up and penetrates the moving average, investors move money from the MMF into the mutual fund. When the mutual fund's price line penetrates the moving average, share prices are expected to continue moving up.

Investors remain invested in the mutual fund for as long as the daily or weekly closing share prices remain above the moving average. But, if the market slows and reverses, the closing share price line penetrates the moving average. At that point the investor moves from the mutual fund back to the MMF. In a price-reversal, trend-following market timing system, investors do not get out at the top and they do not get in at the bottom, but they pick up most of the move in both directions.

A single moving average can generate whipsaws, when the closing price penetrates the moving average on an up move and then drops back. On an upward penetration, the investor moves money from a MMF to a stock mutual fund. A day or a few days later, share prices drop back and the investor switches back to the MMF, usually at a loss. Market timers have developed different tactics to reduce whipsaws, even though they have not completely beaten them. One tactic is to use more than one moving average. If mutual fund prices penetrate a reference moving average to the up side, an investor might not switch until the upward trend is confirmed by a similar move of the DJIA and its moving average, similar to the Dow Theory confirmation. Or, a buffer band may enlarge the neutral zone. A penetra-

tion must move past the moving average by a small margin, such as 1 $\frac{1}{2}$ percent of the value of the moving average. A similar buffer zone protects the moving average on the lower side. A 3 percent buffer zone means penetrations must be stronger than if the difference is a single line. A strong penetration is less likely to be reversed quickly than one that barely makes it past the moving average.

Moving average timing systems typically underperform a buy-and-hold strategy during long-term bull markets. A buy-and-hold strategy calls for buying stocks or mutual funds and holding them for years through ups and downs. Timing works best in a market that moves up and down in broad, medium-term cycles in the order of four to five years from crest to crest. A cycle is one complete move up and then down to near the original starting level. By moving out of a stock mutual fund into a MMF in response to a timing signal, an investor avoids the loss of capital in the stock fund and earns interest on the money parked in the MMF. When the trend swings upward again, the investor moves back into the stock fund at a lower share price and holds until the moving average timing system signals another switch into the MMF. A timing system has the advantage in this case because losses hurt more than gains can remedy. If a mutual fund loses 50 percent of its value in a decline, it must gain 100 percent to reach its former level. For example, suppose Fund M drops in share price from $10 per share to $5 per share. It has lost 50 percent of its value. But the share price must double or gain 100 percent to reach its former level of $10 per share.

Mechanical Systems

A system follows a fixed agenda, one that tells you when to invest and when to get out. Using a system as a mechanical crutch for investing avoids a primary hazard to investor success—emotion. Emotional investing (buying and selling according to how you feel about the market) permits the disciplined professional to earn fabulous profits at your expense. Part-time, emotional investors tend to buy when new highs create excitement in the market. When the emotional investor is buying, the disciplined pro is selling out the shares he or she bought when prices were lower. On the downside, emotional investors, fearful of losing even more of their capital than a sliding market has already cost them, sell out at or near the bottom. Meanwhile, the pro is picking up shares at bargain prices. Later, when the market recovers and reaches another peak, the pro unloads again. This pattern repeats itself in every market cycle.

A system that substitutes logic and discipline for emotion can and does work, even with some limitations. The problem with systems is the same one that plagues investors without a system; lack of discipline. Investors attempt to override the system's discipline by substituting how they feel about the market for the system's discipline and thus eliminate alleged advantages of the system. Two of the recognized systems that work are dollar-cost averaging and value-cost averaging.

Dollar-cost Averaging

Dollar-cost averaging (DCA) has a proven history of beating the market. An engaging attribute of DCA is its simplicity. A demanding attribute is its need for strict discipline. Like most systems, DCA pays off only over a long term.

Basically, DCA calls for you to invest a specific number of dollars on a regular schedule. The vehicle—stocks, bonds, or mutual funds—is not important except for costs. Since DCA involves numerous small purchases, the commissions for buying small odd lots of stocks or bonds increases costs. By far the most attractive vehicle for DCA is one or more no-load mutual funds. After meeting the initial deposit minimum, small quantities of mutual fund shares, including fractional shares, can be bought.

A DCA program might begin by investing $100 every second Tuesday in shares of XYZ Stock Fund. Every second Tuesday you call XYZ Stock Fund and direct the customer representative to switch $100 of your cash on deposit in XYZ Money Market Fund into shares of XYZ Stock Fund. Regardless of what happens to prices, every second Tuesday you call and switch $100. If you believe you might forget or if you do not have enough savings to maintain a second account in XYZ Money Market Fund, arrange with XYZ Stock Fund to draw $100 from your bank checking account on the regular biweekly schedule, a process called drafting. You can see from Table 12B what happens.

As share prices drop, your $100 buys more shares. As prices rise, your $100 buys fewer shares. For example, for the second investment the fund NAV (share price) drops to 10.45 from 10.86 and the $100 buys 9.57 shares. The reverse occurs when NAV rises. Over 26 investment periods, your 26 investments will have bought shares at an average lower price per share, 9.00 (2,600.00 ÷ 288.854 = 9.00), than the average of prices at the time of purchase, 9.12 (237.05 ÷ 26 = 9.12).

Dollar-cost averaging suffers two potential problems:

1. When the market continues declining, you may be tempted to hold off buying.

You may think that next Tuesday you can buy shares even cheaper than this Tuesday. Or, you may believe that the market's decline could cost you money. If you allow these thoughts and emotions to interfere with the strict discipline of investing $100 every second Tuesday, then DCA will not work for you. The effectiveness of DCA comes from buying shares during declines, but

TABLE 12B	DOLLAR-COST AVERAGING	
Cumulative Investment At $100.00 per period	Mutual Fund NAV	Shares Bought
$100	10.86	9.21
$200	10.45	9.57
$300	10.18	9.82
$400	9.60	10.42
$500	9.55	10.47
$600	8.96	11.16
$700	9.14	10.94
$800	8.80	11.36
$900	8.60	11.63
$1,000	7.98	12.53
$1,100	7.84	12.76
$1,200	7.60	13.16
$1,300	8.20	12.20
$1,400	8.20	12.20
$1,500	8.32	12.02
$1,600	7.84	12.76
$1,700	8.16	12.25
$1,800	8.28	12.08
$1,900	8.38	11.93
$2,000	8.82	11.34
$2,100	9.14	10.94
$2,200	9.60	10.42
$2,300	9.95	10.05
$2,400	10.30	9.71
$2,500	10.94	9.14
$2,600	11.36	8.80
Total	237.05	288.854
Average cost per share	9.12	9.00

this is exactly the time when many investors lose heart and waver. Dollar-cost averaging is discipline; give that up and DCA won't work for you.

2. Lack of a sell discipline, or knowing when to get out of the market, could hurt your investment program if you need money when the market is down. Suppose you use DCA to build a college fund for your children. If the market is down during the September when your first child is due to register at college, you could lose some or all of the benefit of a DCA program. Some financial planners recommend switching out of a DCA program three to five years ahead of retirement when the market appears near a high or has been advancing for several months or more. Protecting the gains from a low average cost per share may call for switching to a MMF or a bond fund for income ahead of retirement.

Value-cost Averaging

Value-cost averaging (VCA) is a variation of dollar-cost averaging that works better than DCA but is more complex. Instead of investing a specific number of dollars on a regular schedule, such as the $100 every second Tuesday, VCA calls for increasing the value of your mutual fund portfolio by a fixed amount each period. Note the values in Table 12C. In this example, $100 buys 9.208 shares at the beginning.

At the second week, the net asset value (NAV) has dropped to $10.45, and the number of shares needed for the portfolio value to reach the total $200 at the $10.45 price

totals 19.139 shares. However, since 9.208 shares were bought with the first $100, the number of new shares needed to reach the new investment total of $200 is 9.931 shares. At $10.45 per share, the amount invested is $103.78 ($10.45 × 9.931). This amount would be transferred from your associated MMF. Note the different amount of new cash called for at each new investment point. This is where VCA gets complicated.

You will note from the details of each transaction in Table 12C that, as the price of shares declines, you must put up more than $100 to maintain the pace of increasing nominal portfolio value by $100 each period. As the value of previous purchases declines, you must put up more money to compensate for the lower NAV share prices. This discipline increases the amount of money you invest during downtrending markets. To maintain the value, the VCA system calls for selling shares at times—exactly what you should be doing—buying low and selling high.

Results of VCA are impressive compared to DCA. At the end of 26 weeks the value of your portfolio using VCA gained $617.68, or 31.2 percent ($2,600 − $1,982.32 ÷ $1,982.32). DCA using identical share prices over 26 periods produced a 26.2 percent gain and a dollar increase of $681.38, as summarized in Table 12D on page 199. The difference in dollar gain between DCA and VCA represents the substantial difference in the number of dollars invested. If $2,600 had been committed at the beginning, $617.68 would remain in the associated MMF after 26 periods with VCA, and the interest earned would increase total gain for the VCA program. Additional interest in MMFs associated with

TABLE 12C	VALUE-COST AVERAGING			
Cumulative Investments (Portfolio Value)	Mutual Fund NAV	Shares Owned	Shares Bought	Amount to Invest
$100	10.86	9.208	9.208	$100.00
$200	10.45	19.139	9.931	$103.78
$300	10.18	29.470	10.331	$105.17
$400	9.60	41.667	12.197	$117.09
$500	9.55	52.356	10.689	$102.08
$600	8.96	66.964	14.608	$130.89
$700	9.14	76.586	9.622	$87.95
$800	8.80	90.909	14.323	$126.04
$900	8.60	104.651	13.742	$118.18
$1,000	7.98	125.313	20.662	$164.88
$1,100	7.84	140.306	14.993	$117.54
$1,200	7.60	157.895	17.589	$133.67
$1,300	8.20	158.537	0.642	$5.26
$1,400	8.20	170.732	12.195	$100.00
$1,500	8.32	180.288	9.557	$79.51
$1,600	7.84	204.082	23.793	$186.54
$1,700	8.16	208.333	4.252	$34.69
$1,800	8.28	217.391	9.058	$75.00
$1,900	8.38	226.730	9.339	$78.26
$2,000	8.82	226.757	0.027	$0.24
$2,100	9.14	229.759	3.002	$27.44
$2,200	9.60	229.167	−0.593	($5.69)
$2,300	9.95	231.156	1.989	$19.79
$2,400	10.30	233.010	1.854	$19.10
$2,500	10.94	228.519	−4.491	($49.13)
$2,600	11.36	228.873	0.354	$4.02
Total investment				$1,982.32
Average Cost per Share				$8.66

DCA and VCA would also accrue during the program but is not calculated. If the total $2,600 had been invested at the initial share price of $10.86 and left for 26 weeks before selling at $11.36, the gain would have been 4.60 percent.

Complexity arises with VCA because the amount you invest each period changes. You must first calculate each periodic investment amount, and then buy the shares on the regular day. A mutual fund will not draft your bank for a variable amount each period, so you must continue to be actively involved. The simplest way of continuing a VCA program is to set up part of your savings in a fund family's MMF, as noted earlier. On the investment day, call the fund and request the specific amount you calculated be transferred. The process is simple, but you must do it as regularly as

TABLE 12D	DCA versus VCA	
	DCA	VCA
Shares bought	288.854	228.873
Average cost	9.00	8.66
Total value	$3,281.38	$2,600.00
Amount invested	$2,600.00	$1,982.32
$ Gain/(Loss)	$681.38	$617.68
% Gain/(Loss)	26.21	31.16

If $2,600 had been invested initially at $10.86 per share and held for 26 weeks without selling at $11.36, gain would be 4.60 percent.

$$\frac{(11.36 - 10.86)}{10.86} = 4.60\%$$

the sun rises in order for the program to be successful.

VCA suffers the same lack of a sell discipline as DCA. Take similar precautions to avoid having to cash out when the market is down.

Conclusion

Few activities around the world occupy so many bright and analytical minds as how to earn more or gain more from one's investments. Basic tools are available—fundamental analysis, technical analysis, and mechanical systems—all approaches attract hosts of disciples. Risk management is a key ingredient in any successful investing program. You manage stock risk through diversification, market risk through market timing, and event risk through selection of assets. Regardless of the tools you elect to use in helping manage your investments, be patient. The wisdom derived from the tale of the tortoise and the hare applies to investing; slow steady progress with risk-controlled investments does better than high-risk attempts at quick profits. Finally, disciplined investing beats emotional investing. If you learn discipline, you will be a better investor.

CHAPTER THIRTEEN

Six Steps to Successful Investing

KEY TERMS FOR THIS CHAPTER

tax-deferred
annuitized
withdrawals
straight life annuity
10-year-certain annuity
capital spending
interest-free loan
10-year reversionary trust

risk tolerance
recreational investor
stock risk
market risk
event risk
asset allocation
price reversal
recovery period

While knowing about Wall Street and how it works can be helpful, know-how alone does not guarantee investment success. A planned program of investment can maximize your chances of winning at the investment game. Generally, successful investors tend to be serious, conservative, and involved. While there is no guarantee—ever—the following six-step program can be expected to produce positive investment results over a long term—at least five years.

Define Objectives

To say simply, "I want to make as much money as possible," isn't enough. You need to think through the options and decide why you wish to invest. What are your goals for spending the money once you get it? Are you investing for your retirement? To accumulate cash to pay for university educations for your children? To finance the start of your own small business? While these are common objectives, they differ in their time and cash commitments, and thus require different implementation strategies.

Retirement

How you invest for retirement depends on several variables: when you start, which in turn governs how long you have to accumulate assets; whether income from your retirement assets will supplement a pension and Social Security income or substitute for a pension; your age when you expect to retire—65, 62, or earlier; how quickly your savings grow (that is, how much of a return you expect from assets); and whether you expect to spend capital as well as income from your retirement fund. Let's look at each of these parameters in turn to see how they impact your investment plans.

When to start. An early start is critical if you expect to collect a substantial pool of assets for retirement. For example, you may invest up to $2,000 in an Individual Retirement Account (IRA) each year. Whether the $2,000 per year is tax deductible or not is less critical than the tax deferral of all income.

For a graphic example of how time affects an IRA, refer to Table 13A. Three options are compared, starting at ages 30, 40, and 50. Each of the three options requires an investment of $2,000 per year for 15 years, for a total investment of $30,000. Each $2,000 investment grows at an average 10 percent rate compounded annually. If you begin at age 30, then by age 65 the 15 investments of $2,000 each on successive years total $517,273. If you wait until age 40 before beginning the 15-year program, the $2,000 invested each year for 15 successive years will grow over 25 years to $199,431 at age 65. Waiting to begin a 16-year program at age 50 produces a minimal $79,089 at age 65. The only difference between the programs is the time your money works for you. Compound interest is interest paid on interest, and the longer it has to work, the more powerful it is.

While money deposited in an IRA compounds at **tax-deferred** rates, all of the money is taxable when withdrawn unless the original $30,000 was from after-tax money. Money in an IRA may not be withdrawn without penalty before age 59½ except under an **annuitized** program. You must begin withdrawing IRA proceeds in the year you reach 70½ and yearly **withdrawals** must be programmed to exhaust the total amount within your life expectancy or the life expectancy of you and your spouse or other person. Withdrawal rules permit refiguring the minimum withdrawal rate at the beginning of each year to avoid running out of money.

Income from assets. Retirement plans, like the three-legged stool, typically depend on three supports:

1. Social Security (SS) credits accrue during one's working lifetime. At age 62 you become eligible for reduced SS benefits; full benefits are not available until age 65. Even with full coverage, SS provides only subsistence benefits. It is not intended to provide enough cash to support what most of us would consider to be an acceptable lifestyle.

2. Only about half of the workers in industry and government are eligible for pension income. If the organization you work for or the labor group you are a member of does not support a pension or profit-sharing program, you must replace that leg of your retirement program with personal savings.

3. Income from accumulated assets may supplement SS and pension benefits. Deferred compensation or a personal pension plan (such as a Keogh plan for

TABLE 13A   EFFECT OF TIME VALUE OF IRA

Begin Age	Amount Con-tributed	Total	Annual Earn-ings*	Year-end Total	Amount Con-tributed	Total	Annual Earn-ings*	Year-end Total	Amount Con-tributed	Total	Annual Earn-ings*	Year-end Total
30	$2,000	$2,000	$200	$2,200								
31	$2,000	$4,200	$420	$4,620								
32	$2,000	$6,620	$662	$7,282								
33	$2,000	$9,282	$928	$10,210								
34	$2,000	$12,210	$1,221	$13,431								
35	$2,000	$15,431	$1,543	$16,974								
36	$2,000	$18,974	$1,897	$20,872								
37	$2,000	$22,872	$2,287	$25,159								
38	$2,000	$27,159	$2,716	$29,875								
39	$2,000	$31,875	$3,187	$35,062								
40	$2,000	$37,062	$3,706	$40,769	$2,000	$2,000	$200	$2,200				
41	$2,000	$42,769	$4,277	$47,045	$2,000	$4,200	$420	$4,620				
42	$2,000	$49,045	$4,905	$53,950	$2,000	$6,620	$662	$7,282				
43	$2,000	$55,950	$5,595	$61,545	$2,000	$9,282	$928	$10,210				
44	$2,000	$63,545	$6,354	$69,899	$2,000	$12,210	$1,221	$13,431				
45		$69,899	$6,990	$76,889	$2,000	$15,431	$1,543	$16,974				
46		$76,889	$7,689	$84,578	$2,000	$18,974	$1,897	$20,872				
47		$84,578	$8,458	$93,036	$2,000	$22,872	$2,287	$25,159				

Age											
48	$93,036	$9,304	$102,340	$2,000	$27,159	$2,746	$29,875				
49	$102,340	$10,234	$112,474	$2,000	$31,875	$3,187	$35,062				
50	$112,574	$11,257	$123,831	$2,000	$37,062	$3,706	$40,769	$2,000	$2,000	$200	$2,200
51	$123,831	$12,383	$136,214	$2,000	$42,769	$4,277	$47,045	$2,000	$4,200	$420	$4,620
52	$136,214	$13,621	$149,836	$2,000	$49,045	$4,905	$53,950	$2,000	$6,620	$662	$7,282
53	$149,836	$14,984	$164,819	$2,000	$55,950	$5,595	$61,545	$2,000	$9,282	$928	$10,210
54	$164,819	$16,482	$181,301	$2,000	$63,545	$6,354	$69,899	$2,000	$12,210	$1,221	$13,431
55	$181,301	$18,130	$199,431		$69,899	$6,990	$76,889	$2,000	$15,431	$1,543	$16,974
56	$199,431	$19,943	$219,374		$76,889	$7,689	$84,578	$2,000	$18,974	$1,897	$20,872
57	$219,374	$21,937	$241,312		$84,578	$8,458	$93,036	$2,000	$22,872	$2,287	$25,159
58	$241,312	$24,131	$265,443		$93,036	$9,304	$102,340	$2,000	$27,159	$2,716	$29,875
59	$265,443	$26,544	$291,987		$102,340	$10,234	$112,574	$2,000	$31,875	$3,187	$35,062
60	$291,987	$29,199	$321,186		$112,574	$11,257	$123,831	$2,000	$37,062	$3,706	$40,769
61	$321,186	$32,119	$353,305		$123,831	$12,383	$136,214	$2,000	$42,769	$4,277	$47,045
62	$353,305	$35,330	$388,635		$136,214	$13,621	$149,836	$2,000	$49,045	$4,905	$53,950
63	$388,635	$38,864	$427,499		$149,836	$14,984	$164,819	$2,000	$55,950	$5,595	$61,545
64	$427,499	$42,750	$470,249		$164,819	$16,482	$181,301	$2,000	$63,545	$6,354	$69,899
65	$470,249	$47,025	$517,273		$181,301	$18,130	$199,431	$2,000	$71,899	$7,190	$79,089
Total accumulation	$470,249		$517,273				$199,431				$79,089

*At 10 percent annually

This table illustrates the dramatic benefits of beginning an IRA at an early age. Over a 15-year period of investment, an IRA begun at age 30 will be worth two and a half times that of an IRA started at age 40, and more than six times that of an IRA started at age 50.

self-employed persons, 401(k) joint contribution plan between you and your employer, 403(b) plan available to employees of nonprofit or government organizations), and IRAs help by deferring taxes during accumulation periods. Without a pension your personal savings and investment program must provide two of the three supports.

Age at retirement. How long you work directly affects financing options for retirement. Early retirement impacts your retirement planning two ways. First, you may receive a smaller pension; and second, you must stretch your resources over a longer period. If life expectancy is 80 and you retire at 55, your pension (possibly reduced as much as 35 percent to 40 percent) and income from invested assets must carry you to at least age 62, the age when minimum SS benefits are available. At 62, SS benefits will be 80 percent of the level you would receive at age 65. If you continue working after 65 and postpone receipt of SS benefits, their value increases 3 percent per year up to age 70. Assets deferred from taxes in an IRA, Keogh plan, deferred compensation arrangement, 401(k), or 403(b) plan may continue to compound to age 70½ before withdrawals must begin. Early retirement, unless greatly enhanced by a munificent golden handshake, can put considerable pressure on your financial resources.

Risk versus earnings. Earnings from investments accumulated for retirement may earn considerably different rates of return depending on how they are invested. Generally, the higher the risk, the higher the expected return. Tables 13B and

13C show how different average rates of growth affect the bottom line for the IRA program beginning at age 30. If your earnings average 8 percent over the 35 years, expect a total accumulation of $295,227. If earnings average 12 percent, the total accumulation at age 65 climbs to $902,192. Similar differences would affect IRA programs beginning at ages 40 and 50.

The growth figures noted in Table 13A assume an average rate of 10 percent. This is close to the 10.3 percent compound rate of growth for stocks over the past 65 years from the beginning of 1925 through the end of 1989, according to results from Ibbotson Associates (see Resources). Other investments and other strategies may produce higher compound rates of return, possibly with greater risks.

A higher risk, while promising greater earnings, also entails greater possible losses. If you elect to avoid all risks, keeping your money in bank certificates of deposit (CDs) will possibly earn an average of 6 percent or 7 percent, depending on how the government manages its finances. Considering federal income taxes only, a 28 percent tax rate reduces the 7 percent return to 5.04 percent. Deduct the loss for inflation of 5 percent or thereabouts, and your investment barely breaks even.

Suppose you elect to invest in something only a bit riskier, such as Government National Mortgage Association (GNMA) certificates. You could probably earn an 8 percent return, or 1 percent more than an after-tax, after-inflation breakeven (ATAI) 7 percent. Increasing your return to 9 percent by investing in growth-income mutual funds would double your ATAI return.

TABLE 13B	EFFECTS OF DIFFERENT INTEREST RATES ON EARNINGS				TABLE 13C	EFFECT OF DIFFERENT INTEREST RATES ON EARNINGS		
Age	Amount Invested	Total	Interest Earned*	Year-end Total	Age	Amount Invested	Total	Interest Earned*	Year-end Total
30	$2,000	$2,000	$240	$2,240	30	$2,000	$2,000	$160	$2,160
31	$2,000	$4,240	$509	$4,749	31	$2,000	$4,160	$333	$4,493
32	$2,000	$6,749	$810	$7,559	32	$2,000	$6,493	$519	$7,012
33	$2,000	$9,559	$1,147	$10,706	33	$2,000	$9,012	$721	$9,733
34	$2,000	$12,706	$1,525	$14,230	34	$2,000	$11,733	$939	$12,672
35	$2,000	$16,230	$1,948	$18,178	35	$2,000	$14,672	$1,174	$15,846
36	$2,000	$20,178	$2,421	$22,599	36	$2,000	$17,846	$1,428	$19,273
37	$2,000	$24,599	$2,952	$27,551	37	$2,000	$21,273	$1,702	$22,975
38	$2,000	$29,551	$3,546	$33,097	38	$2,000	$24,975	$1,998	$26,973
39	$2,000	$35,097	$4,212	$39,309	39	$2,000	$28,973	$2,318	$31,291
40	$2,000	$41,309	$4,957	$46,266	40	$2,000	$33,291	$2,663	$35,954
41	$2,000	$48,266	$5,792	$54,058	41	$2,000	$37,954	$3,036	$40,991
42	$2,000	$56,058	$6,727	$62,785	42	$2,000	$42,991	$3,439	$46,430
43	$2,000	$64,785	$7,774	$72,559	43	$2,000	$48,430	$3,874	$52,304
44	$2,000	$74,559	$8,947	$83,507	44	$2,000	$54,304	$4,344	$58,649
45		$83,507	$10,021	$93,527	45		$58,649	$4,692	$63,340
46		$93,527	$11,223	$104,751	46		$63,340	$5,067	$68,408
47		$104,751	$12,570	$117,321	47		$68,408	$5,473	$73,880
48		$117,321	$14,078	$131,399	48		$73,880	$5,910	$79,791
49		$131,399	$15,768	$147,167	49		$79,791	$6,383	$86,174
50		$147,167	$17,660	$164,827	50		$86,174	$6,894	$93,068
51		$164,827	$19,779	$184,606	51		$93,068	$7,445	$100,513
52		$184,606	$22,153	$206,759	52		$100,513	$8,041	$108,554
53		$206,759	$24,811	$231,570	53		$108,554	$8,684	$117,239
54		$231,570	$27,788	$259,359	54		$117,239	$9,379	$126,618
55		$259,359	$31,123	$290,482	55		$126,618	$10,129	$136,747
56		$290,482	$34,858	$325,340	56		$136,747	$10,940	$147,687
57		$325,340	$39,041	$364,380	57		$147,687	$11,815	$159,502
58		$364,380	$43,726	$408,106	58		$159,502	$12,760	$172,262
59		$408,106	$48,973	$457,079	59		$172,262	$13,781	$186,043
60		$457,079	$54,849	$511,928	60		$186,043	$14,883	$200,927
61		$511,928	$61,431	$573,359	61		$200,927	$16,074	$217,001
62		$573,359	$68,803	$642,163	62		$217,001	$17,360	$234,361
63		$642,163	$77,060	$719,222	63		$234,361	$18,749	$253,110
64		$719,222	$86,307	$805,529	64		$253,110	$20,249	$273,358
65		$805,529	$96,663	$902,192	65		$273,358	$21,869	$295,227

* At 12%   * At 8% Annually

A 9 percent return less 7 percent leaves a 2 percent ATAI return.

Spending capital. Prudent financial planning calls for conservation of capital as a prime objective in retirement. If you lose capital after retiring, you can no longer replace it by working harder, longer, or smarter. Once you lose capital in retirement, it may be lost forever—a problem if leaving an estate for heirs is one of your priorities. Thus, you need to balance the need for income against the risk of capital loss.

Still, you may choose to improve your golden years by judiciously spending portions of your capital. If so, you can choose one of two routes to avoid running out of money.

1. Buy an annuity from an insurance company. Annuities come in various sizes and shapes. **A straight life annuity,** for example, pays a specific amount each month for as long as you live. If you should die within a few months, the insurance company pockets the remainder of your invested cash. A **10-year-certain annuity** guarantees to pay you or your beneficiaries a specific amount each month for a minimum of 10 years or for as long as you live. A 10-year-certain annuity will pay less per month than a straight annuity based on the same investment. Other options are also available.

   Two variables affect the amount you receive each month from an annuity, regardless of which plan you accept: your age and how much money you invest in the annuity. The older you are, the fewer years the insurance company

figures it will be obligated to pay benefits; so, monthly amounts can be higher. If you invest $200,000 in an annuity, monthly amounts will be twice as high as if you invested only $100,000.

Annuities have two weaknesses. First, once you start receiving the fixed amount each month, regardless of the option, there is no turning back. You are locked into that amount for life. Second, fixed monthly amounts have no built-in protection to counter the effects of inflation.

2. Manage your own **capital spending** program. You may decide to spend half, or some other part, of your asset base when you begin retirement. Computer-generated charts are available to tell you how much of your capital can be spent each month without running out of money. For example, you may decide when you retire at age 65 to spend half of your capital over a 20-year period. The amount you can spend each month for 20 years depends on the earning rate of your assets and the size of your asset base. Suppose you begin with $100,000. If those assets earn an average of 10 percent each year, you could withdraw $937 each month for 240 months, or 20 years, before the assets would be gone. If you spent only the 10 percent interest income, you would be limited to $833 per month ($100,000 × .10 = $10,000 ÷ 12 = $833.33 per month). Both figures are before taxes. (A complete chart that covers withdrawal periods from 1 through 50 years by year and effective yields on assets from 5 percent through 25 percent is available from Capital Withdrawal Charts. See Resources.)

Running your own capital spending program, rather than buying an annuity, could be advantageous for two reasons. First, you retain access to your capital. If an emergency should arise, such as a medical crisis, you could withdraw more funds than the usual monthly rate. Second, if you should die before the projected period, any capital left over remains in your estate.

Paying for College

Accumulating cash for college is a common goal for parents. At the same time that college expenses are mounting at annual rates higher than inflation, the number of options available to parents is shrinking. Loans to finance college educations are more difficult to get, and the rates of interest on student loans are rising as subsidies decline. More and more graduates are finding that paying off college loans is a heavy burden for years after graduation.

Changes in the tax laws have complicated saving for college. Until a few years ago, parents could shift assets to minors either with an **interest-free loan** or by setting up a **10-year reversionary trust** (Clifford trust). Children could invest the transferred assets and pay little or no taxes on the income. In the late 1980s, however, interest-free loans were outlawed and 10-year reversionary trusts were severely restricted by tax code revisions. Only $500 of unearned income (income from investments) for minors under 14 is tax-free; the next $500 is taxed at their personal rate, currently 15 percent. Any unearned income exceeding $1,000 is taxed at the parents' highest marginal income tax rate. Af-

ter age 14, minors pay taxes on all taxable income at the same rates as single adults.

Investment strategies for accumulating cash for college differ markedly from those aimed at building a resource base for retirement income because time is limited. Some of the strategies for investing to accumulate savings for college are the same as those to achieve short-range objectives or specific goals.

Saving for a Specific Goal

Accumulating cash for a specific goal, such as start-up financing for your own small business, a year's sabbatical, or a boat to sail around the world, involves two tasks: spending less of your current income and investing savings for growth. These limited objectives differ from saving and investing for retirement because periods are shorter and you need the cash by some specific date. If you would like to start your new business three years from now, for example, compounding of investment returns has little time to work. If you invest savings in an aggressive growth stock mutual fund, a cyclic downturn could leave you with less than you started with just when you need the cash. Accumulating cash to pay for college can be an intermediate-term goal if you start when the child is born.

Approach investing the cash you save to achieve short-term goals by either sticking with income-producing investments or buying stock mutual funds that practice defensive strategies.

1. Investments with a high rate of return include intermediate-term bond funds,

those that invest in government or corporate bonds with 3- to 10-year maturities, and GNMA no-load mutual funds. These income-producing investments are safer than stock funds and avoid the problem of needing to withdraw cash when the market may be in the doldrums.

2. A growing number of mutual funds practice a form of value investing that professionals call internal market timing. These funds select stocks for their portfolios on the basis of value. When the general market is depressed, many stocks are available at attractive prices. The portfolio manager selectively adds these stocks to the portfolio at bargain prices. When the market rises and appears to be near a top for the cycle, stocks in the portfolio will be selling at much higher prices and are no longer good values so the stocks are sold. If good values in stocks are not available, as they typically are not at market tops, the portfolio manager leaves a major portion of the assets in money market funds or U.S. Treasury bills (T-bills). A mutual fund that practices similar defensive strategies is unlikely to be badly depressed at any time you might need the cash.

Assess Risk Tolerance

Assessing your tolerance to risks is important because it affects any investment strategy you might adopt. Few guidelines are available to help you define the level of risk you can live with and remain free of stress. Here are a few ideas for helping you assess where you fit in on the scale of **risk tolerance.**

● Age makes a difference. People from their mid-20s to mid-40s tend to be more tolerant of risks. If a young person buys a volatile stock, he or she may not worry about a decline in price. Time may bring the price back, and young people have time. Further, if they lose, they still have time to work to replace losses.

Some young people may even enjoy the thrill of investing at the edge, of taking extra risks in search of the adrenaline surge that comes with winning. They may seek out the risky investment as an adventure. These risk-taking speculators are sometimes called **recreational investors.** They may play in the commodities, futures, or options arenas for kicks and use money as a means of keeping score.

Older and presumably wiser investors tend to shun risks. They may have found, as statistics bear out, that conservative investment programs tend to produce better results over time than riskier strategies. Investors approaching retirement recognize that preservation of capital is as important as return on capital. People actually in retirement tend to become even more risk averse, as they can no longer replace lost capital with working income.

● Gender affects tolerance to risks. Women generally are more risk averse than men. Brokers and financial planners report that women are willing to accept lower returns if such actions mean avoiding losses. While this strategy has merit, concentration of assets in low-return investments limits the potential for building capital. About $450 billion remains invested in bank savings accounts earning only $4\frac{1}{4}$ percent to $5\frac{1}{4}$ percent because owners believe these accounts are insured against losses.

● Home environment, workplace influences, and peer contacts make a difference. If you grew up with parents who were overly risk averse (who hesitated to cross the street if a car was in sight, for example), then you were conditioned to avoid risks. Risk conditioning can be a form of behavior modification either way—you can learn to accept risks easily or avoid them at all costs.

Assessing risk tolerance requires more than a generalized statement of your feelings, and—make no mistake—risk tolerance involves you emotionally rather than intellectually. The gut-wrenching reaction to a loss is totally emotional.

You can assess your risk tolerance level on your own, as shown in the box on page 210. In this assessment, you state your reaction to various investments based on your evaluation of the risks involved. Your bank savings account, for example, is totally liquid; you can withdraw money any day the bank is open with no loss and without affecting the level of interest rates. Bank savings accounts are guaranteed by the Federal Deposit Insurance Corporation (FDIC). Mark your risk assessment of each investment on a scale of 0 to 10. A total score is meaningless, but you might want to limit your investments to those opportunities you marked at 5 or less.

Choosing Securities

The choices you make when implementing your investment program relate to your objectives, your risk tolerance, whether you will be making the decisions yourself or allowing a money manager or broker to pick investments, and how closely you expect to monitor performance and change course.

Costs

The least expensive securities are likely to be no-load mutual funds or U.S. Treasury bills, notes, and bonds purchased directly from a Federal Reserve Bank or a branch. No security is totally cost free, however; when you buy mutual funds, individual stocks, or bonds from a broker, the commission you pay is compensation for his expertise and his time involved in buying or selling securities for you. In addition to helping you decide where and how to invest, a broker takes care of the paperwork associated with transactions. For many types of investing, such as buying shares of companies in the market, you need a broker's help.

If you elect to invest in no-load mutual funds, you assume the tasks you would otherwise pay a broker to do for you. To invest in no-load mutual funds you must deal directly with the fund organization, thereby eliminating the middleman. You will need to research the various funds to study their objectives and assess performance records. You must find the telephone number or address of a mutual fund that interests you and request a prospectus and application. Thus, you have a choice— pay a broker or spend your own time. Either is a cost.

A course elected by many savvy investors is to spend time deciding on a course of action and then seek out one or more newsletters with information on the per-

RISK ASSESSMENT PROFILE

How do you feel about the risks of the following investment instruments?

On the graphic scale to the right of each investment instrument indicate how risky you perceive each to be. Circle NF if you are not familiar with the instrument.

Instrument		Lowest Risk					Highest Risk
		0	2	4	6	8	10
Bank savings account	NF						
Credit union shares	NF						
Bank CDs	NF						
S&L CDs	NF						
Money market mutual fund	NF						
U.S. Treasury bill	NF						
Corporate bond	NF						
Municipal bond	NF						
Mutual fund—stock	NF						
Mutual fund—bond	NF						
Mutual fund—tax-free	NF						
Common stock shares	NF						
Tax-deferred annuity	NF						
Real estate	NF						
Limited partnership	NF						
Options, listed	NF						
Commodities	NF						
Futures, contracts	NF						
Collectibles	NF						

formance of mutual funds—load and no-load. (See Resources for a selected list of mutual fund newsletters.) A yearly subscription to a newsletter may range from $100 to $250, but you can compare that cost to the commission on a block of load mutual fund shares. If the load is 6½ percent, the commission on a $5,000 investment would be $325. Commissions range up to 8½ percent on some stock mutual funds.

Buying U.S. Treasury securities directly from the Federal Reserve Board (the Fed) is limited to original issue bills, notes, and bonds. If you wish to buy bills, notes, or bonds on the secondary market—that is, after issuance and before maturity—you must buy them through a broker who will charge a commission. Notices of forthcoming issues of treasury notes and bonds appear about two weeks ahead of issue dates in *The Wall Street Journal* and the business sections of many metropolitan newspapers. You may also ask the Fed that serves your area about future issues. Once you purchase treasury bills or notes, you can roll them over at maturity into new issues by completing a form the Fed sends you. Treasury bills and notes are kept in data entry format; you no longer receive actual certificates; instead you receive a computer confirmation. Treasury bonds are issued in certificate form due to their long-term maturity.

Tailoring Investments to Your Objectives

The securities you choose need to be tailored to meet your objectives. The following are suggestions only, as different investors will follow varied routes to reach their objectives.

Retirement. Building a retirement fund calls for securities that will grow at rates faster than inflation. A goal of many financial planners is to invest for a total rate of return equal to 1 percent to 3 percent more than inflation after taxes. Growth stocks and growth stock mutual funds are the most likely candidates for long-term growth.

Along with returns you must consider three risks:

• **Stock risk** is the chance you may pick a bum stock. If you pick XYZ Corporation and the stock turns out to be a loser, your investment program takes a direct hit. The time-honored method of minimizing stock risk is diversification. If you are working with $500,000 or more of investable funds, you can buy enough round lots of different stocks to achieve reasonable diversification. Then, if one of your stocks turns sour, your portfolio loses only a small percentage of its value. With fewer dollars to invest, mutual funds offer the quickest and least expensive method of achieving instant diversification. When you buy one share of a mutual fund, you buy small pieces of as few as 20 companies and as many as 1,500 depending on the size and investment policies of the funds. A prudent suggestion would be that unless you have at least $500,000 to invest, stick with mutual funds, preferably no-loads.

• **Market risk** is the second risk that concerns prudent investors. Regardless of how carefully you may pick an individual stock or mutual fund, a decline in the overall market will probably depress its value. Just as a rising tide lifts all ships, an ebbing tide lowers all ships. About 70 percent of the direction of price changes results from market action; the remaining 30 percent is due to the individual stock or mutual fund. The answer, imperfect as it may be at times, to market risk is some form of market timing. A good market timing program will get you out of downtrending markets and keep you in uptrending markets. Market timing also works better with mutual funds than with individual stocks. Sticking with no-load mutual funds reduces the cost of moving into and out of funds according to timing signals.

• **Event risk** is a third risk. The assassination of President Kennedy, President Eisenhower's heart attack, the invasion of Kuwait by Iraqi forces, and similar earth-shaking events can send markets crashing worldwide. Event risks can be troubling because they strike with little advance warning. Your defense against event risk is a portfolio diversified into different kinds of securities. This is called an **asset allocation** strategy. A portfolio assembled to prosper in an imperfect world would contain gold bullion, stocks, bonds, T-bills, and Swiss francs. Theoretically, if forces in the world hammer stocks, then the gold and Swiss francs will prosper and compensate for the stock losses. The quantity of each type of investment you might have in such a portfolio is subject to argument. Mutual funds based on asset allocations have done well at times and lagged the market at other times.

Portfolio make-up may depend on how far you are from retirement. If you are 30 to 35 years from retirement, your best opportunity for building assets is with common stocks and stock funds. At younger ages you could consider structuring your portfolio to include 60 percent to 70 percent in growth stocks, 20 percent to 30 percent in bonds, and 10 percent in money market mutual funds (cash). As you approach retirement, gradually reduce the proportion of growth stocks by switching more funds into bonds or balanced mutual funds. Also called all-season funds, balanced funds include a mix of income-producing stocks and bonds to increase income and minimize volatility. When you get to within five years of retirement, watch the market closely. You want to avoid retiring at a time when the market is in a down cycle. Rather than risk a loss of portfolio value within the five-year period ahead of retirement, move your funds out of stocks and into balanced funds or money market funds (MMFs). You could retain as much as 40 percent of your portfolio in balanced funds.

Building a college fund. Saving and investing to build a college fund calls for a different approach. You may elect to give your minor children money in a Uniform Gifts to Minors Act (UGMA) trust. Minors may not own stocks and mutual funds in their own names; UGMA trusts permit a trustee or custodian, to manage the funds for a minor. A parent may act as trustee, but once money is put into the trust, it belongs irrevocably to the minor. At maturity, which may be at 18 or 21 in different states, the minor owns the UGMA assets and may do with them as he or she wishes. Some parents prefer to keep money in their own names, paying taxes on earnings at their marginal rate, to avoid giving up control.

Within a UGMA trust, investments differ according to the child's age. Since earnings over $1,000 per year could be taxed at the parents' marginal rate until the child reaches 14, investments may be keyed to growth with minimum income while a child is young. Even growth mutual funds trade internally, and in an uptrending market may generate capital gains, which are taxed at a maximum 28 percent rate. Dividends could be taxed at the parents' marginal rate up to 31 percent.

When the child reaches age 14, investments can be switched to earn high income and to avoid a loss of share value if the market turns down. High-income mutual funds tend to hold their value better than growth funds in a down market. Your goal should be to end up with as much cash as possible by registration time. A part of the UGMA portfolio may logically be in a MMF where the capital value of shares remains at $1 per share.

Series EE Savings Bonds (EE-bonds) offer two opportunities for financing children's education.

1. Parents may buy EE-bonds in their own names (not the child's name) and defer interest as usual. After a minimum of five years, the EE-bonds may be cashed and the principal, plus accrued interest, may be used to pay tuition and fees directly to the college. Under these specific conditions, the interest earned on the EE-bonds is tax-free at the federal level. All savings bond interest is free of state income taxes. Some family income limits apply and may reduce the advantages of this plan. Only EE-bonds purchased after December 31, 1989, qualify.
2. Instead of investing in growth stocks or mutual funds, cash may be used to buy EE-bonds in the child's name with a parent as beneficiary. Earnings are de-

ferred until the child reaches 14. EE-bonds could then be redeemed, taxes paid on the interest, and the remainder invested for asset buildup over four years prior to college registration. Taxes would be payable on the accrued interest at the child's rate after age 14.

Investing for a short-term goal. Investing for some short-term goal (such as starting your own business, taking a sabbatical, engaging in an educational experience, or embarking on a world-girdling trip) calls for yet other types of securities. If the time is not critical, growth stocks or growth mutual funds will probably create assets faster than fixed-income securities. Cashing out securities when their value is high could be timed to coincide with the beginning of your venture.

If a specific time is critical, then picking securities with low volatility, such as bond funds or even MMFs, could be the best choice.

Develop a Timing Plan

Looking at investment alternatives from time to time could prove a prudent course for building assets. Different strategies work better in different markets. During strong uptrending markets, buy-and-hold strategies may work better than a timing system. In other markets, a plan for avoiding or minimizing losses using market timing could protect your assets and leave you with a stronger base on which to build. In some markets, nothing appears to work.

Three major systems for timing offer the investor a choice of strategies. They include price reversal, forecasting, and relative strength.

Price reversal, or trend-following, systems depend mainly on moving averages to provide signals for moving into or out of the market. Multiple moving averages may be combined for confirmation of these signals. Your easiest option for using a timing system is to follow the signals from a market timer published in a newsletter or given by telephone hot line. Two prominent timing newsletters are the *Telephone Switch Newsletter* and *The Fund Exchange.* (See Resources for addresses of these and other market timing newsletters.) You can also compute your own moving averages with the help of a computer (see Chapter 12 for an in-depth discussion of moving averages). Once the format has been set, the addition of weekly, biweekly, or monthly data requires only a few minutes for each update. Although it is formidably technical, the definitive reference for building market timing systems is *Stock Market Trading Systems* by Gerald Appel and Fred Hitschler (see Resources).

Interest rate changes, rather than a moving average of mutual funds, are the keys to the Donoghue timing system. Signals appear in the *Donoghue's MoneyLetter* biweekly. MMF average interest rates are smoothed with a 25-week moving exponential average. An explanation of how the interest rate signal works and how a moving exponential average is computed are detailed in *The Donoghue Strategies* by William E. Donoghue with Robert Chapman Wood (see Resources).

Forecasting is another approach to looking for leads on where the market is headed. Forecasters may use a variety of indicators and analytical devices for predicting future market moves. Some gurus are better at it than others, but the record for forecasting has not been outstanding. Forecasting involves too many variables to be weighed with more than human judgmental accuracy that the strategy overwhelms guru capacity—so, inconsistent results. A key newsletter practicing forecasting is the *Mutual Fund Forecaster* (see Resources).

Relative strength is the key to a highly successful system for earning consistent profits with mutual funds. Using a relative strength system requires extensive data collection and analysis. A relative strength system collects data from as many as 600 mutual funds. Total return is the key and includes dividend and internal capital gains distributions plus changes in net asset value (NAV) for the most recent month, as well as the past 3, 6, and 12 months. Averaging these performances yields a score for each fund; you begin by investing in the fund with the top score. By remaining invested in the top fund until it drops below the fund with the fifth score, investors have earned more than 20 percent compounded annually. Using results published in a newsletter is almost mandatory because of the massive amount of data that can only be analyzed efficiently with a computer. One of the newsletters that analyzes the continuing performance records of more than 600 no-load mutual funds is *NoLoad Fund X* (see Resources).

Monitor Performance

Tracking or monitoring how your investments are performing calls for more than checking the closing prices of stocks or mutual funds when the mood strikes. On some regular basis—monthly or quarterly—check what has been happening to your stocks and mutual funds. At least once a year, at the end of the year, compute the total return for each of your stocks, bonds, and mutual funds as outlined in Chapter 11. Unless your bonds are listed, you will need to call your broker for a quote on their current value.

Absolute performance may not be enough. If your mutual funds gained 9 percent when the overall market—represented by the Standard & Poor's 500 Index (S&P 500)—grew 15 percent, you could rate your funds' performance as disappointing. But a 9 percent gain compared to the overall market gain of only 3 percent would encourage you to keep your money in the fund. At least once a year compare your securities with other measures of market activity, such as the S&P 500 and the Dow Jones Industrial Average (DJIA).

Changing Course

Just as few people today expect to continue with a single company or organization for their entire working lives, neither should you expect to stick with the same securities forever. Companies' fortunes ebb and flow as the public's tastes change: Managements mature and retire, products age and are replaced by new products, and world economies change. Few companies maintain a top financial position decade after decade. Short-term conditions vie with long-term changes to produce a need for changing your investments from time to time. The following conditions might indicate a change of course.

● Deteriorating performance of a company or mutual fund. This can be detected by monitoring your securities. When one or more of them fall behind, don't hesitate to change. A common fault among stock owners is that they fall in love with their stocks. They become accustomed to its ups and downs—when it is up they exult and when it is down they look forward to its recovery. A long-standing maxim on Wall Street is, "cut losses short and let profits ride."

When you review the performance of your securities and compare them to averages or indexes, decide unemotionally which losers to dump and which winners to keep. Problems develop with securities in the middle range for profits. Are they likely to improve or remain mired in mediocrity? Generally, if you can't decide, replace them with securities that appear more promising.

● Economic growth or recession. The economy affects some securities more than others. A company in a cyclical industry, such as steel or chemicals, will suffer more in a declining economy than a company that supplies food or energy. If the economy is emerging from a recession, growth stocks will likely outperform the stocks of companies furnishing basic products, such as food. Relating the performance of your stocks and mutual funds to the economy and where it appears headed can be a reason for changing your investments. Don't allow lethargy to trap you.

● Your age. Growing older can be a strong incentive to change course. Assuming higher risks when one is young has the potential for building a bigger asset base for achieving some goal, such as retirement. Faced with the prospect of financing a child's college education, a change from growth stocks or mutual funds to securities that promise more immediate income would appear reasonable. Later, in the **recovery period** (that period between the time when children clear college and you retire), changing direction toward building and holding onto more assets for retirement makes sense.

• Your level of affluence. If you are fortunate enough to acquire enough assets to be considered affluent, you may need to change investment strategies to defend earnings against taxes. At high marginal tax rates, tax shelters and tax-free municipal bonds can increase spendable returns, that is, after-tax dollars.

Tax effects may also call for a change in investment policy if you move from a no- or low-tax state to a high-tax state. U.S. Treasury securities, even EE- and HH- bonds, are free of state taxes. Gross earnings from stock or mutual fund investments might exceed the total returns from treasury securities, but avoiding a state tax could change the net return. Money market mutual funds that invest only in U.S. Treasury securities are exempt from state income taxes in nearly all states.

• Changing tax laws. A change in the tax laws could cause you to change the course of your investment strategies. Until 1986 capital gains taxes were only 40 percent of taxes levied on ordinary income. Since then, federal income taxes on ordinary income and capital gains are the same, except that federal income taxes on gains are capped at 28 percent. When those changes went into effect, prudent investors altered course to avoid high-risk adventures into limited partnerships and real estate and began investing in enterprises oriented to income and growth. If the tax laws should change radically in the future, investment strategies could be influenced again.

Conclusion

Solid investment results depend on eliminating emotion from the decision-making process. Beginning with clear goals, knowing one's tolerance for risk, and monitoring investment performance is a multi-step program that has served prudent investors for decades. Adopting a similar program with a full understanding of how the financial markets function can produce important benefits for you as well.

CHAPTER FOURTEEN

Money—The Common Denominator

KEY TERMS FOR THIS CHAPTER

barter
scale of value
inflation
money supply
M_1, M_2, M_3
monetary aggregates
reserves
reserve limits
monetizing

mint
velocity of money
Consumer Price Index
broker loan rate
prime rate
inflation bias
discount rate
federal funds rate

Money is one of those terms that need no definition; we know what money is. But let's define it anyway: Money is the coins that jingle in your pocket, the currency you carry around in a billfold or purse, and the balance in your checking account. Money is something that is immediately available, generally acceptable as a medium of exchange, easily recognized, difficult to counterfeit, uniform in quality, and easily calculated.

Since money is so essential to everything we do and directly affects so many of our decisions, you should understand how it is regulated and how those regulations affect saving and investing. Managing your money is equivalent to managing your life.

Three Roles of Money

Money plays three distinct roles in our lives and in the economy.

Money is a medium of exchange—it facilitates the exchange of goods and services. You have cash and you exchange it for a lunch, a bag of groceries, or whatever. As a medium of exchange the dollar is readily recognized and universally accepted in the United States. In a country outside the United States, the dollar is subject to the relative value of that country's money. If we did not have money, we would need to **barter**—a bushel of wheat for a replacement auto part, an hour's time behind a counter for lunch, and so on. Russia must barter in many of its out-of-country transactions because the ruble is not convertible; that is, the United States and other countries do not accept the ruble as a medium of exchange.

Money is a measure of value. When goods and services are priced in dollars, they are measured against each other in a dollar value system. A wheelbarrow, for example, carries a price, and that price may be equivalent to the price of a dinner in a restaurant. Both dollar figures represent positions on a **scale of value.** A man's suit priced at $450 is almost certainly better than a suit priced at $250. These two suits represent two points on a value scale where one appears better than another because of the price difference. Similar value scales exist for products and services as compared with other products and services. Salary and wage differences stated in dollars per hour measure variations in the worth of people's services, even if such measurements are inexact and subjective. We would live in a troubled world if there was no way of measuring the worth of one product against another or the value of services against products. Money serves that purpose, if not always perfectly.

Money is a store of value. A stash of cash, such as a balance in a savings account, represents a store, or cache, of purchasing power to be utilized at some future time. If money were a reliable store of value, then a specific sum, say $1,000, would buy the same bag of goods and services today as it did 10 years ago. That is not the case, as **inflation** continues to degrade the purchasing power of the dollar and other world currencies. Thus, of the three roles money plays, its role as a store of value is the least satisfactory. Gold, on the other hand, continues as a basic store of value that is little affected by inflation. An ounce of gold would buy about the same amount of bread today as it did in 1900. By comparison, a dollar today buys only a small fraction of the amount of bread it bought in 1900. Inflation is partially due to the increased number of dollars available today compared to the number of dollars in earlier times. The number of dollars available is recognized as the money supply.

Money Supply

The Federal Reserve System controls monetary policy in the United States, mainly through its regulation of the **money supply** and indirectly through the control of interest rates. Three levels of money supply are monitored and reported weekly.

1. Money narrowly defined is called M_1 and includes currency, coins, and demand deposits in commercial banks other than domestic interbank and U.S. government entities, not including cash items in the process of collection. Briefly, M_1 is quick money you can spend immediately.
2. A broader category is M_2, which includes all of M_1 plus money in savings accounts, certificates of deposit (CDs), deposits in money market mutual funds, and deposits in similar depositories where it cannot be used immediately.
3. More inclusive still is M_3 which includes both M_1 and M_2 plus financial instruments and capital of institutions

that cannot be readily converted for immediate spending.

All three of the Ms are referred to as **monetary aggregates,** or totals, and serve as means of measuring how much money is out there. The amount of money available affects prices and interest rates directly. The Federal Reserve Board monitors how much money is circulating and attempts to regulate the health of the economy by controlling the money supply.

The Federal Reserve Board

The Federal Reserve Board (the Fed) was established in 1913 as a semi-independent agency of the U.S. government to give the country an elastic currency, one that can expand to foster economic activity or contract to help control inflation, to provide facilities for discounting commercial paper, and to supervise banking. In its role of providing the United States with an elastic currency, the Fed regulates the money supply, mainly by injecting money into or withdrawing money from the monetary system.

To increase the money supply the Fed buys outstanding U.S. Treasury bonds and credits the banks supplying the bonds with cash balances called **reserves.** With higher reserves a bank can then lend out from two to six times (or more) the value of the Federal Reserve credits. If a bank receives $1,000 in payment for a bond or a deposit from a customer, it may retain a reserve, possibly 7 percent to 10 percent, and lend out the rest. If you borrow $900 and deposit that in the bank, and 9 percent is retained in reserve, $810 can be lent out again. This pyramiding of checking account deposits available through bank loans increases M_1.

Another tool in the Fed's arsenal is control of **reserve limits.** The Fed may increase the reserve limit from 8 percent to 9 percent. Immediately, banks have less money to loan because more of their capital is tied up in reserves. If the Fed wants to loosen money, it may decrease the reserve limit.

Monetizing a portion of the national debt is akin to printing money to pay for goods and services the government buys. The idea of a printing press run amok is simplistic but not far off the mark. What actually happens is that the Fed buys outstanding U.S. Treasury bonds to put more reserves into the banking system. The banks can then buy more bonds being offered by the U.S. Treasury. The key is the credits transferred to banks, as this is made money, like printing more dollar bills at the **mint.**

Inflation

Monitoring the money supply is important. When too much money is created without a similar expansion of goods and services, prices increase inflation. Excessive expansion of the money supply accounts for the double- and triple-digit inflation rates in some countries, particularly in South America. A mini-expansion of the money supply continues to feed inflation in the United States.

The Fed attempts to keep a rein on inflation by increasing the money supply only as necessary to support growth in the economy. The Fed's task is complicated when the federal government engages in deficit spending, that is, borrowing money to pay for spending that exceeds tax revenues. The additional borrowing effectively increases the money supply and pushes prices up by decreasing the purchasing power of each dollar. Charts 14A and 14B show the rising money supplies in M_1 and M_2 categories.

Velocity of money also affects inflation and is something the Fed can do little about. Velocity is the turnover rate of money, or how many times a dollar changes hands during a year. Velocity affects inflation because it increases or decreases available spending power. If $1

billion turned over once a year, then the effective money supply (purchasing power) would be $1 billion. But if $1 billion turned over four times a year, then the effective money supply would be $4 billion. With more purchasing power available, prices rise, leading to inflation.

Individual actions affect the velocity of money. When inflation is running at rates above the earning capacity of money in relatively risk-free investments, such as bank CDs, people tend to spend freely, figuring that the longer they hang onto their money, the less it will buy. After World War I, German employers paid employees

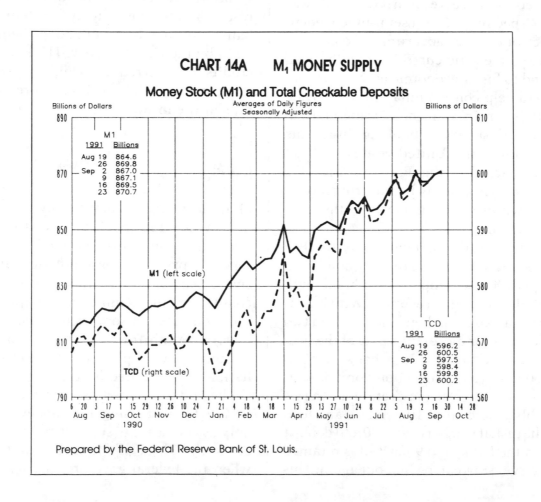

Prepared by the Federal Reserve Bank of St. Louis.

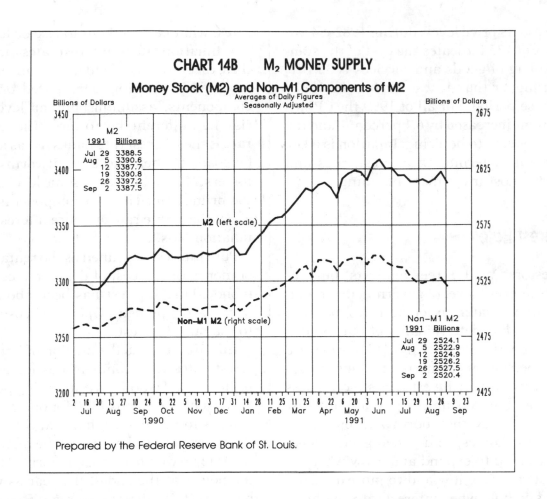

CHART 14B   M₂ MONEY SUPPLY

Money Stock (M2) and Non-M1 Components of M2

Averages of Daily Figures
Seasonally Adjusted

Prepared by the Federal Reserve Bank of St. Louis.

twice a day to enable them to spend their earnings before prices rose and decreased the purchasing power of their wages. Velocity is a measure of that tendency. During stable times people leave some of their money in savings or investments because they prefer to spend later and are less concerned about the decrease in purchasing power with time. The money they set aside earns more than the inflation rate.

The Fed has no tools to control the velocity of money because velocity results from millions of individual decisions. Velocity tends to make inflation worse by rising at the wrong times. When people sense inflation is rising and believe their dollars will buy less next week than they will today, they rush to spend the dollars they have. The cumulative effect of these actions tends to push inflation even higher. The reverse occurs when inflation appears to be declining. As people sense inflation declining, they are more apt to hang onto dollars, thus lowering velocity and helping the decline of inflation.

Inflation measures tend to be imprecise. The most common measure of inflation is the **Consumer Price Index** for Urban Consumers (CPI). The CPI records the increase in the rate of inflation by relating the cost of a bag of goods and services today to a base. Currently the base equals 100 and represents price levels during 1982–84. An index of 135 indicates the cost of the standard bag of goods and services is 35 percent higher than it was during the 1982–84 base period. For all of 1990 the CPI for all items increased by 6.1 percent—and the rate appears to be rising. Inflation is a key factor in determining interest rates and affects most investment planning.

Interest Rates

Investors, Wall Street analysts, bureaucrats at every level of government, and individuals watch interest rates because they are key determinants of our money-related activities. When interest rates are low, persons in retirement living on interest from their investments receive less income, but consumers pay less interest on the money they borrow to buy automobiles, homes, and other goods. Businesses tend to expand and grow when interest rates are low and to put expansion plans on hold when interest rates are high. Interest rates affect stock prices directly. As interest rates decline, stock prices tend to rise. When interest rates are high or climbing, stock prices tend to fall.

One of the key interest rates affecting investor actions is the **broker loan rate,** the interest rate stockbrokers charge customers for money borrowed to buy stocks on margin. A high broker loan rate discourages investors because the stock they buy must move faster and farther to pay the higher cost of margin interest. A low broker loan rate encourages investors to leverage stock purchases by borrowing more money to buy stocks on margin.

With so much depending on interest rates, what causes them to rise or fall?

• Inflation affects interest rates through the expectations of lenders. A banker sets an interest rate for loans based on two components, assuming similar levels of risk for different borrowers. The **prime rate** is the interest rate banks use as a base for loans to their most creditworthy customers. Most loans are at some level above the prime rate. The two components that affect the prime rate are pure interest and inflation bias.

Pure interest is defined as the rental cost of money or the cost of delay in receiving money. Pure interest has been about 2½ percent to 3 percent. Operating costs add to the pure interest.

Inflation bias is the portion of bank interest rates that compensates for an expected loss of a dollar's purchasing power. When a banker lends $100 for one year, he expects to be "made whole" at the end of the year—that is, he expects the money he lends to be worth as much in terms of buying power at the end of the year as when he lends it. If inflation averages 5 percent, the $100 would have to grow to $105 to buy the same bag of goods and services as $100 bought the day he loaned it. This allowance for inflation is the inflation bias, based not on what inflation has been but what bankers expect it to be during the period of the loan. Thus, as inflation expectations rise, so do interest rates.

• Money supply affects interest rates according to whether the supply is increasing or decreasing. If the money supply is growing, more money is available to make loans. If, however, lenders see the Fed pumping excess reserves into the system, they can reasonably expect, on the basis of experience, that the additional money will push up inflation. And as inflation rises, so do interest rates because of the inflation bias. Thus, pushing too much money into the system can cause interest rates to rise rather than fall. The Fed is aware of the constraints on trying to reduce interest rates too much or too quickly.

• The **discount rate** set by the Fed affects interest rates directly. The discount rate is the rate member banks pay when they borrow money from the Fed. If the discount rate rises, the cost of funds to banks also rises, and interest rates rise in tandem. Interest rates fall when the Fed lowers the discount rate. Stock market watchers monitor the Fed's actions on discount rates, as stocks tend to rise dramatically following a cut in the discount rate and to fall following a rise in the discount rate.

The Fed raises or lowers the discount rate according to how it sees the economy. If business is brisk and inflation appears to be heating up, the Fed may raise the discount rate to cool things off. To head off a slump, the Fed may reduce the discount rate.

• The **federal funds rate** (FFR) is a commonly watched interest rate that banks charge each other for use of funds over-

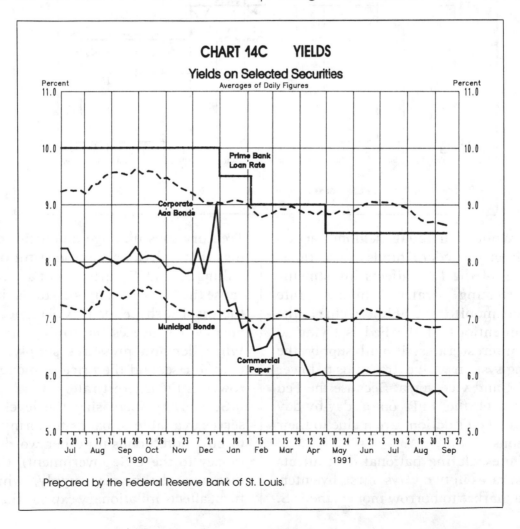

CHART 14C   YIELDS

Yields on Selected Securities

Averages of Daily Figures

Prepared by the Federal Reserve Bank of St. Louis.

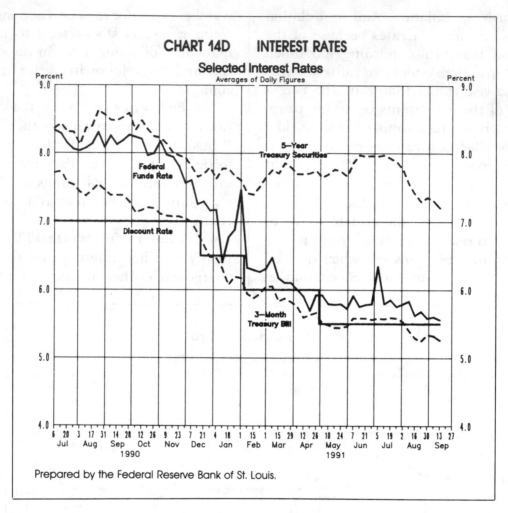

CHART 14D   INTEREST RATES

Selected Interest Rates

Averages of Daily Figures

Prepared by the Federal Reserve Bank of St. Louis.

night. While individuals seldom participate directly in federal funds transactions, the level of the FFR affects investments and investing strategy. Interest rate watchers monitor the FFR as a clue to the Fed's intentions. If the Fed is trying to lower interest rates, it will supply the banking system with extra funds to lower the FFR and vice versa. Because the Fed can control the FFR on a day-by-day basis, the Fed's actions are a clue to their intentions.

• The escalating national debt affects interest rates in two ways. First, by entering the market to borrow money, the U.S. Treasury sops up huge quantities of savings that individuals and institutions are willing to lend. Security is not a factor because the U.S. Treasury's credit is the best there is. The sheer quantity of money being borrowed squeezes the supply, however. When demand pressures supply, prices tend to rise, and the price of money borrowed is the interest rate.

Second, by increasing the level of reserves available to banks to permit them to buy more bonds (in other words, lend money to the U.S. government), the Fed increases the money supply, which in turn, affects inflationary expectations and causes interest rates to rise. The Fed walks a fine line between accommodating the government's need for money and keeping inflation under control.

• Interest rates for various purposes—such as credit card finance charges, housing credit, corporate and U.S. government bonds—are constantly fluctuating as a result of supply and demand in relation to the economy. Charts 14C and 14D reflect yields and interest rates as monitored by the Federal Reserve Bank of St. Louis. Yield is the return an investor expects from an investment. It does not include appre-ciation. Interest on a savings account in a bank is a simple example of yield.

Conclusion

Money and how we use it affects inflation. In turn, inflation, by itself or in concert with interest rates, affects what happens on Wall Street. Numerous other factors also affect prices of stocks, bonds, and mutual funds, but money and its national and international roles are major concerns to investors.

Glossary

Acquisition cost Cost for shares of stock; it includes the price of stock plus commissions and fees, if any. Also known as the cost basis for calculating capital gains or losses for income tax reporting.

Advance-decline line The number of advancing stocks compared to declining stocks as a percentage or ratio. More advancers than decliners is positive; more decliners than advancers is negative.

Agency securities Bonds or certificates issued by an agency of the U.S. government. A few agency securities, such as Government National Mortgage Association certificates, are guaranteed by the federal government. Other agency securities, while not specifically guaranteed, carry a moral obligation of security from the U.S. government.

American Depositary Receipt (ADR) A security issued by a bank in the United States that represents stock from a foreign country.

Annualization Extension of a short-term return to an annual rate for the purpose of comparison.

Annuitization Receipt of regular payments under a contract, usually for life or for a limited number of years.

Appreciation Increased value of an asset over time.

Arbitrage Simultaneous purchase of similar securities to take advantage of different prices in different markets or for different time periods (e.g., the purchase of a futures contract and the group of underlying securities, as in program trading). Also applicable in buy-outs and mergers where market price differs from tender price.

Arbitrageur An investor who practices arbitrage.

Arbitration A format for settling disputes between a broker and client that is quicker and less expensive than a suit in a court of law.

Arithmetic average The simple mean calculated by totaling an array of numbers and dividing the total by the number of entries.

Asset allocation A system of investing that distributes assets to different investment opportunities.

At the market The exercise price for an

option that equals the price of the underlying security.

Average An indication of central tendency, or a figure that represents the middle position of a range of numbers or values. There are three methods of calculating averages: arithmetic, geometric, or exponential; each method produces a different result.

Average maturity The total time for each security in a money market fund to mature divided by the number of securities in the portfolio.

Balance sheet The statement of a company's assets, liabilities, and shareholder equity.

Barter A system of exchange for trading products without the use of money.

Base value The starting point or level for an index. Prices or values are related to a base to determine relative value.

Benchmark The known reference point from which other values can be calculated and mutually related.

Beta A system for quantifying volatility by relating stocks or mutual funds to the volatility of the Standard & Poor's 500 Index.

Bottom line A colloquial expression for the amount of after-tax profit or loss on a corporation's Statement of Income.

Break-out The movement of share prices out of a trading range on the up side through the resistance level or on the down side through the support level.

Broker A licensed salesperson for stocks, bonds, and other securities.

Brokerage A firm engaged in the promotion and sale of securities; a firm that hires brokers to sell securities.

Broker loan rate The interest rate brokerages charge clients for loans to buy shares on margin or for trading in commodities, futures, or options.

Buy-back A company program for buying its own shares in the market for use in management incentive programs or to influence stock prices.

Call option Right but not obligation to buy 100 shares of an underlying stock at a stipulated exercise price on or before an expiration date.

Call provision Clause in a bond indenture that gives the issuing company or government organization the right to redeem the bond at a stipulated price, possibly with a penalty, after a fixed date or a certain number of years after issue.

Call writer An investor who sells a call option.

Capitalization The combination of equity and debt that makes up a company's capital. Also, the value of a company obtained by multiplying the number of shares of stock outstanding by the share price.

Capital spending A program in which a company adds to its asset base by spending earnings or borrowed money on improvements or additions that increase the company's capabilities.

Certificate of deposit (CD) A contract between banks, savings & loan associations, and credit unions and savers that provides a fixed rate of interest for a specific period. Interest rates are usually higher for longer periods. Early withdrawals may be penalized.

Churning The frequent selling and rebuying of securities within a client's portfolio by a broker to increase his or her commission income.

Clearing corporation A support organization for commodities, futures, and index trading to process paperwork, monitor margin levels, and facilitate trading.

Closed-end fund One form of mutual fund in which a fixed number of shares are issued in an initial offering. Shares of closed-end funds trade on an exchange or over-the-counter.

Closing price The price of a stock or other security on the final trade of a session.

Cold calling A method used by some brokers to gain customers. A broker may call individuals on a list without any previous contact or introduction.

Commercial paper IOUs issued by corporations to raise money. Commercial paper is not collateralized—that is, not backed by assets—and ratings depend on the creditworthiness of the company.

Commodity pool A group of investors who contribute cash into a pool to be used by a broker-manager for investing in commodities, futures, or options.

Common stock Shares in a corporation documenting partial ownership interest. Common stock conveys voting rights; stockholders participate in earnings if dividends are declared, and they are behind bondholders and preferred stock owners in access to assets of a corporation at dissolution.

Composite tick A tick is a move up or down in a stock or mutual fund price. A composite tick summarizes the number of upticks and downticks, usually at the close. A positive composite tick forecasts an up opening of the market at the next session. A negative composite tick forecasts a down opening.

Composite transactions Reports of stock prices on the NYSE Composite that reflect high, low, and closing prices on any of its eight associated markets.

Compounding The payment of interest on interest.

Confirmation A notice sent to an investor following a trade to document details of the transaction.

Consumer Price Index Known as CPI or cost of living index, this index is compiled by the U.S. Bureau of Labor Statistics to document changes in prices of a standard bag of goods and services over time.

Contingent redemption Fees or penalties that are imposed when or if an investor redeems shares, usually in a mutual fund.

Contract A trading vehicle for commodities and futures that precisely defines what is being traded. A contract for wheat is 5,000 bushels of a specific grade.

Convertible An instrument that may be converted into some other investment, as a convertible preferred stock may be converted to common shares under specified conditions.

Cost basis For a security, such as stocks or bonds, cost basis is the original price paid plus the commission or other acquisition cost. It is the basis for figuring capital gains or losses.

Cumulative provision A provision in preferred stock contracts requiring payment of all past dividends before dividends can be paid on common stock.

Currency exchange value A constantly changing rate at which the currency of one country may be exchanged for the currency of another.

Data entries A method of documenting ownership of securities in which entries are recorded in a computer and evidence of ownership is a computer-generated confirmation.

Debenture A bond issued by a corporation without collateral, based on the general credit of the corporation.

Declaration date The date a company announces a dividend to be paid on its stock.

Discounting The process of reducing the price or value of something on the basis of perceived future value.

Discount rate The interest rate charged by Federal Reserve banks on loans to member banks.

Diversification Owning a variety of securities to spread the risk of possible loss.

Dividend The income distribution to stockholders from a corporation's earnings.

Dollar-cost averaging (DCA) An investment system that calls for investing the same dollar amount in a given medium on a regular schedule over long periods.

DRIP A dividend reinvestment plan whereby dividends paid by a company or mutual fund are automatically reinvested in additional shares.

Entry price The price paid for a futures or index options contract.

EPS Earnings per share, a factor used in evaluating stock prices.

Equity Ownership interest in a company, as distinct from a position as debtor or lender.

Eurodollar Dollars traded or deposited outside the United States, mainly in (but not limited to) European countries.

European Currency Unit ECU is the name for a currency based on 12 currencies issued by European countries. It is expected to be the currency for trading after the 1992 consolidation of the Common Market in Europe.

Event risk The possibility of loss due to some unforeseen catastrophic event, such as a presidential assassination.

Exchange A place where investors and traders get together to transact business.

Ex-dividend date The first date following a declaration of a dividend when a share of stock is not entitled to receive a dividend, usually five business days before record date.

Execution The transaction of finding a buyer or seller and effecting a trade of stocks or bonds along with follow-up paperwork.

Exercise To call a stock in an option contract.

Exercise price See strike price.

Exponential average A method of averaging a series of numbers, such as closing prices of NYSE Composite Index, for the purpose of charting a moving average; an exponential average gives greater weight to more recent numbers in the series. See also moving average.

Federal funds rate The interest rate charged by banks on overnight loans of excess funds to other banks.

Fill The completion of a trade, as in a trade filled at some price.

Financials A corporation's financial statements that include an income statement, balance sheet, and flow of funds statement.

First in-First out (FIFO) A method of pricing inventory or determining the cost basis of shares for tax purposes.

Float, currency The amount of currency in the hands of traders and consumers.

Float, stock The number of shares outstanding that are available for trading.

Flower bonds A special series of U.S. Treasury bonds that are accepted at par value in the settlement of estate taxes when owned by a decedent prior to death.

Form 1099-B Information returns filed by brokers to report gross sales of securities to the IRS.

Form 1099-DIV Information returns to the IRS filed by corporations and mutual funds to report dividends paid to shareholders.

Fractional share Less than a full share of stock, usually in a mutual fund but also in dividend reinvestment plans.

Fundamental analysis The study of a company's financials, marketing strategies, management, and profitability as a means of determining the worth of its shares.

Futures Contracts for the delivery of a product at a specified future time.

Geometric average An average of a series of numbers calculated by taking the *nth* root of *n* numbers multiplied together.

GNP deflator An index of gross national product compared to product prices stated in constant dollars; a measure of inflation.

GTC Good 'til canceled, a term used in placing limit orders to buy or sell stock. (See also limit order.)

Hard currency Currency of a country that is readily convertible into the currency of other countries.

Hedging A mechanism used in commodities and futures markets to control risks related to future price movements.

Income statement A corporation's statement of earnings for a specified period of time.

Index An average of stock prices, commodities prices, or other series of numbers related to a base.

Index fund A mutual fund that buys stock in companies in proportion to the companies' representation in an index, such as the Standard & Poor's 500 Index.

Index option An option based on one of a number of indexes, such as an index option based on the Standard & Poor's 100 Index.

Indicator A fact, event, or number derived from analysis that may be used in deciding when to move into or out of the market.

Inflation Increasing price levels in an economy that reflect a decreasing value of the currency.

Inflation bias That portion of bank interest rates designated as compensation for an expected loss of a dollar's purchasing value before the loan is repaid.

Initial public offering (IPO) First time sale of a company's stock to the general public. After the IPO, the company is a public corporation and shares trade regularly.

Insider trading Sales and purchases of shares by a company's officers and/or directors based on information not available to the public.

Interest-free loan A loan by someone without interest.

In-the-money An option purchased at an exercise price lower than the current trading price of the underlying security.

Intrinsic value The difference between a strike price and the current trading price of an option less the time value of option. See strike price.

Inverse relationship A situation in which one value moves in an opposite direction to another; for example, the price of bonds rises when interest rates decline and vice versa.

IRA Individual Retirement Account, a means for deferring taxes on current income and investment gains.

Keogh A plan available for the tax-deferred accumulation of retirement assets by self-employed individuals.

Laying off risk Jargon for transferring risk from a hedger to a speculator in futures and commodities trading.

Leverage Investing with debt to compound gains or losses, for example, buying stocks on margin.

Limited partnership An organizational form consisting of general partners who accept personal unlimited liability for debts of the operation and limited partners whose liability is limited to the amount of their investment.

Limit order An order placed with broker stating a price or some other condition which a security must attain before the order may be executed.

Liquidity The ability to buy or sell a security quickly and at a price that will not disturb the price for other owners.

Listed Stocks, bonds, or other securities that are traded on an organized exchange are said to be listed on that exchange, as differentiated from an unlisted security, which trades over-the-counter.

Load Jargon for the sales commission charged on the sale of mutual fund shares by brokers.

Long A position which an owner holds with the expectation that prices will rise.

M_1, M_2, M_3 Three measures of the U.S. money supply.

Make-out basis A method of trading over-the-counter in which a market maker does not hold shares in inventory but knows where shares are available at certain prices.

Margin The amount of cash put up as evidence of good faith in futures and commodities trading. Also the amount that may be borrowed from a broker in purchasing shares of stock.

Market A term that refers to all the exchanges, traders, investors, and others involved in effecting the transfer of goods and securities.

Market indicator An index, average, or other mark of activity that appears to forecast the direction of the market.

Market maker A brokerage firm that functions as a mini-exchange in the buying and selling of shares in a company that is not listed on one of the exchanges.

Market risk A possible loss resulting from movements of the overall market as distinct from potential losses from fluctuations of an individual stock or bond.

Market timing A system aimed at reducing market risk by calculating the best time to get out of bear markets while remaining invested in bull markets.

Mark to market To revalue securities at the end of the trading day based on prices established during the trading session.

Mint A U.S. government facility for printing currency and producing coins.

Monetary aggregates Totals of various forms of money, including deposit accounts, represented in M_1, M_2, and M_3 totals.

Monetization An action by the Federal Reserve Board to increase the amount of money in the system in order to pay off part of the country's deficit.

Money market instruments   Short-term investments, such as certificates of deposit, treasury bills, bankers acceptances, and commercial paper, used to facilitate business. Also, investments held by money market mutual funds.

Money supply   The amount of currency, deposits, and other forms of money in circulation at any one time.

Mortgage bonds   Bonds collateralized by liens on property.

Moving average   An average computed on a regular schedule that moves forward with time, dropping earlier components as later ones are added.

Multiplier   The number used in compiling index option contracts. For example, the S&P 500 index option is 100 times the value of the Standard & Poor's 500 index.

Municipals   Bonds issued by states, cities, and local taxing districts whose interest is free from federal income tax.

Naked call   A contract to sell 100 shares of a stock that the seller does not actually own.

Negative correlation   The relationship of two series of numbers that work in reverse; as one series advances, the second declines in a known proportion or relationship.

Net asset value (NAV)   The NAV of mutual fund shares is computed daily by dividing total assets by number of shares outstanding.

Odd lot   The number of shares other than 100, which is a round lot.

Open-end funds   Mutual funds in which the number of shares is not fixed. As investors put up more money, the fund issues more shares, and as investors redeem shares, the number of shares declines.

Open interest   The total investments outstanding in commodities, futures, and options which must either be delivered or closed out.

Open outcry   An auction system used in trading commodities and other securities in which buyers and sellers communicate with a combination of shouts and hand signals.

Option   The right, but not the obligation, to buy or sell an underlying security.

Out-of-the-money   An option purchased when the price of the underlying security is less than the strike price.

Payment date   The date on which a company mails a dividend.

Penetration   Jargon for the point where a price line for a stock or mutual fund crosses a moving average in an upward or downward direction. Used in market timing to determine when to buy or sell.

Penny stock   A stock that sells for less than $1 per share. Some brokers consider stocks that sell for less than $3 or $5 per share to be penny stocks.

P/E ratio   Ratio of price to earnings, an important indicator of a stock's price.

Pink sheets   The prices of OTC stocks published on pink paper by the National Quotation Bureau, Inc.

Portfolio   A collection of securities.

Position   Owning securities, as in taking a position in a company's stock.

Preemptive right   A right to buy additional shares in proportion to current ownership; this permits a shareholder to retain a percentage ownership position and preempts the rights of other investors to buy shares of a new issue.

Preferred stock   Shares in a company that pay a stated dividend, which is paid ahead of common stock dividends. An owner of preferred stock also holds a preferred position in case of the liquidation of the company's assets.

Premium   The payment for an option.

Price limit   The amount by which the price of a commodity may advance or decline in one day before trading stops.

Price reversal   The mark point at which a stock's price changes direction. It is used in trend-following analysis for market timing.

Price weighting   A method used in compiling an index of security prices without regard to number of shares issued.

Prime rate   The interest rate banks charge on loans to their most creditworthy customers.

Principal   The capital portion of an investment or loan.

Program trader   A major investor or brokerage firm that buys and sells collections of securities to gain a profit from the difference between aggregate price of the collection of securities and the value of a futures contract.

Program trading   Trading groups of securities against a futures contract for those securities.

Prospecting   Jargon for brokers' searching for new clients.

Prospectus   A document that discloses relevant facts about a stock or mutual fund.

Proxy   A transfer of voting authority by a stockholder to another person. Also designates an index fund that appears to move in a pattern similar to the market and that is, thus, a stand-in (proxy) for the market itself.

Put option   The right, but not obligation, to sell shares at an agreed strike price on or prior to a specified expiration date.

Record date   The date when shareholders of record will be entitled to a dividend.

Recovery period   The period between the time a person's children complete college and the time when that person retires, usually the most productive period for collecting assets to be used in retirement.

Recreational investor   A person who invests for the fun of playing the game and for whom profits or losses are a means of keeping score, similar to a gambler in a casino.

Relative strength   A statistical indicator of a company's stock price performance relative to other companies.

Relative value   A system for rating the investment potential of mutual funds based on recent performance.

Reserve limit   A percentage of deposits that must be retained by banks in accordance with Federal Reserve Board regulations.

Reserves   Cash or deposits retained by a bank to cover possible losses from loans.

Resistance   A level of stock prices that appears to be a limit on upward movement of prices, as in the upper limit of a trading range.

Return on investment (ROI)   A factor used in the fundamental analysis of a company.

Reversal   A function of a moving average that is useful in market timing systems for marking when to get into or out of the market.

Reverse stock split   The consolidation of shares in which a specified number of a company's shares are exchanged for a smaller number: a 10-for-1 reverse split would require shareholders to submit 10 shares in exchange for one new share.

Risk tolerance   An investor's willingness to accept some level of risk in exchange for a possibly higher return on investment.

Round lot   100 shares of a company's stocks. Some stocks with prices over 200 may trade in lots of 10 shares.

Round turn   Jargon for a buy and subsequent sale of a security.

Scale of value   A yardstick for evaluating different products or services. One of the functions of money is to serve as a scale of value.

Seat   Jargon for membership in an exchange. When a firm has a seat on the NYSE, the firm is a member of the NYSE.

Sector funds   Mutual funds that invest in a single industry, such as companies involved in medicine.

Securities   Stocks, bonds, options, and other equity or debt investments with inherent and prospective value. A security involves a money transaction—it is part of a common enterprise—and it is a contract entered into with the expectation of profit.

Security analyst   A person, usually employed by a brokerage, who follows the operations of companies or an industry to track performance and advise investors on prospects.

Sentiment index   An index based on the percentage of financial writers who believe the market is headed higher or lower.

Settling   The completion of a commodities, futures, or option contract with a payoff in exchange for cancelling the contract.

Shareholder   An investor who owns shares in a corporation.

Short   The position of investor who sells borrowed shares.

Short selling   The process of selling shares borrowed from a broker with the expectation of replacing them later at a lower price and profiting from the difference.

Simple mean   An average calculated by adding a series of numbers and dividing the total by the number of entries.

Sinking fund   Money deposited by a debtor into a fund for paying off notes or bonds.

Soft currency   Currency issued by countries used for internal transactions but which is not readily convertible into the currency of another country.

Specialist   An exchange member who acts as a broker to brokers in trading designated issues of stocks with the objective of facilitating trading and maintaining an orderly market. A specialist also holds limit orders and maintains a book of offers to buy and offers to sell at varied prices.

Speculator   An investor who is willing to accept large risks in exchange for the possibility of increasing capital.

Spot market   Trading for immediate delivery and payment, as opposed to trading in futures.

Spread trading   A strategy in commodities, futures, and options that entails trading in two different but related securities to reduce risk while retaining opportunity for profit.

Stock certificate   A document evidencing ownership in shares of a corporation.

Stock index futures Contracts for trading futures based on an index of stocks.

Stock risk The risk that a stock will decline in value.

Stock split The process of increasing the number of a corporation's shares without affecting the overall value of the shares, even though the cost basis and the price of additional shares will be lower. A common split is two new shares for each current share.

Stock symbol A one- to four-letter abbreviation for a company's stock to facilitate quick reporting.

Stop order A limit order placed to protect share value from significant decline. If prices for a stock decline to the level set in the stop order, it becomes an active order that is executed.

Straight life annuity A contract to pay a fixed amount regularly, usually monthly, for as long as the owner lives.

Strike price The price at which an option holder may call or put shares to a speculator holding the opposite side of the option. Strike prices are set by the exchange in regular intervals. Also known as the exercise price.

STRIPS An acronym for Separate Trading of Registered Interest and Principal of Securities, referring to the interest portion of U.S. Treasury bonds separated from the bond and sold to investors interested in income.

Support The level of trading prices at the lower end of a trading range.

Tax-advantaged Refers to securities (such as municipal bonds) that are not taxed at the federal level and to programs (such as IRA and 401(k)) that permit deferral of taxes until withdrawal.

Tax-deferred Investments under IRA and similar umbrellas that permit deferral of taxes.

T-bills U.S. Treasury bills.

Technical analysis The study of patterns of past price and volume movements to determine possible future price movements.

Technician An analyst who practices technical analysis.

Tender offer An offer by a company or an outsider to buy shares of the company's stock at a fixed price outside an exchange.

10-year certain annuity A contract to pay a fixed amount regularly, usually monthly, for life or for a minimum of 10 years, even if the owner dies before the 10-year period is up.

10-year reversionary trust A trust that transfers assets to another person for a minimum of 10 years, after which the assets may be passed on to someone else. Although still legal, 10-year reversionary trusts now forbid the original grantor from reclaiming the assets. Also known as a Clifford trust.

Tick The minimum price difference permitted for a trade at a new price compared to the existing price.

Ticker tape Formerly printed reports of transactions on ribbons of paper. Now transactions are reported on an electronic reader board, still referred to as a ticker.

Time value The remaining value in an option prior to expiration.

Trend The long-term direction of the market. Over past decades the market has trended up at about 6 percent per year.

Trend following A system of market timing based on analysis of moving averages. See also market timing, moving averages.

12b-1 fees Fees charged by some mutual funds against asset base to pay for marketing and distribution costs.

Underlying stock Used with options, underlying stock is a share of a company's stock that is the base for an option. If a call is exercised, the underlying stock will be delivered to the holder of the call on demand.

Unit A combination of securities, for example, a share of stock, warrant, and a piece of bond. Traded together, they form a unit with one price for the group.

Unit trust A pool of bonds used as a base for issuing certificates of ownership, usually in $1,000 increments.

Unweighted Numbers or prices used in an average without giving more or less significance to some entries as opposed to others.

Value-cost averaging (VCA) A system for investing differing amounts on a regular basis, usually in a mutual fund, to increase the value of the investment. A variation of dollar-cost averaging.

Velocity of money The rate at which money turns over from one owner to another. A high velocity rate has the effect of increasing the effective money supply and can be inflationary.

Volatility The rapidity and range of the price movement of stocks and/or mutual funds.

Voting issue Shares of common stock that carry rights to elect the board of directors and vote on other quotations.

Warrant The right to buy shares at a predetermined price, similar to a call option but exercisable over a longer period, in some cases in perpetuity.

Wash sale The repurchase of a security within 30 days of a sale of that same security to establish a loss.

Weighted average An average weighted by size of company, price, or date.

Weighting A system for giving some numbers in an average or index more influence on the result than others.

When issued A stock issue declared but not yet issued, even though it is open to trading. A *WI* symbol indicates the stock will be priced at the trade price when issued.

Wire house A branch office of a large brokerage organization tied to the main office by telephone or data link.

Withdrawals Redemptions of shares or checks written against an asset base.

Yield Income, usually interest, paid by a security on a regular basis. Yields are usually annualized, i.e., converted to an annual basis for comparability.

Yield to maturity (YTM) Applicable to bonds, particularly those bought at a premium or discount to face value where the difference between purchase price and redemption value is calculated but not distributed annually.

Resources

Exchanges

American Stock Exchange, 86 Trinity Place, New York, NY 10006

Boston Stock Exchange, One Boston Place, Boston, MA 02108

Chicago Board Options Exchange, LaSalle at Van Buren, Chicago, IL 60605

Chicago Board of Trade, LaSalle at Jackson, Chicago, IL 60604

Chicago Mercantile Exchange, 30 S. Wacker Drive, Chicago, IL 60606

Chicago Rice and Cotton Exchange, LaSalle at Jackson, Chicago, IL 60604

Cincinnati Stock Exchange, 49 E. Fourth Street, Suite 205, Cincinnati, OH 45202

Coffee, Sugar, and Cocoa Exchange, Inc., 4 World Trade Center, New York, NY 10048

Commodity Exchange, Inc., 4 World Trade Center, New York, NY 10048

Kansas City Board of Trade, 4800 Main, Suite 303, Kansas City, MO 64112

MidAmerica Commodity Exchange, LaSalle at Jackson, Chicago, IL 60604

Midwest Stock Exchange, 440 S. LaSalle Street, Chicago, IL 60605

National Quotation Bureau, Inc., Harborside Financial Center, Jersey City, NJ 07302

New York Cotton Exchange, 4 World Trade Center, New York, NY 10048

New York Futures Exchange, 20 Broad Street, New York, NY 10005

New York Mercantile Exchange, 4 World Trade Center, New York, NY 10048

New York Stock Exchange, 11 Wall Street, New York, NY 10005

Pacific Stock Exchange, 301 Pine Street, San Francisco, CA 94104

Philadelphia Stock Exchange, 1900 Market Street, Philadelphia, PA 19103

Spokane Stock Exchange, N. 20 Post, Suite 206, Spokane, WA 99201

Toronto Stock Exchange, 2 First Canadian Place, Toronto, ONT, Canada M5X 1J2

Vancouver Stock Exchange, Stock Exchange Tower, 609 Granville Street, Vancouver, B.C., Canada V7Y 1H1

Newsletters

Bob Nurock's Advisory, Box 988, Paoli, PA 19301

California Technology Stock Letter, 1620 Montgomery Street, Suite 200, San Francisco, CA 94111

Dessauer's Journal of Financial Markets, Box 1718, Orleans, MA 02653

The Dines Letter, Box 22, Belvedere, CA 94920

Dow Theory Forecasts, 7412 Calumet Avenue, Hammond, IN 46324

The Elliott Wave Theorist, Box 1618, Gainesville, GA 30503

The Fund Exchange, Paul A. Merriman & Associates, 1200 Westlake Avenue N., Suite 700, Seattle, WA 98109

The Granville Market Letter, P.O. Drawer 413006, Kansas City, MO 64141

Growth Stock Outlook, Box 15381, Chevy Chase, MD 20825

Donoghue's Moneyletter, Box 8008, Holliston, MA 01746

Investment Quality Trends, 7440 Girard Avenue, Suite 4, La Jolla, CA 02037

Mutual Fund Advisor, One Sarasota Tower, Suite 602, Sarasota, FL 34236

Mutual Fund Forecaster, 3471 N. Federal Highway, Ft. Lauderdale, FL 33306

Mutual Fund Investing, 7811 Montrose Road, Potomac, MD 20854

The No-Load Fund Investor, Box 283, Hastings-on-Hudson, NY 10706

NoLoad Fund X, DAL Investment Co., 235 Montgomery Street, San Francisco, CA 94104

Personal Finance, 1101 King Street, Suite 400, Alexandria, VA 22314

Professional Tape Reader, Box 2407, Hollywood, FL 33022

Standard & Poor's Outlook, 25 Broadway, New York, NY 10004

The Volume Reversal Survey, Box 1451, Sedona, AZ 86336

The Zweig Forecast, Box 360, Bellmore, NY 11710

Periodicals

Barron's, 200 Liberty Street, New York, NY 10281

Forbes, Forbes, Inc., 60 Fifth Avenue, New York, NY 10011

Investor's Daily, 1941 Armacost Avenue, Los Angeles, CA 90025

Kiplinger's Personal Finance Magazine, Kiplinger Washington Editors, Inc., 1729 H Street, N.W., Washington, DC 20006

Money, Time, Inc., Time & Life Bldg., Rockefeller Center, New York, NY 10020

The Wall Street Journal, 200 Liberty Street, New York, NY 10281

Books

Analysis of Financial Statements. 3d ed. Bernstein, Leopold A. Homewood, IL: 1990

Computerized Investing. American Association of Individual Investors. Chicago: Annual editions

The Donoghue Strategies. Donoghue, William E. and Robert Chapman Wood. New York: Bantam, 1989

Dow Jones-Irwin Guide to Stock Index Futures and Options. Nix, William E. and Susan W. Nix. Homewood, IL: 1985

Dow Jones-Irwin Guide to Trading Systems. Babcock, Bruce. Homewood, IL: 1989

Encyclopedia of Technical Market Indicators. Colby, Robert W. and Thomas A. Meyers. Business One Irwin. Homewood, IL: 1988

Financial Futures—Fundamental Strategies and Applications. Schwarz, Edward W., Joanne M. Hill, and Thomas Schneeweis. Business One Irwin. Homewood, IL: 1986

Financial Options From Theory to Practice. Figlewski, Stephen, William Silber, and Marti Subrahmanyam. Business One Irwin. Homewood, IL: 1990

Forecasting Financial Markets—Technical Analysis and the Dynamics of Price Movement. Plummer, Tony. Wiley. New York: 1990

Getting Started in Options. Thomsett, Michael C. Wiley. New York: 1989

Handbook of Financial Market Indexes, Averages, and Indicators. Berlin, Howard M. Business One Irwin. Homewood, IL: 1990

Handbook of Financial Markets—Securities, Options and Figures. 2d ed. Fabozzi, Frank J. and Frank G. Zarb, eds. Business One Irwin. Homewood, IL: 1986

Handbook for No-Load Fund Investors. Jacobs, Sheldon. The No-Load Fund Investor. Hastings-on-Hudson, NY: Published annually

The Individual Investor's Guide to No-Load Mutual Funds. American Association of Individual Investors. Chicago, IL: Published annually

Options—Essential Concepts and Trading Strategies. The Option Institute. Business One Irwin. Homewood, IL: 1990

Stock Market Trading Systems. Appel, Gerald and Fred Hitschler. Dow Jones-Irwin. Homewood, IL: 1980

Stocks, Bonds, Bills and Inflation. Ibbotson Associates. Published annually. Chicago, Ibbotson

Technical Analysis Explained. 2d ed. Pring, Martin J. New York: McGraw-Hill, 1985

Trader Vic's Method of a Wall Street Master, Sperandeo, Victor. Wiley. New York: 1991

Capital Withdrawal Charts, available only by mail from Merle G. Dowd & Assoc., 7438 S.E. 40th St. Mercer Island, WA 98040. $3 per set

Useful Address

U.S. Treasury, Bureau of the Public Debt, Division of Securities Operations, Washington, DC 20239–0001

Index